3

studies in jazz

Institute of Jazz Studies, Rutgers University
General Editors: *Dan Morgenstern & Edward Berger*

In the Mainstream

Studies in Jazz No. 11

Metuchen, N.J., & London, 1992

The Scarecrow Press and the Institute

In the
Mainstream

18 Portraits in Jazz

Chip Deffaa

of Jazz Studies, Rutgers University

British Library Cataloguing-in-Publication data available

Library of Congress Cataloging-in-Publication Data

Deffaa, Chip, 1951–
    In the mainstream : 18 portraits in jazz / Chip Deffaa.
       p.   cm. — (Studies in jazz ; 11)
    Includes bibliographical references and index.
    ISBN 0-8108-2558-9
    1. Jazz musicians—United States—Biography.   I. Title.
  II. Series: Studies in jazz ; no. 11.
  ML385.D32   1992
  781.65′092′273—dc20
  [B]   92-8173

To Joe Franklin

Contents

In the Mainstream

DAN · MORGENSTERN

Editor's Preface

This is the third collection of Chip Deffaa's profiles of jazz musicians to be published in book form, and the second in this series, which proves that Chip is a diligent laborer in the vineyards of jazz. And a good thing that he is. Everyone has a story to tell, and no one is going to be around forever—though Doc Cheatham may yet prove me wrong. As one who once plied Chip's trade, I could kick myself blue all over for the chances I missed to get some of those irreplaceable stories, thinking that there'd be plenty of time, or that someone else would do the job.

Chip doesn't make those mistakes: he seizes the day. As before, he has cast his net wide—Mahlon Clark and Bill Dillard are just two of the people in this book you're not likely to know much about. And also as before, Chip's chosen subjects are all "in the mainstream," which is where his heart for music lies. As I said in my preface to *Swing Legacy*, Chip's pieces are a significant contribution to jazz oral history, and as such belong in what is essentially a series of scholarly books. The lives and thoughts of the music makers are the meat that sits on the bones of scholarship, and there is many a nugget to be gleaned here by future researchers: insights on the Savoy Sultans from George Kelly, discographical corrections from Ray McKinley, and uncommonly benign views on Benny Goodman from Sonny Igoe and Ken

Peplowski, as well as not-so-kind ones of Lionel Hampton and Harry James from Joe Wilder and Jake Hanna, respectively.

For some reason, the drummers (Hanna, Igoe, McKinley, and my man Oliver Jackson) seem to be particularly keen observers and commentators, but all the 19 subjects collated herein have something to tell us, and we are grateful that Chip Deffaa was there to listen and pass the message on. Grateful, too, that he never inserts his own opinions or ego, but lets the musicians speak for themselves—something that may look easy but is not.

DAN MORGENSTERN
Director
Institute of Jazz Studies
Rutgers University

In the Mainstream

Introduction

The musicians profiled in this book have all contributed to and have, for at least a portion of their careers, seen themselves as being part of the jazz tradition. Not all of their work was in jazz, to be sure, for everyone has to make a living and jazz is not always the most financially remunerative of fields. Some of these musicians were notably more jazz-oriented than others, but an interest in jazz is one unifying thread. And, broadly speaking, we can view them as being part of a *mainstream* jazz tradition. The term mainstream jazz, James Lincoln Collier writes in *The New Grove Dictionary of Jazz,* is commonly used today to refer to "any jazz improvised on chord sequences in the essentially solo style developed by Louis Armstrong in the late 1920s." Most of these musicians wouldn't have much interest in fusion, free or avant garde jazz. But all do share an appreciation for—to mention one name repeatedly volunteered by musicians themselves—the contributions of Louis Armstrong. And although it's unlikely you'd ever actually find these disparate musicians in the same place, they all could, if need be, jam together and find some common ground. They're comfortable working in a jazz tradition that pre-dates Charlie Parker. (Perhaps Bill Challis, Bob Haggart, or George Kelly could sketch out arrangements to keep things orderly in that hypothetical jam.) Their specific individual preferences in music naturally vary, reflecting their respective ages, backgrounds, and temperaments, but they all favor jazz that's got a certain respect for melody, jazz that's accessible to the layman. Most have had big band experience.

Nearly all of the musicians in this book also have one other thing in common: they have never before been profiled in a book. And that was a factor to consider. If you start listing the musicians who've been profiled in books by such conscientious writers as Stanley Dance, Whitney Balliett, and George T. Simon (to name but three), you'll have a good-sized list. This collection aims to cover some fresh ground, which is one goal of any serious writer. Doc Cheatham, of course, *has* been profiled nicely before, but in my talks with him I was pleasantly surprised to discover just how much of what he had to tell me had not appeared in any previous profiles—and it's well worth setting down in print.

I don't want to overstate the common bonds these assorted musicians may share, though. This is a collection of profiles and the reader should not expect to find too many unifying threads. The truth is, I'm as interested in the differences in these musicians' lives as in any similarities. Because they started at different points (the oldest, Bill Challis, was born in 1904; the youngest, John Pizzarelli Jr., in 1960) and worked in different bands and explored different directions, collectively they have more to tell us about American musical history than a more tightly cohesive group would. This book is not a comprehensive study of a milieu, but is intended to complement my two previous collections of profiles, *Swing Legacy* and *Voices of the Jazz Age*, giving the histories (mostly in the musicians' own words) of some fine, and in certain cases overlooked, contributors to mainstream jazz. Not all of the musicians are well known; but you may discover that even musicians you've barely heard of have valuable insights into the music business to share. I've sought out these musicians because I've enjoyed the music they've made and have been interested in the stories they have to tell. I've gone about my work with a certain sense of mission, too—a feeling that if I didn't profile some of these musicians, I didn't see anyone else who was likely to do so. My contemporaries in the jazz writing field focus mostly on younger players. But I think you'll find a good bit of history here worth preserving.

Cheatham and Challis offer contrasting views of the black and white jazz scenes of the 1920s (and those scenes were pretty much divided by race then). In the mid '20s, Cheatham was in Chicago, soaking up the sounds of King Oliver and Louis Armstrong. He went on to play lead trumpet with Sam Wooding, Cab Calloway, and others before finally blossoming as an articulate, lyrical soloist late in life. While Cheatham was digging Oliver and Armstrong, pioneering big band arranger Challis was scoring music for the two leading jazz-inflected white orchestras of that era, Jean Goldkette's and Paul Whiteman's, and working closely with some of the greatest white jazzmen then alive, including Bix Beiderbecke and Frank Trumbauer. Ray McKinley drummed for the big bands of the Dorsey Brothers and Jimmy Dorsey before making his marks with his own bands, the Glenn Miller Army Air Force Band, and as leader of the Glenn Miller Band of the 1950s and '60s. Bob Haggart was a seminal figure in Bob Crosby's big band of the 1930s, which sought to preserve the spirit of New Orleans jazz well after most bands had moved on to a more streamlined brand of swing; he remains a highly respected bassist-composer-arranger today. Trumpeter Bill Dillard recalls, among other things, what he learned in travels to Europe in the 1930s. Trumpeter Erskine Hawkins, billed as "the Twentieth Century Gabriel," shares stories behind the creation of several of his big band's best-remembered numbers. Clarinet star Johnny Mince offers recollections of two leading white bands of the Swing Era: Ray Noble's and Tommy Dorsey's; he played in both bands when they were at their peaks. Tenor saxist George Kelly, whom you might have seen in the movie *Moscow on the Hudson*, recalls the heyday of Harlem's "Home of the Happy Feet" where Lindy Hoppers and jazz players inspired one another, the Savoy Ballroom. Clarinetist Mahlon Clark, drummer Sonny Igoe, and trumpeter Joe Wilder offer not only impressions of such band leaders as Will Bradley, Ray McKinley, Woody Herman, and Lionel Hampton, but worthwhile commentary on the more commercial music fields in which they toiled after the big bands faded. Buddy Morrow achieved success as a trombonist

5

in other musicians' bands during the Swing Era, then leading his own rhythm-and-blues-tinged big band after the Swing Era, and finally returning to the sounds of his youth as leader of the Tommy Dorsey Band for the past dozen or so years. Oliver Jackson, in demand as a drummer with both small groups (Earl Hines and Erroll Garner) and big bands (Hampton and Goodman), offers his perspectives on his craft. Bucky and John Pizzarelli talk of their unique father-and-son guitar partnership; Bucky's comments on today's musicians echo those I've heard from any number of musicians of his generation and before. Ken Peplowski, a younger "keeper of the flame," details his rise from sideman with Buddy Morrow to well-respected solo clarinetist. Dick Hyman, who's produced and emceed concerts that could comfortably use the talents of all of the musicians in this book (and have in fact used the talents of a number of them), has happy memories of both the bustling New York studio scene of the 1950s and '60s and of his re-emergence onto the jazz club and concert scene (as a pianist/composer/impresario) in the years since then. And drummer Jake Hanna speaks out—try and stop him!—on subjects ranging from Woody Herman and Harry James to music on TV and records in recent times.

Earlier, shorter versions of most of these profiles originally appeared in *The Mississippi Rag*. I previously wrote about Sonny Igoe and Oliver Jackson for *Modern Drummer*. And I've done brief pieces about various musicians in this book for an assortment of other publications. The profiles of Bob Haggart, Johnny Mince, and Dick Hyman are appearing for the first time in this book. All profiles are written in the present tense; conditions described are those at the time of the original interview (the date of which will be found at the end of each profile). Concise updates have been appended to some profiles as needed.

The paths of the assorted musicians in this book have crossed on occasion—sometimes in ways you might expect (working in the same bands or at jazz festivals), occasionally in ways you might not expect (in 1974, for example, Bucky Pizzarelli drew Bill Challis out of virtual retirement to arrange a unique album, *The Bucky Pizzarelli Guitar Quintet Plays Beiderbecke/Challis*, on Monmouth Evergreen). Some of the musicians profiled in this book

INTRODUCTION

have never met—much less worked with—one another. Yet in a broad sense, all of these figures—despite the diverse directions they may have chosen—may be viewed as coming out of a long, and continuing, American musical tradition. Let's listen to the recollections of these varied musicians "in the mainstream."

—CHIP DEFFAA
January 1991

A "Bright Future Star" from Nashville

"We've had a request for 'Jubilee,' " declares Doc Cheatham. He leans back, elbows jutting outward, trumpet pointed toward the ceiling, and begins to blow, the individual notes coming sure, clean, and jaunty. He creates an illusion of gaining momentum as he plays. And then he sings, beckoning us to "come and join the jubilee" in a voice high and cheery, the words enunciated with a decorous precision. He picks up the horn again for another chorus. I like the *sound* he gets, golden, nicely rounded, radiating a quiet joy. Not enough musicians today pay attention to the sound of their horns; such masters as Armstrong and Beiderbecke won you with their sounds, not just their phrasing and ideas.

Now, however, Cheatham's playing grows softer. Is his energy beginning to flag? (He is, after all, in his 80s.) Or is he pacing himself, saving up his strength for the finish? It seems the latter, for suddenly his notes rise upward with unexpected drive. The highest notes that he hits can be hit by many young trumpeters with little apparent effort—and also with little drama. Cheatham gives you the drama, creating more impact by hitting his high C than many trumpeters would by hitting higher notes. His higher notes retain a sunny wholeness; they never screech.

He greets acquaintances in the house at Sweet Basil, the

8

Greenwich Village jazz club where he plays at brunch every Sunday—musicians of varying abilities, whom he soon has sitting in with his quartet. But he remains the show. He plays "It's Been a Long, Long Time" thoughtfully, offering us that sentiment-rich melody like a gift. When he sings "I Can't Get Started" (which he enunciates with an almost British inflection as "I cahn't get started"), he alters one line to "Maxine Sullivan has had me to tea." Aficionados know it is a tribute to a singer he admired from the first time he worked with her, early in her career, to their frequent team-ups in her final years. When he plays a Billie Holiday song, some may know he played behind Holiday on records in 1944 and on TV in 1957. He mentions he was attracted to her ("I tried to hit on her several times, but I wasn't fast enough"). When he drops a reference to Ma Rainey, he is not just conjuring up a name from an almost mythical "Jazz Age," he is remembering a blues singer with whom he recorded in 1926.

Some people are no doubt here simply because Cheatham's music is so accessible, so together, and so appealing in a down-to-earth way. In his mid 80s, Cheatham is still making lyrical music with an unassuming charm that I can't imagine anyone completely resisting—and still coming up with energized final choruses of surprising verve. And some people are no doubt here because they're fascinated by the jazz history Cheatham represents. The little anecdotes he'll occasionally tell between songs are part of his appeal, no less than the music that he creates.

To learn more of his history, I got together with Cheatham at his tidy Lexington Avenue apartment. We sat at the kitchen table in those high-backed wooden chairs that demand good posture, and Adolphus Anthony Cheatham, as he was actually named when he was born on June 13, 1905 in Nashville, Tennessee, reflected on his lengthy career.

"There was no music in Nashville at all, during those days. It's a college town—nothing but schools there," Cheatham recalls. "We had in our neighborhood a fellow who was a dean of a little church, a chapel. He had an idea that he would like to form a club for the kids in the neighborhood called 'The Bright Future

Stars.' I got about six or seven of us kids together—I must have been about 12; we were all very young—and he got us some used, beat-up, old instruments that were given to him, maybe from some of the local stores. I think he had a trombone and he got a cornet and drum, and a violin—that's about all. And my father bought me a used cornet of my own. Our club would meet once a week at this little frame church. This dean wasn't a musician; he just had an idea that he wanted to do something for the kids. Now a lot of circus musicians lived in Nashville. When the circus season was over, they'd come home. And so he had one of the trumpet players from the circus band come by once a week to give us instructions. He was a heavy drinker and we smelled whisky on his breath. Those circus musicians drank a lot, you know. We'd give him like 25 cents apiece whenever he'd come to teach us. I wanted the drum but he said, 'No, with your lips you would make a better cornet player than a drummer.' I accepted that.

"And we went along, practically taught ourselves. He helped us a lot, but he didn't give us music theory; he just did the best he could and made that little money. But I was very anxious to learn; I think two or three of us out of the group were really interested in learning to play music. We got where we were sounding pretty good for kids. We had little uniforms made and we played around for like the neighborhood fair, the church picnic, the county fair. We were playing mostly overtures. The music we had was written for kids, it wasn't nothing heavy. We played little simple marches and things. After about a year, we decided to try to play some jazz. There was no jazz around there. But we wanted to play some 'hot music,' as we called it. But the dean disapproved of that. The church disapproved of that. The whole neighborhood, the whole town disapproved of what we were trying to do. We were sounding like hell, I know that; we were blowing all kind of crazy things. We wanted to do it but he disapproved of it. He broke up the whole club, took the instruments away from the kids. He didn't take mine.

"Only two of us continued with our instruments. When we got to high school, we had a high school band. A saxophone, a trumpet, a violin, and a piano—that's about all we had playing in the high school in Nashville. I can't describe how bad it was. We just played at the high school, to bring the kids into the auditorium. We sounded like hell but I was very interested. I played all day when I was at home and I learned to play cornet very well." (One photo Cheatham has of Nashville's Pearl High School Orchestra shows nine members, one of whom, clarinetist Jerry Blake, three years Cheatham's junior, would in later years play professionally with Cheatham in several bands.)

Cheatham was soon playing two instruments. "My father bought me a B-flat soprano saxophone so I learned to play both the saxophone and the cornet by ear. At church I would go up and play a solo. You know, the people would encourage me. But they didn't like the idea of my playing hot music. They would disapprove of that. There were a lot of simple solos written for cornet—no jazz. I learned these things although I didn't learn to read music. I didn't want to learn to read music because my ears were so good, I didn't think I needed to."

Cheatham adopted then the heroic stance for which he's become well known, his head thrown back, his horn aimed towards the heavens. He recalls: "I have an aunt who was a vocal teacher in Tuskegee University. And she was an opera singer, like. She used to tell me, 'Hold your chest out and your throat back and open your throat.' It feels better, because it opens your throat. A lot of trumpet players hold their horns downwards, and their throat is closed. And you get a better sound when it's open. It's like singing." His aunt told him to use the posture used by singers of opera she admired, such as Galli-Curci and Black Patti.

The Cheatham home was very near the campus of a black college in Nashville, Meharry. "During that time, they had like a little symphony at Meharry Medical College. Out of the bunch of freshmen that would come to the school each year, there would be some guy that could play piano. He would be studying pharmacy or dentistry, but he could also play piano. And there was a drummer, there was a violinist, and that was about all. Because I almost lived right on the campus, I would go up to Meharry and join this little group that played every Sunday. These other guys who were students there didn't know if I was a student or not. We had a guy named Bill Tyson on violin, who was studying medicine. We had a guitar player named Smith, who was studying pharmacy. And Herbert Bloom from New Orleans, a wonderful pianist, was studying pharmacy. They were all students at Meharry. I joined the band because they didn't have a cornet and I wanted to play. They called me Doc—Doc Cheatham: 'This is Doctor Tyson, this is Doctor Cheatham.' They didn't know I wasn't a student. See, that's the way I got the name Doc. And my parents took it up. My mother took it and called me 'Little Doc.' That's how I got that name. I must have been about 15, something like that. My father disapproved of my playing, of course, because he could see the circus musicians— every now and then they would parade and they were drunk, and he disapproved of that. So I had that to contend with. But I just continued to play.

"Our mathematics teacher at the high school was a pretty good piano player. And he managed to get little jobs around town through Vanderbilt University, a white school. So he would go out and play once in a while, like on a Saturday, for a fraternity somewhere in Nashville. And he took me along because I was playing pretty good. I played with him all the time I was in high school. And that's the way I really started to play popular things, in what they called ragtime tempo. That was the style then.

"And then, I went down to the Bijou Theater; all of the famous black artists would come to the Bijou once a week. They were traveling on the T.O.B.A. circuit—that really stood for the Theater Owners' Booking Association but the actors and musicians said it stood for 'Tough on Black Actors.' Shows traveled all the ways in the south from Georgia and Alabama up to Newark, New Jersey, and out to Chicago and St. Louis. These big black artists had no other way to make a living, other than going around this circuit. It would be one week in Atlanta; then after the last show, they'd get on a train and come to Nashville and do a week there. Then they'd go to probably St. Louis and do a week, and Alabama, and places like that.

"Sometimes, when the acts would come to the Bijou Theater, they'd have a piano player, sometimes they'd have a small group. When Ethel Waters came to the Bijou, she had Fletcher Henderson playing the piano with her. Bessie Smith had her pianist. All those blues singers had their pianists. But I was playing saxophone in the pit. The only musicians in the pit were a drummer, a cornet player from New Orleans named Jefferson, the pianist, and myself. I wasn't getting paid, I was sitting in. I wanted to play and there was no other place to play—maybe a dance once a year. I couldn't read a note, but I could fake like hell. So when these acts came in, I would augment what they had. That's how I learned to play with all the blues singers. And I played with all of them: Bessie Smith, Clara Smith, Trixie Smith, Ethel Waters, Ida Cox, and a lot of others that I don't even remember their names.

"The Bijou Theater was the only theater where the black people in Nashville could go. See, that was down in the bottom— we called it the bottom part of the town. It was a nice theater but a very old theater. And that was the only entertainment the people had in Nashville, to go to the theater once a week and see these shows. All these great shows came through Nashville and played the Bijou Theater. I mean Miller and Lyles, and all these big names. There was no other place for them to play but the circuit."

Cheatham had little idea of how hot music may have been developing in other parts of the country.

"We had no way of hearing anybody," he notes. "We were close to New Orleans but we didn't know anything about New Orleans then. So the only thing we could hear was maybe a record would come out, that we could hear that was played once in a while over a radio station. I think Johnny Dunn was the first jazz trumpet player I ever heard in Nashville. Because he was a sensation. He made a record of 'Bugle Blues'—that's 'Bugle Call Rag' [December 21, 1921] and he was the first musician that ever played double time—I mean double tempo—on the blues. He picked the blues up slow, then he played it double time. He's the first one to do that. And he made a record, a 78, which was a sensation—it was what you call a hit record—back in those days. So I heard his record. Then I heard, Paul Whiteman made a recording back in those days and he had a trumpet player by the name of Henry Busse. And Henry Busse and Johnny Dunn—I was inspired by what they were playing. So I copied from them. I started playing what I heard from there. There was nothing else for me to hear. There was no radio back in those days. A crystal set—that's all. And I had one. And I could hear KDKA and all that . . . And I could hear the bands, like Alphonso Trent from Dallas. He had a big band at the hotel, a black band. And I could hear them over my crystal set. And all of these things came and kind of encouraged me. And then I would get, sometimes, a job playing saxophone down in a saloon in Nashville, like on a Saturday night."

Cheatham, at that point, had never heard of King Oliver or Louis Armstrong. "Oh, no. I wasn't hearing about anybody, anybody other than what was there in Nashville. We had a piano player at the barbershop in Nashville who played by ear—and only on the black keys—Dan the Barber. He had one wooden leg. He would go and play by himself at fraternities. There was no other music for the people out there to hear. And he started carrying me out with him to play these fraternities, like at the Peabody College and Vanderbilt. And the students at the college, they enjoyed our duo. There was no one else they could hear. There was nobody. So that went on for a long time and I played at the Bijou for long time. And my father raised hell because I wouldn't go to a college, a medical college! I didn't want to be a doctor."

His father had made quite a good living as a barber—he owned his own home, car, and the three-story building in which he worked, which was unusual in that era—and he wanted his children to be the best they could be, professionally. Cheatham notes: "My brother was a doctor, and my father's two brothers were doctors, and my sister was a supervisor of nurses at the hospital there. All my people were in medicine. And they wanted me to be in it. But I just didn't want to be in the medical profession. My father was very much against what I was doing. My mother just kept quiet; I think she was in my corner. But my father, he didn't like it at all.

"My father had a barbershop right in the middle of Nashville. All of his trade was white. It was a very nice shop—three floors. And he was getting like 35 cents for a haircut, 15 cents for a shave; I don't remember what a shampoo went for, or a massage. On the first floor he had four chairs. On the second floor there were two bathtubs. On the third floor was a tailor shop. A customer could come in there looking like hell, and get a shampoo, shave, haircut, and go up and take a bath—and while he was doing that, his clothes would be cleaned and pressed up on the third floor. And that's the way my father ran that shop. And out of that 35 cents a haircut and 15 cents a shave, he sent my brother to dental school—my brother was a dental surgeon—he sent *his* two brothers through medical school, he sent my adopted sister to college.

"I was the only one left. And I saw my father failing. My father was working like eight, nine hours a day down at that barbershop. And he would spend all day Sunday going to the homes of customers that were sick, that couldn't come to the shop, cutting their hair and shaving them. I said, 'How in the hell can my father send me to school? He's getting old and failing. He's working too hard. All he did for his family—that's enough.' But I didn't say anything."

Cheatham concentrated on his music. He remembers going to see the bands of Paul Whiteman and Ted Lewis—both of whom were major draws throughout the 1920s—when they came to Nashville. "Ted Lewis and I became friends. Because I would always go to hear him. He used to come to Nashville with his group. I'd heard his records before that, actually. I ran into him here in New York a couple of times before he died [in 1971], and he had never forgotten me. He always was nice to me." In addition to the singing for which he is most remembered today, Lewis played clarinet and alto sax; his records sold so well in the early and mid 1920s that he was probably the best-known reed player player in the country.

Cheatham, meanwhile, "stayed at the Bijou Theater. Once in a while a show would come in, and they would want me to play in the band. Like they had a jazz band on stage and they heard me play in the pit, and they'd say, 'Get that doctor up there!' So I'd go up and play with them," he recalls. "Then they wanted to take me on the road. And I went on the road with two or three of those show bands. It was tough because you never got your money. They would give you like $10 or $12. We didn't worry about sleeping because you could get a room for $2 or $3 a week. And people would feed you, just out of sympathy for us. So we wasn't worried about that and we went on the road. But things got so bad with one show, headed by a comedian—I forget his name—it had to break up because no one was getting paid and I went back to Nashville." Bandleader John "Bearcat" Williams and pianist Mary Lou Williams—who were not yet married to each other—were among the musicians in one show with which Cheatham toured, he recalls. One of Cheatham's trips took him up to Atlantic City, New Jersey, where he tried to join Charlie Johnson's band at the Paradise. However, his reading skills were not good enough yet to execute Johnson's charts and he only lasted one night with the band. He picked up other jobs when he could.

Cheatham remembers touring with a show starring Clarence Muse, who went on to make a name for himself as an actor in black motion pictures, and another built around "Sunshine Sammy," a black child actor in early silent "Our Gang" comedy film shorts. "I'd only tour with a show for a few weeks because when they were getting to pay you, they had no money. They'd give you like $5 or $6, and you could live on that. The very last show I traveled with was Sunshine Sammy's Review. Sunshine Sammy—his real name was Ernie something—was a hell of a dancer. His father decided to take him on the road because he was a big star of the 'Our Gang' comedies. And he formed a unit to take on the T.O.B.A. circuit, with a singer and a comedian and maybe a couple of chorus girls dancing. But on payday, his father would always come up short with the money. He was looking out for his son, see what I mean? It looked like he had plenty of money. But they didn't pay us. They would just give us handouts. And when we got to the Grand Theater in Chicago, he said he didn't have any money—he was lying—and he had owed us money from weeks back. The show broke up in Chicago." He was disappointed—but on the other hand, if a show did have to break up in the mid 1920s, there was no better place for that to have happened than Chicago. Some of the greatest jazz players in the country were concentrated in Chicago at that time. Once Cheatham became aware of the scene, he knew he'd left Nashville for good. It was 1925. Cheatham stayed briefly with an uncle living in Chicago. To earn a few bucks, he "got a job washing dishes in a cafeteria down in the Loop. The dishes got so heavy around about 12:00; I never saw so many dirty dishes in my life. I got to the place where I couldn't take any more of that and I stopped. Meanwhile, Jerome Carrington, who had played piano in our band [The Sunshine Sammy Revue] got a good job with Charlie Cooke's Band, a great big band that played dance music (they didn't know about jazz then) at White City [Ballroom]. And he took me out on the South Side—I didn't know anything about Chicago—and he said, 'I got a room here and you can stay with me. I'm working, and I can help you out when I get to eat.' We'd eat some beans or whatever he could get. So he took me out and I stayed in this woman's apartment. I had no money.

"And he took me to hear—Joe Oliver. [Cheatham pronounces the name with a kind of reverence; Oliver is still, obviously, one of the greats for him.] He took me to hear Freddie Keppard. He took me to hear Jimmie Noone. He took me to the theater where Samuel Stewart was playing, and I heard all those.

"There were *no* Chicago musicians playing in Chicago at that time because the New Orleans musicians had come to Chicago— Chicago was full of them. And they were hiring only New Orleans musicians in Chicago. So I would just listen every night, I would go to hear Joe Oliver. I couldn't go in the clubs, but in Chicago you have alley-ways. So I could go in the alley, and the back of the bandstand would be right there, you know I could sit down and hear. That's the way I heard Joe Oliver and Freddie Keppard and all of the New Orleans musicians." Oliver was a hero to him, a role model. He'd walk behind Oliver. If Oliver wore a cap, then he would wear a cap like him. Keppard was a stronger, louder, rougher player than Oliver; but Oliver, in his judgment, played with more feeling. Both fascinated him; he wishes the talents of both were more fully captured on records.

He had never heard this kind of music before. Certainly he wasn't playing anything at that level then. As he puts it: "When I got to Chicago, I knew that I could forget about it! Because what I was playing was nothing."

Louis Armstrong was playing in New York in Fletcher Henderson's Band when Cheatham arrived in Chicago. In fact, Cheatham has vivid memories of Armstrong's return in November 1925. "Before Louis came, they had trucks with banners with Louis' name on them going all around Chicago: 'Louis Armstrong's Coming Back to Chicago!' They had a record playing all of his things. You could hear it all over the South Side: 'Louis's Coming Back to Chicago.' " When Armstrong got back to Chicago, he began playing in the band led by his wife, Lil, at the Dreamland Cafe. He was soon making his first records under his own name (his previous records had been with Henderson or King Oliver), the Hot Fives. In 1926, he doubled at the Dreamland Cafe and at the Vendome Theater.

In the meantime, Cheatham was trying to get a union card so he could play in Chicago. He went to the headquarters of the union local for black musicians (racially segregated locals were the norm then) and learned that the membership fee was beyond his means. He recalls: "The president of the union was a woman named Lottie Hightower. She said, 'Where are you from?' 'I'm from Nashville, Tennessee.' She said, 'Yeah, I graduated from Fisk University in Nashville. I'll give you a card.' And she gave me one for free! She introduced me to Lillian Armstrong, who had also graduated from Fisk University. Between the two of them, they helped me. Lillian carried me out on gigs with my cornet. And she encouraged me. And then she said, 'I'm going to get you a job.'

"So she told Louis. Louis had just come back to Chicago. Later, that's when they started making the Hot Five records. And what happened was—Albert Wynn [a trombonist from New Orleans] had a band at the Dreamland [in 1926]: Albert Wynn and his Creole Jazz Band. Lil told him, 'If you could help, do something to help this boy from Nashville,' you know. And Louis came to the Dreamland and spoke to Al Wynn. They were talking over in the corner, and then they came over and met me, and Louis said—and he was playing at the Vendome Theater then, he was there for a long time with Erskine Tate's band—and Louis said, 'How'd you like to go and play for me on a Thursday at the Vendome Theater? I'm going to take off that day.'

"I said, 'You can't be talking to *me*.' Because I was hungry, see what I mean. I said, 'Damn, Louis, yes, I will do that.'

"He said, 'You go there and nobody's going to say a damn thing to you. I want you to go over there.' I said, 'OK.' In the meantime, Al Wynn wanted me to be one of his members in the band at the Dreamland. And the manager didn't want to hire me because I wasn't from New Orleans. I was a newcomer in Chicago; he didn't know anything about me. So Louis was very, very in with Al Capone. Louis could do anything he wanted to. Capone loved Louis. Louis was a big shot then. So through Al Capone and Louis Armstrong, they got me a job in the Dreamland, told the manager of the Dreamland to hire me so he hired me. Because Louis and Capone both said to hire me. So that's how I got a job at the Dreamland Cafe with Albert Wynn. Otherwise, I would never get a job in Chicago, because I was not from New Orleans."

Cheatham remembers well his experience at the Vendome. Erskine Tate's orchestra had to accompany the feature film (movies were still silent in 1926), as well as play its own featured bit. "I went over to the rehearsal. At that time they had silent movies only, and the musicians had parts to play, cues to play with the film. So I went to this rehearsal, and I went and sat in the first row, right by the pit. And the guys came in one at a time and took their seats. And nobody said a damn thing to me. They didn't even look at me. So Erskine Tate came in and got up on the stand. In the meantime, Tate had a brother playing lead trumpet in his pit orchestra.

"So I was right here, and Tate was on the rail, and Tate's brother was here. So I said, 'Louis sent me. He won't be able to make it, so he told me to come over and play for him Thursday.' Tate's brother said, 'Well, come on around and sit in the pit.' So I took my cornet and walked around and sat next to him. Nobody else said one word—Tate or nobody. So he would go da-da-da-da-da [Cheatham simulates a conductor rapping his baton to get attention] and they would play the music for the film, little cues, like. I wasn't reading then, but I could fake like hell. I could get in there and play an A, and if I'm supposed to play an F, I'd play it. I couldn't read a note. But they didn't know it. The music was

19

so simple; it was like a cue. [He hums a short phrase.] A certain thing on the film would come up and you'd hear a chord—that's what the music was for the film.

"So, after they rehearsed that, then they rehearsed Louis Armstrong's specialty. Louis at that time featured a song called 'Poor Little Rich Girl.' That was his feature. In the meantime, I had gone to the Vendome to hear Louis as often as I could. I had to go way up to the top balcony for little or no money at all. I would go every day to hear Louis, up in the balcony.

"And so now we rehearsed that. Tate, he had a beautiful arrangement on it. And the band would come up with that big introduction to 'Poor Little Rich Girl.' And then Louis would stand up in the pit and the spotlight would hit him. And then he'd play 'Poor Little Rich Girl.' Solo. And the people—you couldn't get in that theater the whole time Louis was there, it was standing room only because of him. He was the biggest thing in the world. I mean, nobody had ever heard anything like this guy.

"So, I rehearsed. No one ever said anything to me. They played the introduction, and Tate said, 'You're supposed to stand up after the introduction.' I said, 'Oh, I know.' Because I had been there. So then I played the solo—*my* way, you know. Nobody ever said a damned thing to me. I went home, came back Thursday to play the gig for Louis, went and sat in the pit. Still, nobody came over and said, 'What's your name?' Or 'What are you doing here?' I just told Tate's brother that Louis had told me to come. Louis had told me, 'Man, nobody's going to say nothing to you.' And they didn't. So that Thursday, I got in the pit and we played the music for the film. Then the overture came. This place, this theater was packed, jammed. Then we got to Louis' solo, 'Poor Little Rich Girl.' We got to the introduction, and I stood up and the spotlight hit me right here. And the people started *screaming!* That's the way they did with Louis. You couldn't hear one note Louis played until they stopped applauding and screaming. So they did the same thing for me—for about a second, until they realized, 'That's not Louis.' And everything just died down. Man, I felt like hell. I felt like hell!

"I played the number my way. It was the only way I could play. I wasn't *nothing* compared with Louis' playing in Chicago.

But I played the solo. And I got $85. Louis paid me $85. But I didn't do a damn thing.

"And Louis came back again a couple weeks later and said, 'Doc, do you want to play that for me?' I said, 'Sure.' And I did again! I did it twice for Louis. And nobody said a word. Erskine Tate didn't even come over and say, 'Thank you, Doc' or nothing. Because he was afraid. Because Louis was so big. No one said a damn thing. None of those musicians in that pit spoke to me, other than Tate's brother. They didn't come over and introduce themselves. They were being mean! Naturally they felt bad because Louis would take off. They didn't like that. And me? I wasn't known in Chicago. Nobody knew a thing about me. The thing I couldn't understand then was why Louis would ask me. Because there were trumpet players in Chicago then that could have done a better job than I could, and he *knew*. There were trumpet players from New Orleans all over Chicago then. Why did he come to me? Other than I'd say maybe Lil—I don't know, it took me years to find out why. I found out about three years ago when Johnny Guarnieri, the piano player, said to me, 'You know, Louis told me why he asked you. He said it was because he liked you, you were a gentleman, and all the musicians from New Orleans were very jealous of him; they envied him.' Louis didn't want to bother with them because they were giving him a hard time. I never saw too much of Louis after that. But whenever I would run into him, he would call me 'Professor.' I played with him at the Strand Theater—I substituted in his big band with Luis Russell.

"I stayed there at the Dreamland for a while. Then that guy at the Dreamland wasn't paying off either, because Bill Bottoms who had run Dreamland was part of the Capone gang. And when he gave it up, these other guys took it. And then I was working there, and getting handouts for that. The club wasn't doing any business. So like on a Monday or a Tuesday, or whatever days that we would want some money, we'd go in his office and he would open a big ledger, and he would give us like $10, and he would sign Doc Cheatham's name up here, so-and-so a date, and that's all. I signed my name to it. And that's the way we, the band, even Al Wynn, all of us, we wasn't getting paid anything. But I didn't mind, because I was living practically free. I was making a few dollars, and getting some beans and stuff; I managed to live. I was 135 pounds. I've always been thin. But I was eating beans and things like that.

"During that year that I was at the Dreamland, 1926, I made a recording with Ma Rainey, on the soprano saxophone. It was blues. Ma Rainey was singing a whole lot of blues songs, and I was playing soprano saxophone—with Al Wynn's Band. That was the first time I ever had a chance to meet Ma Rainey, and I thought she was all right." Personnel details for some of Ma Rainey's sessions remain hazy. Although Brian Rust's *Jazz Records: 1896–1942* discography does not indicate the presence of Cheatham on any of Rainey's sessions, it seems likely that he participated in the Chicago session that produced Rainey's Paramount recordings of "Sissy Blues," "Down in the Basement," and "Broken Soul Blues," which Rust dates only as circa August 1926; the only player on that session Rust identifies with absolute certainty is Al Wynn on trombone. Rust also indicates Cheatham may have been present on pianist Tiny Parham's first side, "Um-Ta-Da-Da-Da," recorded for the Black Patti label circa June 28, 1927.

Cheatham wasn't working much, but, he recalls: "I was just excited to be in Chicago, in that environment, with Louis and all those guys. The whole time I was there, I wanted to learn. Because I knew I wasn't playing nothing compared with those guys from New Orleans."

Cheatham sold his saxophone and concentrated on his cornet—soon replaced by a trumpet. "After hearing Joe Oliver and Freddie Keppard and those guys, that was it! There were no saxophone players around there doing anything to amount to anything. So it was trumpets. So that's why I just went with the trumpet. I sold my saxophone. And I got rid of the cornet because Louis played trumpet. He *had* played cornet; then he switched [in 1928] to trumpet. So I bought a trumpet—the same kind of trumpet he had.

"I couldn't get any work around there, other than the Dreamland. (And that club got so bad that eventually we had to leave.) But I wanted to learn the New Orleans music. So I stayed almost two years in Chicago, learning. And I went *every night*, I would go to hear one or the other, Louis Armstrong and there was Shirley Clay [trumpeting in the bands of Detroit Shannon and Carroll Dickerson in the 1925–27 period] and there was Bob Shoffner [trumpeting with King Oliver, 1925–27]. I went up to [clarinetist] Jimmie Noone—he was very nice to me—at the Apex Club. I had no money but I didn't have to pay anything because Jimmie liked me. And he would invite me to sit down, and I would sit down and listen to him. Benny Goodman came up there almost every night. And I saw Benny and Bix. I met all those guys. They were going to be there every night to hear Jimmie Noone. And I would listen to him, too." Reuben Reeves had attracted a good bit of attention for his trumpeting with Erskine Tate's Band just before Louis Armstrong returned to Chicago from New York, Cheatham recalls; but after Armstrong got back, everybody seemed to forget about Reeves.

Which trumpet player did Cheatham like the most of those he heard?

"Louis! Louis Armstrong. Of course," he says, as if there could be no question. Certainly he had admired others he had heard in person and on records, but once he was exposed to Armstrong's powers, he knew Armstrong was the king. And a good bit of Armstrong's influence remains evident in Cheatham's phrasing today.

Like most musicians, he had been greatly impressed by cornetists Red Nichols and Bix Beiderbecke when their records first appeared. He recalls, "Red Nichols was before Bix. The problem was, Red Nichols was a sensation but he wasn't too far ahead of Bix. Bix came in, and then the people started listening to Bix. Because Bix had something different, more beautiful than Red. Red was just a gutbucket, corny jazz trumpet player. He had like a jerky style. Bix came in with smooth harmonies and beautiful chord changes no one had ever done before. He was a musician. Red Nichols was a gutbucket. Well, Red and Miff Mole had something good together that had never been done before also; it was their style of jazz. I said Red was corny because after listening to Bix, you had to say that Red Nichols was corny. But he was a sensation. And he started something. The trouble was,

Louis came in so quickly after them that everybody forgot about Bix and Red Nichols. Louis washed them all away! But I liked Bix, I learned a lot from Bix also. I learned a lot from Red Nichols, also, because I used to listen to him. I learned a lot from all trumpet players that I liked to hear."

Cheatham's main priority back then, however, was trying to master the New Orleans style of playing trumpet. "And so I learned all of the New Orleans tunes. The Dixieland players play the same tunes but in a different tempo. And I studied to read music with a woman piano teacher. I caught on right away. I could read like a top, then! But I had no place to play in Chicago. You had to be from New Orleans to get the jobs. But I didn't care, because I realized that I wasn't nothing compared to what I was hearing up there. So I learned all the New Orleans melodies, and how they played them, the arrangements and the forms that they played; I wrote all these things out—I have two books—I wrote all the cues and every damned thing out." The New Orleans musicians, he felt, were serious about their music. There were some white Dixieland bands that wore funny hats, jumped about on stage, playing New Orleans music in a vigorous, crowd-pleasing way that struck him as being a burlesque of the real music.

He learned the real New Orleans music and worked at developing a style of his own. "I had no style because in Nashville it was very corny what I was trying to do. Nashville, you know, was a cow town. So I was trying to learn the New Orleans style of playing cornet. That's why I was listening to Louis—and I listened to Louis all the time. And Freddy Keppard. I listened to Red Allen. And all of them had different ways of playing New Orleans music. You could tell one from the other after you knew them. That's what I wanted to learn to do. And that's what I learned to do. I stayed in Chicago two years. Then one day, a girl from Minneapolis came to Chicago, and asked me would I like to go to Philadelphia. I said, 'I'd never been to Philadelphia.'

"She told me Bobby Lee needed a lead trumpet player for his band in Philadelphia. I said, 'I don't know anything about being a lead trumpet player.' In Chicago, I had never heard

24

anything about a lead trumpet player. Trumpet players played everything—lead, solos, whatever. But I wasn't doing anything and I was getting to the place now where I needed to do something. They sent me a ticket to Philadelphia. I stayed at Bobby Lee's house, and I played lead trumpet two seasons in his 10-piece band at the Sea Girt Inn in New Jersey. Juan Tizol was in that band. And then that place closed or changed policy or something and I was out of that job."

Cheatham played briefly with Wilbur De Paris in Philadelphia but wasn't satisfied with what De Paris paid him, so he moved on to New York, where he played a few weeks in a band on the Keith vaudeville circuit.

"Then Chick Webb heard about me being a great lead trumpet. I was playing hell out of lead trumpet. You know, I forgot all about solos, jazz. I thought I was doing the greatest thing in the world by being a nice lead trumpet player. So Chick invited me to play with him. When I went to the job, all the musicians sat down and they left the first chair open. Nobody wanted to play lead trumpet in New York, because there's no solos attached to the lead trumpet. So I just went on and sat down on that chair. I played this one gig with Chick—a dance somewhere downtown. Johnny Hodges was in his band then. And Chick was crazy about me. He wanted me to join the band. And he had a pretty good band. But I only played with Chick that one night," Cheatham recalls. "What happened was, Sam Wooding's band came to New York from Europe. They had been touring there. And Sam Wooding needed a trumpet player and a drummer and a trombone player and a pianist. So he took [pianist] Freddy Johnson. And he approached me to go to Europe with him. I thought that was a great thing for me—going to Europe with Sam Wooding! So I immediately joined Sam Wooding and went to Europe with him [1928]. And we went to Berlin. Tommy Ladnier was in that band also. And I was happy because Tommy and I became friends. And he was a hell of a New Orleans trumpet player. And that's what I wanted to do. So he and I roomed together. And he would show me a lot of things about playing trumpet, New Orleans style. So I was happy to be in that band."

Wooding's band—which in 1928 was a more prestigious

band to be in than Webb's (which had only been formed the year before)—had first gone to Europe in 1925 as part of an all-black revue, *Chocolate Kiddies*. The show was a hit with European audiences; the band—the best-received part of the show—kept touring on its own after the show itself had closed. Between 1925 and 1927, Wooding had scored hits with his big band, offering a mix of dance music, show music, novelties, and hot jazz, in Germany, France, Turkey, the Soviet Union, Argentina, and a variety of other spots. It played an important role in disseminating American jazz, and paved the way for later European tours by other American bands, such as Ellington's, Armstrong's, and Cab Calloway's. (For more details on Wooding's career, see my profile of him in *Voices of the Jazz Age*.) The edition of Wooding's Band that Cheatham joined also included trombonist Al Wynn, who had led the band at the Dreamland Cafe; clarinetist/alto saxist/vocalist Jerry Blake, who had gone to high school with Cheatham (and had also worked in Wynn's Band and in Bobby Lee's band); clarinetist/tenor saxist Gene Sedric, best remembered today for his longtime association with Fats Waller; and clarinetist/alto saxist/vocalist Willie Lewis, who would later lead one of the most popular big swing bands in Europe.

Cheatham notes: "I stayed in Europe three years with Sam Wooding. I was treated very well. You know, as a newcomer in the band, I wasn't paid as much as the older guys. I was getting $75 a week. The other guys were getting $125. Being young, I didn't worry about that. I played all the lead trumpet. In fact, I held up that band. The lead trumpet player is the most important member of the band, because they depend on him to lead; that's why he's called the lead player. But the audience don't listen to a lead trumpet player; I just realized that in the last few years. Nobody knows who's playing lead; they hear the band, that's all. But the guy that comes out and plays a solo, they notice him. But I was happy with what I was doing. I said, 'Now, I'm probably getting somewhere.' "

Cheatham had just turned 23 when he first arrived in Europe. Unlike a number of other musicians in the band (some of whom, he suspected, probably considered him a bit of a sissy), he wasn't much interested in drinking and carousing. Cheatham's father might have considered him rebellious for choosing to become a musician, but he really hadn't rebelled that much against his upbringing. He behaved as he felt was proper for a gentleman. He was not about to become the kind of "low life" musician his father had warned he'd become.

"I never drank whiskey, I never drank beer. I never drank wine in my life! Because I remember my father said, 'You're going to be just like that trombone player in the circus; he's a drunk, running all over looking like a fool. He hasn't got anything. What has he got? Look at that? That's what you—' My father always told me that," Cheatham recalls. "The only thing I do is smoke cigars. And my father was responsible for that; when he would go to work, I'd go out on the porch and get his cigar butts. But that's the only habit I have.

"When I was in Europe with Sam Wooding, all the musicians and entertainers did was drink. I used to go by the bars. They used to have a favorite bar in Paris—I forget the name—where all the musicians would go. All the entertainers would meet there early in the morning. There'd be these chorus girls with these little thin glasses; one girl would have something pink, another would have something green or blue. One gal had a drink of something that looked like bilgewater: 'That's Pernod. That's a good drink.' I said, 'That looks like bilge.' But I told this girl, 'Let me taste that.' Like to burn my tongue on it. She said, 'That's good for you, to get your appetite together.' Some of them drank that Pernod in the morning. And they'd go work at night and they're drinking at night. You know, oh ha ha, they'd do a show and everybody's happy to go to the bar. [He makes sounds of a drunken reveler.] After you get through working, they'd go and drink. I watched all that stuff. And every one of those people is dead.

"I've played with great guys that suffered from mistreating themselves, that got to where they couldn't play a note. I could see that. Some great musicians I know very well just didn't think. We have one right in the nursing home down here, who was one of the world's greatest jazz trombone players—Sandy Williams. I go there to see him. He started to cry, telling me, 'I was thinking about all those 45 years I was drunk.' He can't play. And during the days when he was flying, he was a great musician. What a pity; they just didn't think that the time's coming. And that was always on my mind. Every time I turned around, I could hear my father's words. So I didn't fool with that."

Wooding's band received red-carpet treatment, Cheatham recalls, playing top theaters and clubs. It was more than just a band, it was a full-fledged entertainment unit, much as Paul Whiteman's Orchestra was. Most of the musicians doubled on instruments, a number of them sang (by themselves or in combinations), some could even offer comedy. The band had so extensive a repertoire, Cheatham says, that if it was booked to do a run at a theater, it could perform a three-hour show nightly—and never give exactly the same show twice. Clubs booking the band could dispense with their own singers and dancers; Wooding's troupe had all bases covered. And the men could kick out with honest hot jazz on numbers like "Tiger Rag" and "Milenberg Joys." Indeed, Wooding's Band was the first introduction to live American jazz for many Europeans (including, for example, two of the first important European writers about jazz, Hugues Panassie and Charles Delaunay). Wooding's band toured to enthusiastic audiences from 1925 to 1931. But being abroad for most of those years cost the band something; it got out of touch with the latest developments in jazz in the U.S.

Cheatham recalls: "In 1930, we were in Paris, and I heard over the shortwave radio, a band playing like hell from America. I said, 'Who is this damned band?' And then they announced it was McKinney's Cotton Pickers from the Graystone Ballroom in Detroit. I said, 'Jesus Christ.' Because being in Europe with Sam Wooding, he had the only jazz band over there. And you know, he had been over there before. And his style was kind of corny. And being over there so long—you know how it is, over here things had progressed; jazz was changing, getting to be a different thing. When I heard the Cotton Pickers, I said, 'I can't believe this. Oh, I'd give anything to play in that band!' That's the way I felt. And at that time, Louis [Armstrong] had just recorded 'I Can't Give You Anything but Love,' which was one of the things that tore up Europe on that same tour. [Wooding's Band recorded that song in 1929. It was Armstrong's first hit pop recording, one of the numbers that helped make him an international favorite.] So I said, 'Hell, I'm going back to New York.' I left Sam Wooding in Paris—the band was playing at the Ambassador—I put in my notice and came back here. I was tired of listening to Sam Wooding all the time."

The first thing Cheatham did when he got back to New York, he says, was to go to the Savoy Ballroom. "And who was up there but Cab Calloway. And I never heard anything, I never saw anything like this guy! I was standing back there at the Savoy, listening. The band was playing like hell. Of course, you couldn't compare his band with any other band because it was a show band; it was Cab's band, playing Cab's music, and everything was written for what he did, jumping and carrying on. It wasn't a solo band or anything—but it was great, so I didn't mind that. I just listened to it and went back to my room overnight." Calloway had not yet recorded the number that would make him nationally famous, "Minnie the Moocher" (that would come the following year), but he had already developed his unique, flamboyant performing style. Cheatham had no idea then that he'd spend more than eight years of his life playing lead trumpet in Calloway's band.

He went to Chicago for a bit with another band. Then, "When I came back to New York, Benny Carter asked me, would I like to go to join McKinney's Cotton Pickers. I couldn't believe that! So he and I went to Detroit. Don Redman was leading the band at that time. I rehearsed with the Cotton Pickers under Redman's conductorship, until he left. Benny Carter was there, getting ready to take over the leadership. I read all that music they played, and they liked me, so McKinney hired me. Then Don left and Benny came and took over in a couple of days. And I stayed with the Cotton Pickers. Man, I loved that band! That was the one band I wanted to play with."

When I asked Cheatham how he'd rate the Cotton Pickers, comparing them to Fletcher Henderson, he exclaimed:

"There was no other band in the world like the Cotton Pickers! This band played at the Graystone. We played a battle of music with Fletcher. We outplayed Fletcher. We outplayed everybody that came in. Because it was an entertaining band. See, Fletcher had a good band but it wasn't an entertaining band. If you know anything about the Cotton Pickers, they did everything. All kinds of songs, and all the beautiful songs that they did that Don Redman wrote and arranged for them. And that was much greater. And they had a good swinging band. They had all the great players. They had Rex Stewart in there when I went there, and Joe Smith and Quentin Jackson—Fletcher Henderson eventually hired those guys out of the Cotton Pickers; he practically broke up the band.

"I was playing lead. I was playing lead from then on, I very seldom had a solo to play. McKinney decided to break up the band to a certain extent because he wanted to get rid of Benny Carter, he wanted to get rid of Billy Taylor, the bass player. Not that he didn't like them—but because the money wasn't coming in to pay those guys. So he wanted to get cheaper musicians. So Benny left and I left. Billy Taylor left. I don't know who else left." Cheatham participated in one recording session by the Cotton Pickers, under the direction of Benny Carter, which yielded the sides "Do You Believe in Love at Sight?" and "Wrap Your Troubles in Dreams" (September 8, 1931).

"In the meantime, before I left, I had a telegram from Walter Thomas, the sax player who was directing Cab Calloway's Band, asking me to come to New York and join Calloway. I came to New York immediately and joined Cab at the Cotton Club. Cab was having all kind of lead trumpet player problems. I sat in the band and played his music right on down, the show music and everything. I was reading like a top. There was nothing I couldn't read." Cheatham married one of the Cotton Club dancers, a marriage that lasted seven years. (Cheatham had previously been married very briefly, shortly after his return to the U.S. in 1930.)

Occasionally, Cheatham got to solo a bit with Calloway ("I've Got the World on a String" and "I Gotta Right to Sing the Blues" are two examples) but such opportunities, he notes, came "very seldom. So all those years passed without my being a soloist." He didn't mind at the time. "I wanted to be a good player. And if it was lead trumpet player, that's what I wanted to do. But it hurt me—it hurt! Because after all those big bands went, what

DOC CHEATHAM

Doc Cheatham (top photo courtesy of Doc Cheatham, bottom photo by Len Kunstadt).

In this previously unpublished photo, taken in Atlantic City in the 1920s, Doc Cheatham is the trumpeter in the back row who's got a saxophone around his neck. He played both instruments in those days. (Courtesy of the Institute of Jazz Studies.)

Doc Cheatham (front row, third from left), playing trumpet in Cab Calloway's Orchestra, 1934. (Author's collection.)

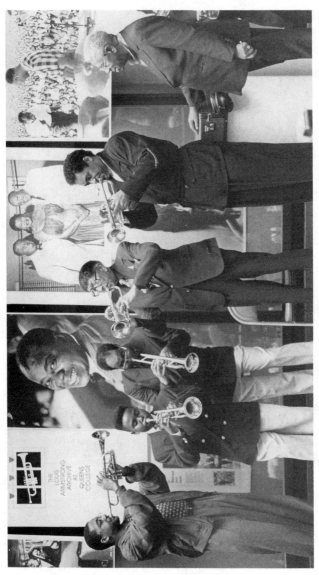

Doc Cheatham leads a stellar group of trumpeters—all playing horns that had once belonged to Louis Armstrong—on "St. Louis Blues" at the dedication of the Armstrong Archive at Queens College, September 5, 1991: (from left to right) Wynton Marsalis, 12-year-old Abate Isles of the Armstrong Middle School, Jimmy Owens, Doc Cheatham, and Jon Faddis; Dizzy Gillespie lends moral support. (Courtesy of Ron Cannava/Queens College.)

was I going to do?" Cheatham played lead on such memorable Calloway recordings as "Reefer Man" (June 9, 1932), "The Man From Harlem" (November 30, 1932), "Kickin' the Gong Around" (December 18, 1933), "Moon Glow" (January 22, 1934), "Keep That Hi-De-Ho in Your Soul" (January 21, 1935), "She's Tall, She's Tan, She's Terrific" (August 24, 1937), "The Jumpin' Jive" (July 17, 1939), "Pluckin' the Bass" (August 30, 1939), "Give, Baby, Give" and "A Bee Gezindt" (both November 20, 1939). Among the musicians of note who played in the Calloway band at one point or another during Cheatham's tenure were Eddie Barefield, Ben Webster, Chu Berry, Milt Hinton, Cozy Cole, and Dizzy Gillespie. They got exposure, but the charismatic Calloway himself was always far and away the main attraction; the band's primary responsibility was to collectively project the same kind of exuberance and gusto he projected. Calloway paid his men top dollar and they traveled in style. They appeared in such motion pictures as *International House* (1932) and Al Jolson's *The Singing Kid* (1936), and traveled to Europe in 1934.

In 1939, Cheatham left Calloway's Band to join Teddy Wilson's recently formed band at New York's Golden Gate Ballroom (Ben Webster, who had known Cheatham from Calloway's Band and who was now with Wilson, recommended him). "Teddy had a wonderful band. And it was already organized when he hired me. He had a lead trumpet player, Karl George, Harold Baker, and myself. He didn't know what to do with me. So he wrote all the lead parts an octave lower, for me. So there were two playing lead. That gave the band a sound that he wanted. I stayed in that band until the band broke up. The band was so good! A lot of people say that the Savoy people bought out the Golden Gate and closed it down so they wouldn't have the competition. So that broke up that band." Cheatham was in the band when it recorded Wilson's classic "Sweet Lorraine" (December 11, 1939).

He then moved on to Benny Carter's Orchestra. He played on Carter's April 1, 1941 recording session when the band, with Maxine Sullivan on vocals, recorded "Midnight," "What a Difference a Day Made," and an instrumental, "My Favorite Blues." He went on to play with Fletcher Henderson's Band, too. But his playing was not up to par. He felt as if he had worn himself out;

35

the taxing pace of so many years on the road seemed to have caught up with him. Anemic and deeply fatigued, he rested at first in a hospital and then at home. His wife kept after him to get up and get back to work, but he hadn't the energy; she finally left him. He didn't bemoan her decision; he felt comfortable being by himself. He took a day job for a spell, until he felt he had regained some of his strength. (It took him many years, however, he says, before he really regained his stamina.)

From September 1943 to 1945, Cheatham found a satisfying spot for himself as the trumpeter in pianist Eddie Heywood's popular sextet (best remembered for their 1944 recording of "Begin the Beguine," although their recording that same year of "I Can't Believe that You're in Love with Me" is the one to check out for a nice sampling of Cheatham's playing in this period). He remembers his days in Heywood's sextet pleasantly, particularly when they played at New York's Cafe Society, along with Billie Holiday and Mary Lou Williams. One recollection he mentions in passing is that "everybody in that group smoked pot. They had a little room off the bandstand, and some, including Mary Lou and Billie, would smoke pot in there. They would put me outside the door, in a chair smoking a pipe that would cover the fumes of the pot," he recalls. "Mary Lou and I used to live in the same building (she was a floor above me) and we would come home together. She would light up. One time she said, 'Take one.' I said, 'Man, I don't want to smoke.' She said, 'Take one.' So I took a little and blew all the smoke out. She said, 'Don't you waste that!' I said, 'Don't give me that! I don't want to be bothered with that. If I wanted to get high, I would drink. I don't think that's good for your lungs anyway. It can't be good, because you don't know where you got it, you don't know what it is.' But you can't tell people nothing. I never bothered with smoking pot. I'm not fooling with narcotics. I'm not saying pot's bad. I don't know a thing about it. But I just didn't do it. Just like I don't drink."

In 1946, as the Swing Era came to a close, Cheatham played for a bit in Claude Hopkins' Orchestra. But jazz was changing rapidly now, and Cheatham, like many of his generation, was growing less certain of where he fit in. The big bands, the main source of employment for a trumpeter known essentially as a lead player, were folding. Cheatham would have welcomed a chance to work steadily in New York with a combo of his own, but he hadn't established himself as a jazz soloist. And plenty of other, younger trumpeters—extroverted stylists with great technical facility—*had* made names for themselves as soloists in the past decade. He recalls: "I tried to play. And there was Roy Eldridge and all these other soloists coming up in the meantime and playing all these things. I said, 'Jesus Christ, I might as well forget it.' I could never learn anything from Roy Eldridge and Charlie Shavers; those guys; they were just too much. They were too fast. You can't learn anything from guys that play all like Roy. Or Dizzy [Gillespie]. Dizzy used to play like Roy. That style I never tried to learn because of my age." (It took him quite a while to even appreciate what Gillespie was trying to do on trumpet, he notes.) In the mid '40s, there was a revival of interest in New Orleans music in some quarters. He acknowledges: "I could play that. But I wanted a *jazz* style. I was listening. And I was confused. I was listening to Roy and Dizzy and Sweets Edison and Buck Clayton. And all these guys I never heard before. They were just as new to me as Oliver and Louis had been when I was in Chicago. And I couldn't play like these guys. No way. Because I didn't know how. So I knew I'd have to learn. I went through hell around here. You know, a lot of guys wouldn't hire me for a long time because I couldn't play solos. A lot of guys put me down."

Developing himself as a jazz soloist became a goal of his. He still wasn't sure where he'd be able to find a niche for himself, though. In the late '40s, many younger players were going all-out for bebop. He knew he could never be part of that scene; it just wasn't him. Other players were getting into rhythm-and-blues; that music didn't lure him either. And in the meantime, he had bills to pay. He couldn't afford to be too picky about what work he took. He recalls: "I joined a little Latin group. Just to keep my chops together. This was an awful band, just playing the mambos. I was doing the best I could."

Throughout the 1950s, '60s, and even into the '70s, Cheatham wound up spending a good deal of his time playing in Latin (or "Afro/Cuban") bands, including those of Marcelino Guerra,

Perez Prado, and Machito. They weren't all he did—he played swing and traditional jazz as opportunities arose, too (with Vic Dickenson and Wilbur De Paris, and as leader of his own groups)—but the Latin bands helped him keep food on the table. The music wasn't what he would have been playing if he'd had his ideal choice (and he didn't believe playing it would help his development as a jazz soloist), but he did feel comfortable playing it, he says. "Oh, I liked the Latin music."

He adds: "In 1950, I went down to South America with Perez Prado's Band, to Montevideo, and we traveled quite a lot in Chile and Argentina. And I met my wife down there, in a little sea resort town in Uruguay. I really fell for her. I guess we fell for one another. We started corresponding. Then when I went back the second time (in 1951, with Cab Calloway), we got married in Santiago, Chile. I brought her back here. We had two kids, four grandchildren. My daughter's teaching down in Florida. She graduated from Hunter College. My son, I couldn't do anything with him. He just went by the wayside. He's trying to get himself together, living somewhere with some girl. But he went to prison a couple of times. Dope and stuff. Even when he was a young boy, we just couldn't handle him. I think he's straightened himself out." Cheatham's wife, Amanda, works as a domestic today, living during the week with the family that employs her; he is used to shopping and cooking for himself when she's away.

Cheatham made additional trips abroad with the bands of Machito (Japan, 1956), De Paris (Africa, 1957; Europe, 1960), Sammy Price (Europe, 1958), and Herbie Mann (Africa, 1960). In 1957, he participated in the landmark CBS TV broadcast, "The Sound of Jazz," along with such jazz trumpeters as Roy Eldridge, Rex Stewart, Red Allen, and Joe Wilder. He felt shy about soloing in such august company, limiting himself to obbligatos as Billie Holiday sang "Fine and Mellow."

For Cheatham, at this stage in his life, there weren't always good jobs to be had. There were even times, he recalls, when he'd think, "Hell, I'm giving up. There's no work in New York—nobody playing anything but bebop, and I can't play that." He could play Dixieland well—it posed few challenges since the repertoire seemed to be limited to tunes he had learned in Chicago in the 1920s—but he didn't want to be perceived as someone who could *only* play Dixieland. He worked with Wilbur De Paris at Jimmy Ryan's Club in New York and on tour. "I stayed with Wilbur a long time, made a lot of recordings. But I wanted to get into jazz—not just New Orleans music—and it was hard. I ruined a lot of dates with people. I did one with Billy Taylor and I failed. I just couldn't do it. You know, I'd lost all of that in all that time when I was a lead player."

He studied the way other soloists played, he recalls. "I'd go around places and sit in, and play and play. Then I'd sit here and write. Or listen to records. I sat all day long listening to Red Allen. I said, 'That man is out of sight.' All of this confusion. Now what do *I* want to do? I'm trying to decide what I want to do."

By the 1960s, Cheatham had begun to blossom as a soloist. In 1961, he recorded a fine album for Prestige with Shorty Baker, *Shorty and Doc*. From 1960 to 1965, he led his own groups in New York. But Doc Cheatham's still was not a well-known name. Society bandleader Lester Lanin once called Cheatham. "He asked me, 'Can you play jazz?' 'I think so.' He said, 'Who do you play like?' I said, 'What do you mean, who do I play like? I'm playing Doc Cheatham.'" Several years passed before Lanin called again, Cheatham recalls—but once he did hire Cheatham for the first time, he began calling him periodically to use him as a featured soloist. Lanin was surprised to find Cheatham knew all of the show tunes Lanin liked to play, not just jazz oldies. (Today Cheatham is too busy to accept all of Lanin's offers.)

In 1966, Benny Goodman heard Cheatham leading a trio at the International Restaurant in New York, auditioned him, and hired him as the trumpeter in his sextet. "I stayed with him almost a year. We went to Las Vegas, and we went to Brussels, and played around Chicago. Sometimes he'd play numbers with symphonies, like the West Virginia Symphony or the Chicago Symphony, then he'd bring on the trio or the sextet, to play jazz. But he was very easy to work with because he was a big shot. He did practically all the solo work. He'd give me a little solo now and then. I didn't mind because I thought, 'This is great, playing with him.' Any little thing that would help me to hear, you know—and listening to him helped me a lot."

Goodman decided to feature Cheatham on "Shine." He asked if Cheatham could play it the dashing way Harry James used to play it in his band (which in turn was adapted from the way Louis Armstrong used to play it). "I knew what Harry James did on 'Shine' because I listened to Harry James; I listened to everybody," Cheatham recalls. "And I know that solo—that long cadenza, and then the drums are supposed to pick it up fast [he scats it]. We rehearsed 'Shine' mostly for the drummer; he would have trouble." But when Cheatham tried to tell the drummer when to pick up the tempo, Goodman said, "I'll tell the drummer what to do; you don't."

Then came a gala at New York's Waldorf Astoria. "Benny says, 'And now Doc Cheatham will take his hat off to Harry James.' I played [he scats the opening cadenza, getting to where the drummer is supposed to explode and dramatically increase the tempo]. Silence! After a while, the drummer starts playing— but *slow*. That's what he gave me, so I played the whole chorus that way. When we got through, I put my horn in the case and went on home. Benny's manager said, 'What happened?' I said, 'I don't need Benny to tell me that I'm fired; I quit.' I called the office just to make sure. I said, 'Am I fired?' He said, 'Yes, you're fired.' It was funny. I laughed. Benny has his little ways. But it meant a lot to me, just to be with him. Later on, he used to come to see me wherever I was playing, and he'd sit and talk with me. He never said any more to me about it."

In the late 1960s, Cheatham went with a Latin band led by pianist Ricardo Rey, no longer playing lead as he had when he had first started working with the Latin bands, but now starring as trumpet soloist. "He recorded me right away with the band and I did all solos, American style—playing American jazz, behind this rhythm he had written out. The album, *Jala-Jala* (Allegre), became a hit, all over everywhere. I was beginning to feel like I was getting back to myself. I began to feel something happening to me. So Ricardo Rey immediately got concerts from all down in Panama, Chile, Argentina, and all through South

America. And I was advertised as a 70-year-old trumpet player. We'd arrive in an airport like in Colombia, and there'd be thousands and thousands of people at the airport and all along the route that we took coming in, throwing flowers as a sign of welcome. The people came out to hear this band, and this 70-year-old trumpet player. Because they knew the solo I was playing, and they liked it. They'd never heard that style solo behind another rhythm before. And all the musicians came out to hear this band. I stayed with that band until it broke up in Puerto Rico."

He did Dixieland gigs with Red Balaban in the early 1970s. He was happy to be playing, but he hadn't attained the recognition or respect he'd long hoped for. He remembers playing one Sunday in Syracuse at a place where Bobby Hackett had worked and being told by the owner afterwards he'd never be hired again because he didn't drink. "The guy said, 'When Bobby was here, every set he came to the bar. By the end of the night, he didn't have any money coming.' They want you to have a bar tab at some places, so that at the end of the week you don't have anything coming!" He laughs at the thought.

Cheatham was inspired to start singing, he says, after listening to trumpeter Red Allen sing. Initially, he was sensitive about people who criticized his singing. "People said I couldn't sing. Then I made an album in Paris with Sammy Price [in 1975]. While they were getting a sound check in the recording studio, I suggested to Sam that we play a song called 'What Can I Say After I Say I'm Sorry?' That was a tune I heard in 1924 in Atlantic City, and I never heard it since. Sam knew the tune. We did that just for the engineer to get the level of the sound to record. Well, I played the shit out of that thing, and then I sang it, and I scatted. And then I listened to the playback. I didn't sound good to myself. I said, 'Oh, the hell with it.' The engineer said, 'Man, that's great! Keep that!' I said, 'I sound like hell.' But the guy said, 'No, that's great.' And, you know, that thing became a hit in France. You'll hear that number on—I think the album's called *Hey Doc* [on Black and Blue Records]. And everywhere I go now in Europe, I have to play that song. And all these groups in

Europe that had never heard that song before are playing it. And they copied my solo. I began to get a little encouragement like that."

In the mid 1970s, George Wein began using Cheatham for various projects—the New York Jazz Repertory Company, jazz festivals, and so on. And that marked a turning point. Cheatham, who had matured into a poised and lyrical trumpeter, was now being seen and heard in all the right places. "The first time I went to the Nice [France] festival, I was put on the same bandstand with Bobby Hackett and Clark Terry, Jimmy Maxwell and Cat Anderson—all on the same damned platform. I almost died! I knew every tune that they were playing, but I couldn't play like them. I felt I shouldn't be there. But I had to solo. I did the best I could. I was very critical of myself. I kept going to Nice— George sent me back there about five more times—and every time I was getting a little better, improved on my solos. I would have records and I would listen to these guys playing—not copying their solos, but just hearing. I wanted jazz to be all in this house, all in my ears, and all that. I began to get some kind of a style of my own. The style I have now is *my* style. I began to feel better. Bobby Hackett was very encouraging; he told me, 'You sound good.' You know, nobody had ever raved about me. I didn't expect it. But it took me all those years to get where I am now.

"Now I go to Europe every year and I play in all these different bands; they throw me in everything. And I have no trouble playing anything. I was out in Elkhart, Indiana's first jazz festival this year. I was thrown in with the Count Basie alumni, with Snooky Young, and I had to play with them a couple of sets. They didn't know that I knew those things. But I knew everything important that Duke or Count played. I knew that. Because I don't sit around here and hold my thumbs. One of the guys starts playing [Doc scats Ellington's "Cottontail"] and I heard one of the guys whisper, 'Do you think Doc knows it?' And Frank Foster says, 'Hey man, Doc knows everything.' And I did, I knew everything they played. It was great. And I played with the Duke Ellington alumni. I know all those things. So that's what I'm doing now. I go to Europe and they throw me in with a Duke group or a Basie group or with Jelly Roll Morton or Louis Armstrong groups. And I get along fine. And I don't think I'll ever do any better than I'm doing now, at my age, but I'm happy that I'm able to do what I'm doing."

He's done salutes to Benny Goodman, Billie Holiday, and many others. Interestingly, one of his more challenging assignments turned out to be trying to mesh with a group playing music he knew some 65 years ago: the famed Preservation Hall band from New Orleans. "I thought those musicians were rude to me. I went to the bandstand at Nice and I said, 'George [Wein] says I'm supposed to play with you this set.' The guy says, 'Well, play, man' [in a very curt tone]. I got up on the bandstand and they all had their seats and I didn't have a seat. There was no space. So I took a chair and sat behind the saxophone player. And then I say, 'When am I supposed to play?' The trumpet player, Kid Thomas, said, 'Well play, man, play!' I said, 'What the hell is this?' So I sat up there and they all played their solos . . . and later on they played 'The Saints' and I played a couple of choruses. I went back to George and said, 'What the hell? Why did you send me to play with these guys? They got their own thing going. I have no business going in there.' He said, 'Maybe they're trying to audition you, because you might be able to join that band when you get old enough.' " The incident made him think of how Louis Armstrong had felt New Orleans musicians could be sort of jealous and clique-ish.

Cheatham has recorded with artists ranging from Sammy Price to Earl Hines to Buddy Tate. The well-recorded, readily available, definitive Doc Cheatham collection has, however, yet to be produced. A fine two-record set on the Jezebel label, *Adolphus "Doc" Cheatham*, is not easy to locate. Even harder to find are two well-recorded albums that Cheatham himself is particularly proud of, produced in 1982 by banjo player Eddy Davis for his New York Jazz label, *Adolphus Anthony "Doc" Cheatham: "I've Got a Crush on You"* and *"Two Marvelous for Words."* Cheatham recorded some of those sides backed simply by Howard Alden's sensitive, pure-toned acoustic guitar, others backed by the Hot Jazz Orchestra of New York, including Davis, Alden, Dan Barrett, Joel Helleny, Joe Muranyi, and Jake Hanna. However, his playing is not as strong on those sides as on more recent ones. (He has since had corrected a recurring hernia problem which, at various periods, had limited how much pressure he could exert as a trumpeter, making his playing sound rather restrained and breathy. There was even a period in the mid '80s when he couldn't play at all and had to limit himself to singing in his performances. But he has fully recovered from those difficulties.) The sound quality on Cheatham's 1988 album, *Doc Cheatham and Sammy Price in New Orleans with Lars Edegran's Jazz Band* (GHB Records), is not as good as on the 1982 New York Jazz albums— it was recorded in a basement, not in a proper recording studio, according to Cheatham—but Cheatham sounds much stronger. He and Price work well together. Their recording partnership dates back to 1958. (Cheatham's tone sounds, to me, generally brighter in real life than on most records I've heard, partly due to less-than-ideal recording facilities used by some of the small companies for which he's recorded, and partly due to the apparent difficulty, even with first-rate recording equipment, of fully capturing the radiance of any fine trumpeter's tone.)

You can find good moments on almost any Cheatham album. For an example of his sensitivity with a ballad, you might check "This Is All I Ask" on the Jezebel set. He energizes W. C. Handy's "Memphis Blues" on *Black Beauty: A Salute to Black American Songwriters by Doc Cheatham and Sammy Price* (Sackville); there's certainly nothing "old man" about his sound (no quaver or weakening of spirit). That same album includes a lyrical reading of "I'm Coming Virginia" which avoids the expected trap of borrowing from the famous Beiderbecke-Trumbauer version; Cheatham approaches it fresh. On the well-recorded Sackville CD, *Doc Cheatham and Jim Galloway at the Bern Jazz Festival*, the vigor of Cheatham's staccato attacks (in tandem with Galloway) near the close of "Limehouse Blues" is startling—hot jazz to make you sit up and take notice—and his incandescent upper-register work near the conclusion of "When It's Sleepy Time Down South" is a joy to hear. Pianist Henri Chaix and some Swedish All-Stars provide a warm cushion for Cheatham on the album *Doc Cheatham: A Tribute to Billie Holiday* (Kenneth Records), which includes an appealing "Moanin' Low"—a reminder that Cheatham is one of very few players left who were active when a song like this was first introduced (1929) and are playing naturally in a style rooted in the era when the song was written.

Cheatham is in reasonably good health today. "I'm enjoying my life. I have my little health problems," he acknowledges. "I have arthritis all over my body but it leaves me after about a few months; it cuts away. I had it so bad last year, I couldn't walk. And it's all gone. It goes away."

For the past decade, he's had a regular outlet, playing Sunday brunches at Sweet Basil on Seventh Avenue South. It's the gig he enjoys the most, he says, "because at Sweet Basil, I can do what I want to do. I can make mistakes, I can experiment, and get myself together. Like I should do. I'm having a good time. I'm having a wonderful time." And that communicates itself very clearly as he works. People feel good being around him. He radiates a certain contentment. And when he raises his horn—a tiny amulet depicting Louis Armstrong dangling from it, so he can see the master as he plays—you smile in anticipation.

He's one of a few trumpeters who've made the transition from respected lead players to respected jazz soloists. He's certainly the only jazz trumpeter ever to have recorded his best work after age 70. He shows me with pride a copy of a recent issue of England's *Jazz Journal International*. His face adorns the cover. He's going to mail it to his daughter, he says. He's delighted at the recognition of his abilities he's gotten in his later years.

"I was so surprised when Wynton Marsalis came down to see me. And *asked* me, would I like to do a concert with him and Sweets Edison, at Lincoln Center. Now that knocked me right out! Because I could never have thought anything like—musicians don't do those things, especially big guys like he," Cheatham notes.

"So one Sunday before the concert, he and Sweets came into Sweet Basil with their horns. I said, 'What the hell is—' They said, 'We came to rehearse.' All three of us got up there. The people in the club, they raved. Wynton Marsalis! All three got on the bandstand and started to play. And the people just shouted. Whatever Marsalis wanted to play. Because it was his concert. He selected the tunes that we were going to play in the concert. So we played and everybody just flipped. And he was very nice. He thanked us and shook our hands. Admiring and all that. Compliments. He liked my tone and all that. He said, 'Gee, I like that tone.' I heard him say that to himself. You know? So I feel great about that. I know he has a pretty tone, too. So we did a concert. Man, the people screamed! We had a hell of a concert. It went over beautifully. And he was very, very lovely. That man was out of sight. He treated us like we were the big shots. And we were treating him like we knew he was a big shot.

"I get a lot of calls these days, a lot of strange things that I go and do. And the people seem to accept me now, when before they didn't. I was in London a couple of years ago at the Pizza Express and I don't think they had two people in there the whole week. Now this year I went to London and I played the Pizza Express, and you couldn't get in! People standing, packed all around the place. Because I did a program for TV about the Cotton Club, called 'The Cotton Club Remembers' or something, with Cab Calloway, the Nicholas Brothers, Adelaide Hall and others. They interviewed us all individually and that show was a hit. And I closed that film with my trumpet, playing and singing an old melody called 'I Guess I'll Get the Papers and Go Home.' And when I went out and sang this song, the people fell out. They fell out! Since then, if I go to London, I have to play that song. At the Pizza Express, you couldn't get in. I went to Cambridge and you couldn't get in the concert, just because of that. Shows you how life is," he muses.

"I went there and those people treated me like a king. So now I'm feeling like I'm kind of, you know, being rewarded for all of these things that I've gone through."

1988

Jazz-Age Orchestrations with Grace

From 1926 to 1929, Bill Challis turned out a series of superior arrangements, first for Jean Goldkette, and then—really hitting his stride, in my opinion—for Paul Whiteman. It was Challis who crafted such Whiteman masterpieces as "Lonely Melody," "Changes," and "Dardanella"—three of the best-known Whiteman works, numbers which define the Whiteman sound at its best.

Other Challis arrangements for Whiteman include "Washboard Blues," "San," "Ol' Man River," "Back in Your Own Back Yard," "Sugar," "Louisiana," "Oh! You Have No Idea," "Tain't So, Honey, Tain't So," "Because My Baby Don't Mean 'Maybe' Now," "Sweet Sue," "I'm in Seventh Heaven," "Oh! Miss Hanna," "Reaching for Someone," and "Great Day"—an incredible list.

Actually, Challis was not Whiteman's chief arranger—Ferde Grofé was—but it is Challis' charts that hold up the best today. The have drama, variety, elegance, and—in contrast to Grofé's— they are jazz-informed. There are times when Challis mixes moods—poignance will give way to exuberance; strings and woodwinds will yield to a brassy jazzband interlude, and then later reappear. Challis knew how to exploit the full range of the Whiteman Orchestra, effectively mixing the semi-symphonic with the hot.

47

For the leaner, nimbler Goldkette Orchestra, Challis arranged such numbers as "Sunday," "I'm Gonna Meet My Sweetie Now," "Hoosier Sweetheart," "A Lane in Spain," "In My Merry Oldsmobile," "Blue River," plus many others which were never recorded. He also arranged such well-known small-group sides for Bix Beiderbecke and Frankie Trumbauer as "Three Blind Mice," "Ostrich Walk," "Borneo," and "Riverboat Shuffle."

These were all pre-Swing Era creations. They were well known to hot musicians of the late 1920s, arrangers and instrumentalists alike, and helped set the stage for the Swing Era that followed. Challis was creating polished, graceful scores—music with foreward movement which was eminently acceptable to the general public and which effectively showcased master jazz soloists.

It is somewhat startling to note that Challis created all of the works listed above when he was between the ages of 21 and 26. He continued arranging for many years thereafter—in fact, he even did some work for the jazz vocal group Manhattan Transfer in the 1970s. And he'd probably be actively arranging today, in his 80s, except for the fact that his vision is now limited. But his most important artistic contributions had been made by 1930, the year he turned 26.

Today Challis lives in Harvey's Lake, Pennsylvania, about 15 miles from Wilkes-Barre, where he was born on July 8, 1904. I drove out to see him for several reasons. He was perhaps the greatest white dance band arranger of the late 1920s, and his story is important in its own right. It seems odd to me that he's never received a profile of his own in any book. In addition, he was an eyewitness to a good chunk of jazz history, one of the few survivors left who was closely connected to Beiderbecke (whom I profiled, drawing upon Challis' observations, in *Voices of the Jazz Age*), Goldkette, and Whiteman at their peak, and their stories are certainly important.

Bill Challis and his brother, Evan (12 years younger), proved to be gracious hosts. And if, occasionally, during the course of several hours' worth of conversation, Bill Challis forgot to mention a detail, his brother was right there to fill in the gaps. Here is Bill Challis' story.

BILL CHALLIS

Challis started on sax when he was 15 or 16, around 1919–20. "I had a violin first, but it sounded like mice," he notes. "I traded it in—I think I got 20 bucks from Wurlitzer—for the C-melody sax that they had advertised in *Etude*. You know, if you were taking up the piano, and my sister did, you bought *Etude*. It had music and articles.

"I liked playing the C-melody. I took lessons in Wilkes-Barre, played in the high school orchestra, played with Guy Hall around town. He was a local bandleader and he wrote 'Johnson Rag.' (Years later, all the big bands made it—Glenn Miller, Jimmy Dorsey.) I had to learn to play it when I got in his band."

Challis also played a few dates in Scranton with the Scranton Sirens, the top band in the region. He got to meet musicians he would later know in the Jean Goldkette Band, including trumpeter Fuzzy Farrar and pianist Itzy Riskin. His gigs with the Sirens were before Russ Morgan, and Tommy and Jimmy Dorsey, whom he would later know well, had joined the band.

"I was in high school, and they wanted me to stay with them, play with them. But I couldn't. You know, my family wanted me to stay in school. So I just picked up the extra bucks." It wasn't jazz he was playing back then, just straight dance music: "At that time, if you had a C-melody saxophone, you stood up and you played the melody."

In fact, he hadn't yet been exposed to much jazz at all. He listened to recordings of popular music by the All-Star Trio. And he heard sides by the Original Dixieland Jazz Band, and by Paul Whiteman's Orchestra—their records enjoyed huge sales. But he did not hear early records by the New Orleans Rhythm Kings, nor by black jazz musicians. (Later in the '20s, he would come to appreciate Bessie Smith, Louis Armstrong, and others. But at this point, his knowledge of music was still rather circumscribed.)

In 1921, he entered Bucknell University. There he led a student band, Challis' Orchestra, from the start of his sophomore year until he graduated in June of 1925. They played dances at the fraternity houses.

Fox trots were popular at Bucknell during those years. Very few students were interested in dancing the Charleston or the Black Bottom. Challis' Orchestra had success playing light clas-

49

sics, such as "Song of India," "To a Wild Rose," and "My Heart at thy Sweet Voice," as well as pop tunes.

It was at Bucknell that Challis began arranging for the first time. He was self-taught. "I had a band and the guys didn't know what to do. We'd buy the sheet music, and I'd have to write parts for the fellows. Otherwise we'd all play the same thing. I wrote chords (symbols) for the piano player and the guitar player. And the rest of the parts I wrote. The bass part. Two trumpets and trombone. And our three saxophones. I had the C-melody. The second guy played the alto. And the third guy played a tenor. There was always somebody in the bands that played all the instruments—and I was the guy. I had a clarinet, a baritone, and I later got a soprano and an alto. The C-melody was my main instrument, though."

In the fall of his senior year, Challis got to hear cornetist Bix Beiderbecke—with whom he was to be so closely associated— "live" for the first time, playing in the Wolverine Orchestra in New York. Bix was beginning to make a name for himself among musicians, if not with the general public.

After graduation from Bucknell, Challis worked briefly in a band led by one Dave Harmon, in Williamsport, Pennsylvania. He tried sending a couple of arrangements to Jean Goldkette, whose Victor recording orchestra was popular with the collegiate set, but his first submissions were not accepted.

"I figured I wanted to go back to school. I planned to become a lawyer. So I quit Harmon's Band and I came back to Wilkes-Barre, and played with Guy Hall again."

And now he sent a couple more arrangements to the Gold-kette Band, which Beiderbecke had recently joined, and *these* arrangements caught on with the band.

"Why, they seemed to like them! The Goldkette Band played one called 'The Blue Room,' which at that time was popular. And there was another—'Baby Face.' I wrote those two and they liked them. So, they came out on the road. Bix and Trumbauer had joined the band [in May of 1926]. And they had five brass. Which in that time was called a big band. It was unusual. Bands were still the Mickey Mouse-type with two trumpets and a trombone.

"Now they were coming through Wilkes-Barre. I had already matriculated at University of Pennsylvania. And a friend of mine—we had played together with Guy—wanted to go down and hear the band. I said, 'Jesus, I got a couple of arrangements.'

"So we went down to the ballroom. And I had a couple of choruses there for Bix. Heh! It was great. And I had some parts for Trumbauer—I mean, not written out, but I allotted some space for both these guys. I didn't write their parts. And it was a kick hearing it, believe me.

"Ray Lodwig had charge of the band. [Later Trumbauer fronted it.] And Fuzzy Farrar was in it, and Irving Riskin, from the Sirens. And Ray asked me if I'd make some more. I told him I was going to go away to school.

"In about three or four days I heard from them. They were up in New England. And he wanted me to join the band. It seems they didn't have an arranger. Some of the guys in the band could arrange. But to play and arrange—they'd rather play." The band had barely more than a handful of completely original written arrangements. They also had some head arrangements that Trumbauer had brought when he had joined. But mostly they were working from published stock charts, sometimes modified by members of the band. "Arranging" consisted of cutting and pasting stocks, maybe adding a new intro or ending. There was a real vacuum for Challis to fill.

"So I thought, 'Well, I won't go to school right now. I'll take a little bit more of the band business.' So I went up to a place called Southboro, Massachusetts [in September of 1926], and joined the band there. Well, when I get up there, they played over 'The Blue Room,' and 'Baby Face' for me, so I could get used to a couple of things, listening to the band, and writing for it. At the time they didn't need any saxophone players, but they needed arrangements.

"Russ Morgan had been arranging for them, but he had a good proposition of his own, in a theater in Detroit. So, they didn't have anybody at the time, and they liked these arrangements.

"They were heading into New York, to play at the Roseland and record. They wanted me to wait—it was just a couple of days—until they got to New York and they would have tunes for me to do, and record. So I went out, just to hear the band a couple nights. And it was an experience for me. Because it was a great band. To hear them work on the job was a pleasure. There they really took their hair down, and played. They played a couple of pavilions, a couple places up there. It was great.

"And then, we came down to New York, and the band played at the Roseland [opening October 6, 1926]. Jeez, what a reception we got there!

"The musicians crowded around the place. They came up there to hear Bix. And to hear Frankie Trumbauer. And to hear the whole band. The band did very well at the Roseland at the time. And playing opposite us was Fletcher Henderson. They liked our band, too. And they had a good band.

"And then we waited around," Challis recalls. Waited for Victor to give them the go-ahead to make records representing what the band was doing nightly at Roseland. But it never quite happened.

The tunes Victor told them to record were mostly dogs, in Challis' opinion. "There was a guy at Victor named Eddie King who had charge of these records. He picked out the tunes for us." Challis wonders if Goldkette and the band's manager, Charlie Horvath, might have had some influence, too. But he doesn't want to believe that, since it would mean that they didn't know "what a good tune was," any more than King did.

At Roseland, the band offered stylish, jazz-inflected instrumental dance music. It was an ensemble band, but Bix and Tram were featured as soloists. It is surprising, though, how little of Bix and Tram wound up on the records the band made.

King felt vocalists would make records by the band more commercially viable, and since the band did not have a vocalist, he brought in Billy Murray, Frank Bessinger, Al Lynch, and the Keller Sisters—whose prime virtue as vocalists was that they all enunciated clearly.

Some of the trivialities the band was forced to record—such as "Just One More Kiss," with a vocal by Lynch, and "Hush-a-Bye," a waltz with a vocal by Bessinger—featured no instrumental solos whatsoever. Others included solos by trombonists Bill Rank and Spiegle Willcox. Others featured solos by Joe Venuti and Eddie Lang.

"Victor got us Venuti and Lang just to make records. They didn't play with us at the Roseland; they were not in the band. I think Joe used to be, before that time. But he was back in New York, and he and Eddie were very busy. And we'd give them a chorus. The band would do this, do that, have spots here and there. But we would feature Eddie and Joe. And they played, Joe particularly, and maybe Eddie backed him up. They sounded great."

But King didn't want Bix featured on the records. "Eddie King didn't want any improvising. Why they let Joe play, I don't know. They could take that," he recalls. But they couldn't take improvising generally—and certainly not Beiderbecke's unpredictable excursions. They felt that if the band wanted to get a hit, it had best adhere closely to the melody as written.

Denied solo space, sometimes Beiderbecke would stand and improvise above the ensemble. And some of that came through effectively, Challis recalls. "But in the meantime, Joe would be playing his chorus, or a half a chorus, earlier on in the arrangement," he notes.

One Challis arrangement, "Sunday," included a three-trumpet chorus, which had originally been a Bix solo. The other two trumpeters harmonized along with Bix. According to Challis, it was the only way to get some of Bix's spirit into the record, since King did not want Bix to be given the solo space. Challis adds that the band had greater freedom on some later recording sessions which King did not supervise.

One reason the band did not get to record some of the superior pop tunes of the day was that other, more-established Victor artists had claimed them, and at that time the company did not want its artists competing with one another.

" 'The Blue Room'—the arrangement that got me the job— I'd like to have recorded that. But Roger Wolfe Kahn had recorded it. And in those days, it wasn't like it was a little bit later, when as many guys as had bands would record a tune. They didn't do that. We had to take the tunes that were assigned to us. Roger was around New York, you know. And Whiteman got anything he asked for. And Nat Shilkret, who worked for Victor, used to do whatever he wanted. So the other bands that recorded for Victor used to get tunes that those bands didn't get.

"Of course, when I got with the Whiteman band it was a different deal. Jesus. We got things like show tunes. We got 'Old Man River,' things like that. Which we never even figured we'd get with the Goldkette Band."

Challis returned with the Goldkette Band to Detroit. "But I didn't hang around the band—very little. Because I couldn't get any arrangements done by hanging around the band. Except to listen. It wasn't like playing with them. See, I'd do my work at home and I'd come over to the band when I'd have it finished, and rehearse it." Challis had the greatest admiration for Beiderbecke as a musician. And they *were* friends. But it wasn't always easy. Beiderbecke was a drinker, and had a reputation for being somewhat unreliable.

"Bix was very friendly with me. We were buddies. We got along well. We would have gotten along a whole lot better, but he could drink. I couldn't drink that way. I don't want to say he was a drunkard, but he was a drinker. And I was sort of a nondrinker. I took a drink now and then. But not to the extent where he and I could go out and bend the elbow at some place. He and I didn't do it.

"The band got a job playing at Atlantic City [in August of 1927]. That was the next to the last job that they did. From there they went up to Roseland for the last time.

"Now Bix and I made that trip, which all the guys thought was very funny. But it really wasn't. Cork O'Keefe, the manager, wanted me to drive his car to Atlantic City from Detroit, and Bix went with me.

"We were supposed to make a 3:00 [a.m.] boat out of Detroit—put the car on the boat and go to Buffalo. And we could leave the boat in the morning, 9:00, and drive down from Buffalo. But the time came around and Bix didn't show up—he didn't make it. I didn't know where he was. Finally he came around, late. We couldn't get on the boat. He told me, 'Somebody rolled me for my money.' He had to go back to the office and get another check. We were all paid so we'd have the money to go to Atlantic City."

Bix got his money, and the two headed off once again. Bix read, as Challis drove south.

"He didn't take a bottle along—but at Harrisburg, where we stopped the first night, he wanted to go out and get, as he called it, a jug. 'I want to go out and get a jug.' 'I want to go to bed. Let's go to bed, get up early, and we'll be off.' Maybe he didn't know the spots in Harrisburg, because he was back in after that. He probably got himself a drink or so. But he didn't get drunk.

"The following morning we left and went the rest of the way. Two guys driving to Atlantic City. . . . And he made it! I think the guys thought that I'd have to take care of him, that he'd be drunk.

"When we got to Atlantic City, we went out that night. I think he knew a girl down there who demonstrated tunes in a Five and Ten store. And he got us a date, and the four of us went to a place. And Jesus, the first thing you know, I see the gin bottle—the big quart.

"The girls would like to drink with him. But he's the guy that wanted to drink—not I. I didn't care much for it. It would have been all right if I'd had one or two. But I could see it building up, you know. And I got hold of the bottle when he was somewhere around, I got hold of the bottle and I dumped it out. We'd all had enough." Beiderbecke tore into Challis for dumping out the liquor. For Challis, it was not an enjoyable night.

"The next day, we were at a rehearsal, and I said to him, 'Jesus, you're a hell of a guy. A fine guy to take a trip like this— to go out someplace.' I told him about, Jesus, last night. And he said, 'I don't remember a thing.' That was his idea of excusing the whole thing. So I didn't say anything more."

Although the cornet was Beiderbecke's primary instrument, he often explored ideas at the piano in his free time. It was Challis who was responsible for setting Beiderbecke's moody, impressionistic piano compositions in permanent, written form.

"You see, in the Goldkette band he played those over for all the guys. They all knew—it wasn't called 'In a Mist' at that time. They had heard him play it, but not the way it was written—not altogether that way, the complete rendition, the way we have it." For Bix's Goldkette colleagues were hearing numbers such as "In a Mist" as they were developing. And he'd play the numbers differently each time.

The Robbins Music Corporation wanted to publish sheet music of Beiderbecke's piano pieces. They realized he'd need a collaborator, someone to transcribe his work and set it in fixed form.

"And now then, working with Bix—they had Hugo Frey do it first," Challis recalls. "Hugo did, I think, about two bars and said: 'This is enough. Get somebody else!' He couldn't find Bix half the time.

"So Jack Robbins came around to me and asked if me I would do it. He knew that we were friends. I said, 'Yeah, I'll do it.' So I took the copy. It took us about six months to get that thing ["In a Mist"] done. It took a long time, anyway. Well, I had to find him, in the first place! He was in the bars, and besides it was not important to him to get it done. It *was* important that he was going to do a piano number. But 'we have plenty of time'—that's the general idea. I'd have to get him on the date. I'd have to get him in some town. I'd have to get him when he's relaxed, to do it. So I did all that.

"And then another thing was, he would play it, play it over, and he would play it differently the second time. It got to the point where I told Jack Robbins: 'Jesus, this guy is tough. He doesn't come around and play it the same way twice.' So we did that, two bars at a time. Two, four bars. And then play it again. And it was up to me, to get him to, to get a whole complete number.

"Robbins told him: 'You might be out someplace playing these numbers and you'll have to play them the same way every time. Nobody's going to listen to them if it's different the second time, and then it's different again the third time.'

"So we went at it and put it down. That's what we had to do. It took a much longer time, and we finally got it done. But by the time we got to the next number, he sensed the value of doing it each time, to put down for print, to put it down the same way.

"So we got it down. 'In a Mist' was first." (Beiderbecke re-corded it on September 9, 1927; the final, written version—which differs somewhat from the recorded version—was copyrighted on November 18th.) "Then 'Candlelights.' And then 'In the Dark.' And 'Flashes' was the last." "Candlelights" was copyrighted August 29, 1930. "In the Dark" and "Flashes" were both copy-righted April 18, 1931. "I knew, I could tell, they were coming more easily. And he was very creative. And he had other things that he could do."

Challis adds: " 'Davenport Blues'—I put that down. I got that from the record [made by Bix on January 26, 1925]. I had to write the final four bars, the end—I had to do that. And I had to do an awful lot of the tune itself—not of the tune, not of the melody, but of his rendition. I had to correct it and make it the same. That was, you might say, that was mine. But the others were his. We got along well and I could tell that gee, he liked to do these things. And when he got out of the band, you might say, that could very well have been his work, you know. Doing short little things like that, on the piano." (Challis' recollection is that he did "Davenport Blues" after Bix's death in 1931.)

Challis also tried to write down Beiderbecke's meandering number, "For No Reason at All in C," which Beiderbecke had recorded (with Trumbauer and Lang) on May 13, 1927. How-ever, Challis soon realized that "For No Reason at All in C"—which was actually Bix's variations on an Al Jolson pop song, "I'd Climb the Highest Mountain," which the Goldkette Band liked to play—didn't have a strong enough theme to make a good written composition.

The Goldkette Band, in the summer of 1927, didn't have much work lined up, and Victor canceled a couple of recording sessions. "At that particular time, the band business was getting pretty bad," Challis recalls. Goldkette tried, unsuccessfully, to get the band a permanent base in New York. Some of its stars felt they could do better financially freelancing in New York than going back out on the road on one-nighters.

In August of 1927, the Goldkette Band was playing at the Million Dollar Pier on the boardwalk in Atlantic City. Challis recalls that Jimmy Dorsey brought Whiteman, trumpeter Henry Busse, Bing Crosby and the Rhythm Boys to see the band; they had driven up from Philadelphia. Whiteman agreed to serve as guest conductor for a couple of numbers. He was leading the men through "St. Louis Blues," and the band was really going over big—Whiteman's showy style of conducting impressed the audience—when Goldkette happened to drop by. He was getting a glimpse of what lay ahead; soon his greatest stars would be working for Whiteman.

"Paul Whiteman said he didn't want to have anything to do with breaking up the Goldkette Band. *But*, if any of the guys wanted a job, they could ask him. And they were welcome to go with him," Challis recalls. On August 28, 1927, Challis went with Whiteman. The Goldkette Band folded three weeks later.

Which orchestra did Challis prefer arranging for—Goldkette's or Whiteman's?

"I enjoyed doing the both equally," he answers. "I had more to work with with the Whiteman band—I could do what I wanted to. With the Goldkette band, although it was a smoother band to work with, you didn't have the instrumental color. So I liked both bands; they were great."

Challis makes it clear that he felt he had more options with Whiteman's Band. The Goldkette Band had just 12 members. Whiteman's had as many as 33 (including vocalists), Challis notes. And he could use as many of them as he wished for making records.

"They had four trumpets that I could work with. They had strings. They had six guys who could sing. And I could do all the vocals I wanted. Whiteman practically gave me carte blanche to do whatever I wanted. When I got in the band, I think we had eight saxophones. We usually recorded with six. Sometimes, I think it jelled down to four. And then we had four trombones. He told me I could use them all."

The Goldkette band gave its final performance on September 18, 1927. By late October, Bix and Tram had joined Whiteman; trombonist Bill Rank followed shortly afterwards. So

BILL CHALLIS

Bill Challis in 1928 (top photo), and in 1990 (Challis, at far right, stands with New Jersey Jazz Society directors Jack Wallace and Jack Stine). (Courtesy of Bill Walters.)

The Jean Goldkette Band, Massachusetts, September 1926. From left to right: Bill Challis, Spiegle Willcox, Itzy Riskin, Bix Beiderbecke, Don Murray, Howdy Quicksell, Doc Ryker, Chauncey Morehouse, Fuzzy Farrar, Ray Lodwig, Bill Rank, Frank Trumbauer, Steve Brown. (Courtesy of Spiegle Willcox.)

Sheet music for "In a Mist," which Bix Beiderbecke composed and Challis set in written form, and for "Since My Best Gal Turned Me Down," one of a number of songs Challis originally arranged for the full Goldkette Band that the band never got a chance to record. Beiderbecke recorded a small-group version.

In 1988, Circle Records released Bill Challis' The Goldkette Project, *a new recording (co-conducted by Challis and Vince Giordano) of 20 numbers that Challis had originally arranged six decades earlier for the Goldkette Band, including several that the band never had an opportunity to record. (Courtesy of Circle Records.)*

Challis now had the same stars to work with as before. He was happy with the setup. Whiteman's Band was huge and could often sound ponderous, but there were enough hot players to keep things interesting. And the other musicians were first-rate instrumentalists who could provide superb tonal blends.

Was Bix happy about being with Whiteman?

"Well, yeah, he liked that," Challis declares. "He was more appreciated, you might say. He had more freedom to play his solos. They made a soloist out of him, actually. He still played the third and fourth parts in the band. But then I always had a chorus for him, here and there. On every tune I did, I think I had a chorus for Bix. Or at least a half a chorus. Jeez, I was lucky enough to be thrown in with Bix—who I thought was, naturally, the greatest.

"He was a drawing card for the band, as far as musicians were concerned. I think every musician in the country wanted to play like him—tried anyway. Same way with Trumbauer. Saxophone players—they wanted to play like Frankie. At that time, it was either Frankie or Jimmy [Dorsey], and they were both in the Whiteman Band."

(Listeners can hear how Bix and Tram sounded in Challis' arrangements, in a boxed set of the complete recorded output of Bix Beiderbecke, newly remastered by the expert John R. T. Davies, released by Sunbeam Records, 13821 Calvert St., Van Nuys, CA 91401. Selected recordings have also recently been released in CD form by both RCA and Columbia.)

Challis adapted many of the arrangements he had previously written for Goldkette for use by the Whiteman Band. And he wrote new arrangements for Whiteman, continuing in the same jazz-informed style he had developed for Goldkette. Challis' arrangements—and the solo contributions of Bix and Tram—helped give the Whiteman band a much jazzier flavor than it had had in previous years.

"I came out of the Goldkette Band and brought as much of that stuff as possible. And then I used as much color and instruments as I could get with Whiteman—which I didn't have in the Goldkette Band.

"We would take certain things and make them a lot like the

Goldkette Band. We had all the instrumental flavor that you needed. Besides good musicians.

"We tried to make it, like you might say, 'dancy.' Well, it was dance music anyway. But, you know, in Paul's case, he was trying to make it more concert-y. American concert. After the *Rhapsody in Blue*. Where I used to use Bix and Trumbauer, Izzy Friedman, Jimmy Dorsey when he was in the band—guys like that. Show them off for a chorus or half a chorus. And that went well.

"Now, take something like 'Dardanella,' for instance—you could dance to that. The beat went right through it, from the beginning to the end. Or on 'Changes,' we used all six vocalists, then we brought Bix in and let him play a half a chorus. And in the meantime, from the beginning unto the end, it was dancy. We competed with the dance bands." (The band did, however, continue to play many of its old standbys in arrangements which made no use whatsoever of the jazz talents of Bix, Tram, and company; those musicians were reduced to playing section parts on those numbers, some of which got rather pretentious.)

Challis credits Ferde Grofé for generously giving him "Old Man River" and other quality tunes to arrange; Grofé, as Whiteman's number one arranger, had first pick. Challis was able to do more with the tunes than Grofé could have. Grofé simply didn't have the interest in jazz that Challis had. Challis viewed Grofé, Whiteman, and Eddie King as being similarly oriented— they liked hearing melodies played straight. Grofé was a pioneering dance band arranger. (Challis, in fact, named him as an early influence.) Grofé's charts had been state-of-the-art in 1920; Challis' were in 1927.

Challis was happy to experiment; he enjoyed trying different effects. His arrangement of " 'Tain't So, Honey, 'Tain't So" (June 10, 1928) was highly unorthodox for its time in that it opened with Bing Crosby singing; there was not so much as one bar of instrumental introduction.

On "Washboard Blues" (November 18, 1927), Challis used strings, woodwinds, and a bass clarinet to help establish one mood, before bringing on a jazz band (with the Dorseys, Bix, and bassist Steve Brown) in the middle, and then finally re-establishing the original mood. He was striving to get a change of feeling as pronounced as if a door were opening, and the listener were stepping into another room and letting the door close behind him.

"Washboard Blues," incidentally, was the first Whiteman record deliberately made without trumpeter Henry Busse. Challis, who much preferred Beiderbecke's modern style of playing to Busse's, had written the arrangement for just one trumpet (or cornet, to be precise)—Beiderbecke's. Busse, who was paid more than Beiderbecke, was not happy about being slighted. After all, he had been featured with Whiteman since 1920; Bix and Challis were newcomers in the band. But Whiteman gave Challis free rein. If Challis could give his band some of the flair of the Goldkette Band, which had proven so popular with the collegiate set, that was great.

Challis continued to showcase Beiderbecke—not Busse—in his charts. Perhaps the clearest sign of the way things were moving came when Challis created a new arrangement of "San," which Whiteman had originally recorded—with Busse on trumpet—in 1924. The new version of "San" (recorded January 12, 1928)—one of the all-time classic Whiteman records—featured just 10 musicians, and Busse wasn't one of them. Bix was joined by such fellow jazz enthusiasts as Tram, Jimmy Dorsey, Carl Kress, Bill Rank—and Challis on piano. By late April, 1928, Busse had quit. Busse felt that the young Turks who had come into the Whiteman Band from Goldkette's had were taking over, changing the feel of the band. He may have been the highest paid member of the band, but he had lost his pre-eminence.

Challis was not the only one creating memorable jazz-inflected scores for Whiteman in the late 1920s, although he created more of them than his colleagues did. Whiteman pianist Tommy Satterfield, for example, arranged "There Ain't No Sweet Man that's Worth the Salt of My Tears" (recorded February 8, 1928) and "That's My Weakness Now" (June 17, 1928); violinist Matty Malneck arranged "Mary" (November 25, 1927) and "From Monday On" (February 28, 1928); and pianist Lennie

Hayton arranged "China Boy" (May 3, 1929) and "Nobody's Sweetheart" (October 9, 1929). Big band arranging was in its infancy and all these arrangers deserve credit as pioneers.

In the late 1920s, bands were racially segregated. There were separate union locals for white and black musicians. The white bands and the black bands drew upon different foundations, and the terms "white jazz" and "black jazz" were used by musicians and laymen alike. Challis was unsurpassed among white big band arrangers of the late 1920s. Don Redman, Fletcher Henderson, and Benny Carter were pioneers among black big band arrangers. They were all working out, in their own styles, ways of giving a large ensemble a jazz feel, and ways to best showcase jazz soloists within arranged music. There was some crossover between the white and black jazz worlds. Whiteman, for example, paid Don Redman to write some arrangements for him, hoping to get some of the sound of the Fletcher Henderson Band, for whom Redman was then arranging. (In 1927, both Whiteman's Band and Henderson's recorded Redman's arrangement of "Whiteman Stomp"; the Whiteman men were not able to swing it the way the Henderson men were.) And Fletcher Henderson bought some arrangements from Bill Challis. (Henderson recorded " 'D' Natural Blues," a Challis arrangement, in 1928, and several others in 1931.) The white arrangers and black arrangers drew upon different backgrounds, but they respected each other. When Benny Carter started arranging, for example, Bill Challis (who had started before him) was one of the arrangers whose work he was taking note of.

The Whiteman Band was at its peak in 1928. It had never sounded better—it had just the right blend of instrumental stars and arrangers—and bookings were solid. Ironically, its tremendous public acceptance, according to Challis, wound up contributing to its decline.

How? The Whiteman Band began going downhill, in Challis' estimation, when it landed its own weekly radio program, sponsored by Old Gold cigarettes, early in 1929. The band got the radio series only because it was so overwhelmingly popular. But Challis soon discovered there was no longer time to craft arrangements as carefully as before. They became merely functional. The band wound up playing more generic "radio music," rather than the quality "dance music" which had earned it such respect.

"When it came to something like the Old Gold Show, we just played the chorus and got out two and a half minutes of it. To satisfy the publishers. Play the chorus—and always have a vocal in there—you have to. And then they got to like Bing's masculine voice. So we didn't use Skin Young. And we didn't use too much of Johnny Fulton, who had a falsetto. We used them where we could. If the tune could call for something like that, we would do it in harmony or somewhere, where we could use the vocal. But they didn't do near as much as they used to do. Because Bing became so popular. Bing had that real masculine voice. He could sing almost anything. Publishers would ask you: 'Can you put a vocal by Bing in there?' " (Challis, incidentally, felt Bing's style in that period was clearly derived from Al Jolson's, although modernized.)

"When we started to do the radio music, you got tunes that came out—Jesus, as often as once a week you'd get a new tune. And you had to play it. And we had 16 of these tunes. We couldn't concentrate on them, like we could on a recording. Where we'd have a few weeks to make a nice arrangement of some good tune that had come out. And we got mostly commercial tunes. As long as you played a few choruses, and got a vocal in, you could take the print orchestration almost and run it down for almost three minutes. And that you were stuck with.

"The band began to lose its appeal by playing radio music. It wasn't the dance music that we used to try to do at first." The band sounded blander. The stress was on quantity—getting as many tunes as possible into a broadcast—rather than quality.

By early 1930, the band was mostly involved in radio, and in making a film called *The King of Jazz*.

"By then Bix had gotten out of the band; they had Andy Secrest in there." Secrest, Challis adds, was a fine trumpeter— but he says he was never able to get as much out of Secrest as he had gotten out of Beiderbecke. "There were a lot of changes. They did the radio show. If you really analyze it, that wasn't the type of band we had, when we first got in it.

"They were booked to come in to the Roxy Theater for three weeks, and Gershwin was supposed to play the piano solo on *Rhapsody in Blue*. And *The King of Jazz* was to be shown then. They were supposed to come back to New York and make a big splash.

"But the picture was a flop. And then the business was, by this time, pretty flat. There was nothing much to do for a band. Now you must realize that for about three years before this, this band was playing in the theaters. I think Paul told me one time that he had 44 weeks a year that he could do theaters. And that's what he did, for the three years. Then when they came back to New York, the picture fell flat. It only lasted one week at the Roxy. Paul made up his mind that he couldn't go any further."

The Depression was on. Whiteman seemed to have lost his cachet. He couldn't get enough bookings to cover his huge payroll.

"So he cut the band down. There were eight guys cut. When I first saw him, I knew what was going to happen. He pointed his finger and said: 'You're fired!' He was just showing off. But then he said, 'Yeah, I'm sorry, Bill. But we got to cut the band down.' So that was the time that I got out."

One wonders if Whiteman had ever fully appreciated Challis' contributions. (Whiteman said he was dissatisfied with Challis' stirring 1929 arrangement of "Great Day." He even mulled having the record recalled.) Challis' tastes were more modern, more jazz-oriented than I suspect Whiteman's were. Whiteman really liked the less imaginative, more symphonic-oriented, offerings of Ferde Grofé.

Challis was in no rush to sign with other bands. He felt he had worked for the two best bands—why should he be eager to commit himself to a lesser band?

He knew the members of the Casa Loma Band, which had originated as a Jean Goldkette unit in Detroit. He could have joined them as a full-time sax player and arranger. "But I didn't want any part of it, because I knew that in a cooperative band [which the Casa Loma Band was], you get 12 different opinions about something. If somebody doesn't like what you do, you've got to change it. He's going to say, 'I don't like this, I don't like that.' You have all those headaches," Challis says.

But he agreed to write arrangements for them, as a freelancer. And he also tried to get Bix into the band. Bix was at loose ends these days. Challis told his friends in the Casa Loma Band that Bix was available. They were delighted. They weren't aware of how bad his drinking problem had become.

"I was thinking of his welfare," Challis recalls. "There were a lot of those guys that he used to hang around with and drink with in New York, but they didn't do him any good. And Bix was the kind of a guy, if he had a couple of bucks, he'd buy a drink for you."

Bix tried, but it quickly became clear he was unable to cut it in the highly regimented Casa Loma Band. "It didn't work out," Challis notes. "I was almost sure that it wouldn't work out. But I was hoping that he'd get himself a paycheck every week and make a go of it—at least for a while."

Challis wrote some NBC radio orchestra arrangements featuring Bix. And—when Bix was in the mood—they worked together on Bix's piano compositions, up until Bix's death from pneumonia (and the effects of alcoholism) in August of 1931.

For the Casa Loma Band, Challis contributed a series of now-forgotten arrangements in the early 1930s, including "Help Yourself to Happiness," "Going, Going, Gone," and "Dardanella." "For You" did become a hit, although the main credit seems due to Kenny Sargent's singing, rather than to Challis' straightforward arrangement. He arranged a number of waltzes, and tunes selected by the band's record label, Decca.

Challis freelanced for a variety of leaders. "I worked for Willard Robison—a real talent, the guy that made 'Tain't So, Honey, Tain't So.' I made some arrangements for Fletcher. Jazz tunes. He was working in Connie's Inn." (Among his 1931 arrangements for Henderson were "My Gal Sal," "Clarinet Marmalade," "Stardust," and "Singing the Blues.")

"I made some for Duke Ellington. (I made 'Stardust' for

him. I've forgotten some things I've arranged.) His boss, Irving Mills, didn't like them. It wasn't flashy enough for him, or something like that. But Ellington wanted to know when I was going to make more for him.

"I worked with Dick Himber. And Charlie Barnet—he wanted 'Ave Maria.' Oh, there was plenty of work."

In the 1930s and early '40s, Challis worked frequently in radio. The pay was good, but the music was undistinguished. Nat Shilkret conducted the orchestras for several big shows, and Challis arranged for him. "They were known by their sponsors' names in those days. He did the Smith Brothers' cough drops. And there was a typewriter show. And Nat had Mobil." He arranged for the Maxwell House Show with Don Voorhees' Orchestra, and for a number of Lucky Strike shows, all based in New York.

The work was commercial, unimaginative. Challis arranged for Kate Smith's popular radio show for three years. All numbers had to follow a set pattern. Smith would sing a chorus, then the entire ensemble would play the melody for 16 bars, and then Smith would sing again.

For each number on the "Lucky Strike Hit Parade," Challis had to write four introductory bars for the orchestra, then the music would fade down—strings here—so that the announcer could give the name of the tune and its ranking on the Hit Parade—and then the ensemble would come up. Challis tried innovating—writing a first chorus without brass, for example—but he was overruled. The sponsors weren't looking for anything too fancy.

On one show Challis was told point blank: he had not been hired to educate the public. He was asked why he couldn't write arrangements like Phil Walls. Walls, according to Challis, could churn out 18 arrangements for radio each week. Challis says Walls' charts looked like something you could write on the subway on your way home from work. He didn't want to create orchestrations that uninteresting. And he was aware, too, that radio producers treated his orchestrations as mere commodities, to be trimmed at will to fit whatever time constraints might develop.

In the mid '30s, Challis recorded some transcriptions—discs

that were not sold in stores commercially, but were distributed to radio stations for airplay. He recalls: "We went up sometimes after midnight, and did a date for about three, four hours. Jesus, I had the best people in the whole business. I had Charlie Margulis, Manny Klein, Wilber Schwichtenberg [later known as Will Bradley], Jack Jenney, Jack Lacy, Artie Shaw. And I had all those fiddle players, you know."

Challis conducted the orchestra, playing his own arrangements, but they were distributed by World Broadcasting under the pseudonym of Bob Carroll—the same initials as Bill Challis—and his Orchestra. (In recent years, record producer George Buck has reissued these sides, properly credited to Challis, on a two-album set on the Circle label entitled *Bill Challis and his Orchestra: 1936*.) The recordings are a bit more middle-of-the-road than the Whiteman recordings of Challis' arrangements.

Challis' goal was to lead a radio orchestra of his own, which would feature his arrangements. He tried to find a sponsor for himself. On several occasions, he felt he came close to finding one. Ford Motor Company, which had previously sponsored Fred Waring's Pennsylvanians, seemed particularly interested in him.

"Ford said, 'Well, what if you had to go out to Detroit and you'd have the whole Detroit Symphony?'

" 'No, I don't really want to do that,' I said. 'Because I've got the guys around here. And they're the best in the business. And if I had a job . . . why, I would have these guys.'

" 'Well, the Detroit Symphony has some of the greatest musicians in the country.'

" 'But not in this racket,' I told 'em. So I didn't even get invited to the next meeting. They wound up with some organist."

For a spell in the mid '30s (perhaps 1935–36), Bill Challis did conduct an orchestra on WOR. The show ran without a sponsor. "It was a standby show, a house show. And I had to take all my arrangements and use whatever I could, and make the rest. Which meant that I was busy doing these things from Monday morning until Sunday night. That was tough. It knocked me out. I couldn't handle it. I wanted to do everything myself. And it was the wrong way to do it. I should have hired the help.

"They gave me some money down there. It wasn't much. I think I paid the singers $10 apiece. . . . The show was a hodge-podge. It wasn't what I wanted to do."

The musicians included such first-rate instrumentalists as Charlie Margulis, Manny Klein, Jack Jenney, Laura Newel, and Artie Shaw—all of whom, in that period, were busy doing plenty of different radio shows.

"Boy, they'd scramble around and come down there when I was ready to go. I remember one time, the guys gave me a hard time about something. And Artie [Shaw] comes up; he goes over in front of the cello and he bangs for the tempo! Heh-heh-heh! I should have done something like that, but I wasn't that type of guy. I thought, to hell with it! But he thought—to help it out, you know—he thought of giving them a beat." Challis simply may not have had the temperament to make it as an orchestra leader.

Challis continued freelancing as an arranger, but he wasn't turning out hits, and he wasn't working for the most popular bands. Not for Benny Goodman or the Dorseys, but for those a rung or two down. He wrote some arrangements for Buddy Clark, Raymond Paige, and Jack Teagarden. He did most of the backgrounds for the Modernaires when they were with Paul Whiteman (before they went on to greater success with Glenn Miller).

Artie Shaw hired Challis to do a few things for his big band with strings in 1941. Challis arranged Shaw's recordings of "Blues in the Night" and "Take Your Shoes Off, Baby" (both featuring Hot Lips Page). Clarinetist-bandleader Jerry Wald, who copied Shaw, hired Challis to make some arrangements for him, too.

Challis also did a couple of charts for Glenn Miller. "But by that time, Glenn didn't like Bix." Why? "I don't know. He probably liked him, but he didn't think much of him," Challis reflects. For Miller looked over the charts Challis had prepared, and said something to the effect that Challis seemed to be trying for a Bixian effect, and today's kids didn't know who Bix was. Miller had no interest.

Challis was doing some arranging for Glen Gray and the

BILL CHALLIS

Casa Loma Orchestra in the mid '40s when Red Nichols joined the band. "He had been working in a factory somewhere and hadn't been playing for two years. Red got himself back in shape in a short while." Nichols started out playing only section parts. After he got his lip back, he began asking for solo spots.

Challis had known Nichols well from the 1920s. "I knew what a talent he was. He knew what to do in the studio, you know. If you gave him a job to do, he could do a fine job. But he was no Bix. He wasn't what I would call creative." (Challis had not been in favor of Nichols joining the Casa Loma Band.)

"But he did a couple of things in the Casa Loma Band that were really great! What was the one that I thought he did as well as he ever did anything? 'Don't Take Your Love from Me.' I just laid out the whole background for him. He ate it up! And then, of course, when he got out of the band—he said we hadn't given him enough good treatment."

Challis was working, but he was not a key player during the Swing Era. Not like Fletcher Henderson or Sy Oliver or Jerry Gray or Bill Finegan. He was more of a peripheral figure.

Did he find it hard to keep adapting as the music changed through the years?

He answers, directly: "Well, I never bothered much with that. I kept on doing what I was doing. I didn't bother about changing any styles, becoming part of what the bands were changing to. I was told by some guys, 'Hey! Time marches on.' It all depended on whom I was with. If I got with a certain group that liked that sort of thing, they played it and would tell you it's a great arrangement. But I suppose there were plenty of guys around that said I was old hat."

Challis worked but sparsely after the 1940s. In the 1950s and early '60s, he contributed arrangements to some TV specials, including one, "Chicago and All that Jazz," which has recently been released on home-video by Vintage Jazz Classics.

By the 1960s, he was something of a forgotten man in the music world. He even took a desk job in an office, wholly unrelated to music, for one year. He also tried giving lessons in arranging. He notes, sadly, sounding hurt by the memory: "There were two guys who came out to the house who tried to get me to give them some instruction without any compensation. I guess they figured that I wanted to keep going or something like that. I didn't think there were guys like that around."

But he had one student he was—and still is—proud of. "Vincent was my star pupil. Vince wanted to get what I had; that's why that was great." Vince Giordano is today a well-known bandleader in New York. His Nighthawks Orchestra, which is dedicated to accurately reproducing dance music and jazz of the 1920s and '30s, works a steady stream of club engagements, society parties, and concerts. He was just 14 or 15 when he first contacted Challis in the mid '60s. Giordano, who had just begun working professionally as a bass saxist, had been thumbing through his newly acquired musicians' union directory when he chanced upon the Challis name. He screwed up all of his courage to dial the number listed and ask: "Are you the same Bill Challis who used to arrange for Goldkette and Whiteman?" He had read about Challis in a book on the history of jazz in New York. For the next few years, Giordano wound up taking weekly lessons from Challis. Ostensibly they were lessons in arranging—but Giordano was interested in everything and anything Challis could tell him about the old days. He immersed himself in that lore.

Giordano organized his Nighthawks Orchestra in the mid '70s, and vintage Challis arrangements were a staple in the band's repertoire from the beginning.

The publication in 1974 of the acclaimed biography *Bix, Man and Legend*, by Richard M. Sudhalter and Philip R. Evans with William Dean Myatt, focused attention on Challis once again, as did the concerts and recordings in tribute to Bix which followed. In 1975, Joe Klee wrote, in a profile of Challis in *The Mississippi Rag*: "Bill Challis would like to record the Jean Goldkette charts again (including some, like 'Blue Room,' which the Goldkette band never recorded), and it's hoped that this project will soon materialize."

It was Giordano who, in 1986, helped this long-held dream of Challis to finally become a reality. He was most eager to do an album of Challis' material. Challis' original charts for the Goldkette Orchestra disappeared many years ago. But Paul Whiteman *had* saved the charts Challis wrote for him—including

74

the expanded versions of Challis' Goldkette arrangements, which Challis had written when he first joined Whiteman's band. These were found in the Whiteman Archives at Williams College. Challis pared down the arrangements, to return them to their original 12-musician form.

In late 1986, Challis conducted an augmented edition of Vince Giordano's Nighthawks, including former Goldkette trombonist Spiegle Willcox, cornetist Tom Pletcher, and reedman Bob Wilber, in 16 of his favorite arrangements from the 1920s. Challis could not have gotten a standard studio band to play them properly. Today's musicians generally phrase much differently than musicians in the 1920s did, and have a hard time getting into 1920s material without making it sound camp. But Giordano has over the past dozen years trained a cadre of musicians who play such vintage music constantly, and have become adept at phrasing it idiomatically. Challis was pleased to be able to work with Giordano's men. *Bill Challis' Goldkette Project* was released by Circle Records in 1988. If this album goes over well, Challis says he'd welcome doing a "Whiteman Project" follow-up.

Would Challis rather be writing brand-new arrangements today?

Problems with his vision limit him, he explains. "It's hard for me to write—anything. So, I haven't arranged in a long time. Now, I'd know what to do. I sometimes want to sit down and do something, but when it goes to write it, I'd have to get too close to the paper. It's not good for me to write. . . . And I do it reasonably well."

1986

ANDY · KIRK

"A Mellow Bit of Rhythm"

The best of Andy Kirk's 1930s and '40s recordings bring us a way of playing big band jazz that's almost been lost—kind of easy, gracious, and charming. He once recorded a number called "A Mellow Bit of Rhythm"—a phrase which for me evokes a good bit of his legacy. He had another memorable number called "Walkin' and Swingin'." A lot of other bands would have made that piece sound more like "Running and Shouting." Kirk never wanted to have the hardest-driving band; he didn't have the aggressive temperament for it, and that wasn't his idea of the best way to make music in the first place. His band's best-remembered sides were made with a total of only 12 or 13 musicians; his band was smaller than most other well-known big bands, and suppler. He had gifted jazz soloists, including lightly rocking pianist Mary Lou Williams and silken tenor saxist Dick Wilson, and he also had vocalists who broadened the band's commercial appeal, including Pha Terrell for ballads and June Richmond for swinging tunes and novelties. His goal was to coax all of his players, no matter what their interests, to perform to the best of their abilities, working together as harmoniously as possible. He wanted a band that was relaxed, warm, and lithe. He didn't much care for the brass-heavy powerhouse approach that became prominent among big bands in the East. His band was long based in Kansas City, and his early years were spent even farther west. (It's probably no coincidence that the only important big band today that emphasizes playing with suppleness and ease rather than with a hard-hitting attack is the 13-man band led by Kansas-born Buck Clayton; the Midwest generally seemed to favor a more relaxed music than did the East.)

The following short profile is distilled from several interviews with Andy Kirk in the once-fashionable, now run-down apartment building at 555 Edgecomb Avenue in which he has lived since 1939. Because Kirk has published an autobiography since these interviews (the recommended *Twenty Years On Wheels,* written with the assistance of Amy Lee), this profile is not a comprehensive recounting of his entire career. It focuses mostly on his formative years and his attitudes as a bandleader. Understanding where Andy Kirk came from is helpful to understanding his music.

Standard reference sources state that Kirk's place of birth on May 28, 1898 was Newport, Kentucky. However, he equivocates a bit about that. "My father said I was born in Cincinnati. I said I was born across the river in Kentucky—see, because my mother was a Kentuckian, and she wanted me to be born in her state. She didn't live very long; she died with tuberculosis when I was about two months old," he comments. One can understand him wanting to feel a connection to his late mother. He was raised by relatives, mostly in Denver. He didn't see his father again for years.

"You see, those days were days where you could catch tuberculosis. Somebody in my family went out to Denver for that clean air; it was just right for tuberculosis. And so that's how I got there. My aunt, who's my mother's half-sister, was out in Denver for her health, for tuberculosis. So I was sent out there. All my schooling was in Denver.

"I didn't meet my father until I'd say maybe five years later. I was brought up in Denver schools. We had everything. We learned to speak German. All right, why? We had a lot of German people out in that section. There were some who came from Germany. And they had it tapered off so well that it wouldn't be a political thing; you know, it was just somebody who knew how to speak German. And they were given the job in the school system. Yeah boy, I was speaking German. I remember when we'd go to German class, she'd say 'Guten morgen, kinder' and we'd say 'Guten morgen, Fräulein. . . .' And we'd go from there, 'Ich bin, du bist. . . .'

"We learned all different songs, European songs. [He sings a song in German.] We had music in the school system. Paul Whiteman's father was the music supervisor in the entire public school system. I played piano then. And it wasn't any problem for us to get around and know other musicians, play together and so forth. Everybody knew everybody. Denver was a small city at that time.

"I wasn't brought up in jazz," Kirk notes. "I was just brought up playing music. Before I knew it, I was playing jazz and everything. And by having jobs with different musical outfits, well, I forgot what kind of music we were playing, because we were playing every kind of music." Kirk eventually learned a variety of instruments, including alto, tenor, and baritone saxophones, tuba, and string bass. He was able to earn money as a musician in the evening, even while working for the postal service in the daytime. "I was a letter carrier out there and we could do most anything we wanted, that is, if it didn't interfere with postal work." By 1917, he recalls, he was playing in George Morrison's Orchestra. He stayed with Morrison for eight years, everything from posh hotel jobs to playing all of the big clubs in town to private parties. Morrison was a role model for Kirk.

"George Morrison was a black man, but he was a violinist," Kirk says. "I was very taken after hearing him because he was a *violinist*, not a fiddle player. The way he played knocked me out. Man, we'd go to a country club and he'd [Kirk hums a light classic, while pantomiming playing a violin]—you know, classics. I learned a lot from him. Because he could play jazz and he could play pretty stuff. I didn't call myself a copy of him, but I learned something from him. He was a fine musician—and man, he had Denver sewed up. The leaders of Denver would say, 'George Morrison, we want you' and such and such. The people in the

78

country club in Denver loved George Morrison. And he would go with *The Denver Post* to Cheyenne, Wyoming every year, you know. We'd get on a train and go up in Wyoming and we'd be playing there. And he wouldn't be saying to anyone, 'What do you want, Mr. so-and-so?' They'd come and pat George on the back and say, 'George, just give me some George Morrison music.' He knew his way around. I remember the end of World War One, the bells started ringing and we all gathered down in front of *The Denver Post*—played in front and formed a parade. I was in that parade, and I was with Morrison's band.

"George Morrison had a big band. But for some functions he'd have just a few pieces. He could take like himself and a piano and a violin and entertain some people if it was not a big affair. Or maybe after a big affair, a few people were going to get together—now maybe they'd need four or six pieces, you know." Kirk opens one of his photo albums and points out his mentor. "That's George Morrison standing. That was his orchestra. At this particular time I was playing the bass violin and tuba. Those are beautiful days. I played tenor saxophone on a small job, you know. Sometimes he had two or three jobs going on one night. And he'd book me on a job and we'd start and people would ask, 'Where's Morrison?' I'd say, 'He said he had something at the house that was going to make him be a little late. But we'll take care of it until he gets here.' "

Their main source of income as musicians, Kirk says, "was the country club. He's on that violin, and we're giving him some background, you know." They played light classics, waltzes, schottisches, one-steps and two-steps. "And then, we had all the new songs, and the country club would be dancing. After the dinner was over, then we started playing dance music, you know. I heard the other kind of music because George Morrison was a fine violinist. And we played jazz, too. Because we had fellows who would go down to New Orleans in the wintertime, you know, and they'd come back to Denver with some new songs. And we weren't thinking of anything but music, then."

The Morrison band traveled to New York, briefly, in 1920. "We were playing with white shows in the theater. We were the house music and we met different orchestras, groups, you know, by being on the bill. One of the acts was a woman with her girls. We used to play the music they'd bring and we'd bring them on stage. And before we'd know it, we were all playing together," Kirk recalls. "Morrison's Jazz Orchestra" recorded "I Know Why (introducing: My Cuban Dreams)" for Columbia during this trip. They made several other recordings, including "Royal Garden Blues," that were not released.

Morrison wanted an orchestra that could play all kinds of music, the way Paul Whiteman's could. Morrison and his musicians were more familiar with the accomplishments of prominent white orchestra leaders such as Whiteman, Ted Lewis, Isham Jones, and Ben Bernie—their records sold well and they toured extensively (Kirk saw all of them play in Denver before he left that city for good in 1925)—than they were with the accomplishments of the best black jazz band leaders of the day. Black bands were less likely to be recorded (and if they were recorded, their records weren't necessarily available in Denver); they could be famous in a given locale (say, New Orleans or Chicago or Kansas City) without having any national impact. Most bands Kirk saw in the early 1920s were white. In fact, the only touring black band Kirk remembers coming to Denver (which did not have a very large black community) was Happy Gene Coy's Black Aces from Texas; their southwestern blues sounded unusual to him. Jelly Roll Morton, the New Orleans-born pianist-composer who liked to claim he was the "inventor" of jazz, played some gigs in the Denver area with a Morrison combo; neither Kirk nor anybody else knew how to stomp the music the vigorous, jazzy way Morton wanted them to. Kirk listened to Alphonso Trent's Dallas-based band after it began broadcasting circa 1924; Trent's was one of the earliest black bands to broadcast regularly, and the only black band Kirk knew of—other than Morrison's, which had worked for quite a while at Denver's Albany Hotel—that worked at a fancy hotel. But Kirk had to travel to fully become aware of how music was developing elsewhere.

Morrison's band made some western vaudeville tours in the early 1920s (even playing in Mexico at one point), sometimes working with Hattie McDaniel, today best remembered for her many portrayals of maids and mammies in movies but then working as a singer and recitalist. They played Kansas City in 1925, where Kirk got his first taste of the infectious way Bennie Moten's group was swinging the blues; he had never heard anything like that. That same year, Kirk married Mary Colston.[1] By now, Kirk had outgrown Morrison's Orchestra. He and his wife went to Chicago, where a sister of Mary's lived. There was far more musical variety here than in Denver. Kirk remembers seeing, for example, Erskine Tate's Orchestra, featuring Louis Armstrong, at the Vendome Theater. And while in Chicago, he got an invitation to join trumpeter T. Holder's Band, which played at a roadhouse just outside of Dallas—a former Morrison musician, now in the band, had recommended him.

By 1929, Holder left the band and the other musicians voted to make Kirk the new leader. That was the birth of Andy Kirk and his Twelve Clouds of Joy; the band made its first recordings that year. Kirk was playing bass in the band then, but eventually he hired another musician to play bass and simply directed. For much of the next seven years, the band was based in Kansas City. Kirk drew upon his background to play a mix of quality dance music and jazz. Equally comfortable playing sweet or hot, he made a name for himself in Kansas City as a first-rate bandleader long before Count Basie (who was still working as a sideman when Kirk was establishing himself as a leader). Kansas City had a far livelier and more varied musical scene than any place he'd been in previously.

"Kansas City! I loved it. I *loved* Kansas City. There was plenty of room for all the bands that they had there. And then the thing about Kansas City—now, there'd be a fiddle player in one band that just had a short gig downtown and he'd come up and say, 'Man, you got room for me?' 'Sure I got room for you.' And we had all kinds of music, you know. Kansas City was beautiful. It was a musical city. Everybody came there because Kansas City dancers liked to dance. And they had different dances. And when you were playing music, they'd dance. Kansas City, man. Oh, that was something! You didn't have to make it—it was

---

[1]Mary Colston Kirk died November 18, 1990.

already made in Kansas City for musicians. There was never a city like Kansas City, as far as music was concerned. Boy, it was something.

"We had so much to do around Kansas City, nobody was in anybody's place. It wasn't that your band was all there was to it. And when you were coming, someone from the other band would say, 'Yeah man!' And they'd get to dancing to your band and they'd talk about it, you know. Count Basie had a top band in Kansas City. And we were good friends. Of course, his band was different from us and he played in different places. We weren't playing those places. I'm playing for the elite, you know, with the classics and so forth. And then after a certain hour, those people who knew nothing but classics, they were hearing some jazz. But we'd start out with what they wanted. What could soften it was, we could play a nice waltz. And the older people would all know how to waltz. So we let them waltz. That was it. You had to have some knowledge of country clubs. And you just had to keep your ears and eyes open. People would come over and say hello to me and the musicians. There's a good feeling between the musicians out there. I didn't know another place like it. Everybody was known by their first names, you know— the Count, Andy my boy. And we'd all be together. Oh, those were beautiful days. I was young and anxious," Kirk says.

Joe Glaser, Louis Armstrong's manager, became Kirk's manager as well. "I didn't like Joe Glaser too much. But I couldn't dislike him, because he was bringing in the money. I played Yale, Harvard, all of them, through Joe Glaser's office," Kirk comments. "He'd say things that didn't sound right, you know. And he's be talking with his chest out. He was puffed up. And he didn't know that much about music. But we'd let it go. He wasn't a bad guy, but he just came up in a different life. It was kind of hard for me to understand him at first. But then I got his way about life, so I said OK. I put him in his corner. I can't really say I disliked Joe, but I can say there were some things that he could have learned about the music business from Louis Armstrong!

"It was through Joe Glaser that Louis and I became good friends. Man, we were tight like that! We had a good thing going together because wherever Louis Armstrong was, I would get a job through Joe Glaser. And at the end of a period, you know, Louis Armstrong would come to where I'm playing and he played with me until two in the morning. He'd hardly say hello; he'd just pick up his horn and say, 'Where do you want me?' I'd say, 'Right here in this chair.' [Kirk laughs happily at the memory.] And he was a drawing force, Louis Armstrong, and he just loved to play whatever I had in my bag. One time Joe Glaser had brought me down to Philly. When Louis would leave the theater, he'd come over to meet with my orchestra where I was playing a dance, and I'd have him blowing. That happened at different times. It wasn't something laid out, but something musicians like to do when we did it ourselves. Louis just loved to play. That's the reason he could play. Oh, he was beautiful. A nice, special person."

Kirk's band came East in 1936, recording steadily now and thus becoming better known nationally. The band scored almost immediately with a hit, "Until the Real Thing Comes Along," crooned by Pha [pronounced Fay] Terrell, whose high clear voice seemed to thrill plenty of women and also put off a certain number of men, some of whom thought he sounded effeminate. Kirk thinks highly of Terrell as both a singer and a person. "Pha was something; he was a natural. And I learned a lot of things from him, just listening to him," Kirk says. "And you know what? That guy was brought up in Kansas City and worked in clubs. His job was to keep people out of trouble on the job. He was a bouncer. But he was a one-punch man. Pow! And the cat's on the floor. Oh, he was something. He wasn't a big-mouthed bouncer, you know. He was some other kind. 'Oh you're getting out of line now,' Pha'd be saying, while patting him on the back. He'd say, 'You and me been friends a long time. Let's go and break it up now. Look man, you know, you and I have been friends a long time. Straighten up.' You'd straighten up. And if you didn't straighten up—boom—Pha had him on the floor. And he'd probably go pick him up, you know. 'Man, you hit me!' 'I didn't mean to hit you hard. Did I hit you hard? But now listen, you had me nervous, man.' He knew what to say. Because he was brought up in that system, you know. Boy.

"I got him out of a club—not for his punching ability, but because he could sing. But he was a natural bouncer because he loved his music and he didn't want nobody interfering with music and the time he spent learning these songs. One time we were playing down in the biggest city in Virginia. Now, these were days, you know, when blacks were here and whites were here, and so forth. Now, we play a black dance down in Virginia. The kids from the University of Virginia—white kids—would sit upstairs; they used to segregate themselves.

"And a great big guy at this dance hated Pha Terrell—thought there was something wrong with him because he could hit a high note, you know. So, this guy, he came up in front of the orchestra and tried to grab the microphone stand—and Pha caught him by the collar and twisted him and dropped him on the floor. And he jumped up and Pha knocked him down again. Pha figured this cat out; he said he was going to have to knock him out. That cat couldn't even hit Pha—Pha was in and out. He knew how to fight. Under this guy's arm and—bam—right in his mouth. This great big guy, six-footer. And little Pha there, waiting for him to get up off of the floor. The cops had to come. Pha had been around characters all his life. And he was a little guy, but he knew his ability as a fighter. And so, when this guy got out of line, Pha was hoping he would get further out of line. He would beat him. And he only needed one punch. And the white college kids sitting up on the balcony were saying, 'More!' Then Pha came to me and said, 'I'm sorry, man.' I said, 'Yeah, that cat you hit is sorry, too.' I'm not supposed to be on that side. Kindness, you know. I don't want no fighting, but I'm so glad Pha hit that cat.

"Pha eventually went to California. I knew his mother and I would see her. When we were in Kansas City, I would go by and say, 'How's your boy acting?' 'Oh, he's all right.' He saved up some money. When we were out in Los Angeles, he saw a house and he bought it. Then he could bring his mother out to live there. So that's where he finally ended up. He was happy with his mother being there," Kirk recalls.

Mary Lou Williams ("the lady who swings the band") was a key member of the Clouds of Joy, as a pianist, composer, and

Andy Kirk. (Courtesy of Andy Kirk.)

Andy Kirk (standing at left) and his Orchestra, featuring pianist Mary Lou Williams and vocalist Pha Terrell (both seated at the piano), 1937. (Courtesy of the Institute of Jazz Studies.)

arranger. "She was something to listen to and she was a nice person. And she could think of ideas which were good to use, you know. Yeah, she was something. She was her own self on piano. There was nothing you could do to make her more impressive. So, we just let her do what she could do best. And we'd make something out of that." He'd teasingly refer to her as "the Pest." "Yeah! She enjoyed it. I appreciated her. I told her, 'I didn't want you to get a head. Hot-headed. You are a pest.' She was all right. Mary Lou was a natural. And [guitarist] Floyd Smith was a natural. All you had to do was tell him. I had some good ones."

He says he first met June Richmond, who became his band's female vocalist in 1939, years earlier. "We worked together out in Denver with George Morrison. Well, she came through Denver and George always had something going, you know. Then, she was a comedienne, too. Aw, she'd keep the house laughing and moving. June Richmond wasn't a musician. But she could sing songs—a certain type." She was an extroverted, vivacious entertainer who pleased crowds with such numbers as "Hey Lawdy Mama," "Hip Hip Hooray," and "47th Street Jive" (sometimes Kirk would join in on the vocal on that one).

"I don't know anybody that worked with me who was bad. I didn't run into any real bad musicians," Kirk says. "They can't all be perfect, you know. But you'll see perfection in somebody somewhere. And then you'll call for that one certain thing, you know. And then build all the rest of them around the way he or she did that one thing that was perfect," Kirk says. He didn't want to be a strict disciplinarian with his musicians, barking orders at them like a drill sergeant. He wanted to encourage them, to gently nudge them with positive reinforcement to go in the direction he believed was best.

"Howard McGhee [the trumpeter who joined Kirk in 1942] was something. And he was a listener. I mean, you could talk to him. You know, my approach with somebody was like this. I'd tell him, 'Man, when you took that solo, that knocked me out.' And I'm telling the truth. I'd say, 'Save that. I'll tell you where I want it. We'll play so-and-so at a certain time, get ready then.' 'Man, I'll be ready.' Nobody's perfect. But you can always improve upon that ability. Even though it's imperfection right here, you can improve upon it. All you have to do is say, 'What was the thing that you did wrong—so-and-so-and-so, all you have to do is play it right.' And so we got along; I got along with all the musicians. Because I'd tell them, 'Man, I can't do it without you. I want you here. You ready to play?' And we'd do it in a little comedy. But still, I'm thinking exactly what I'm thinking—because I've had musicians who were better musicians than I. I didn't tell them, man. But I'd say, 'I can listen to you because I hear some perfection. You brought a thought to my mind. You know the 16 bars you played?' Well, I'd tell him what I liked about that. And why it's better than the first part. 'Yeah man? Well, you mean so-and-so-and-so.' 'Yeah, that. Well, you're the soloist. You know from your heart what you want to play—but these people down there, standing there listening to you, want you to improve on that part there. When they were smiling, I could tell that they loved what you were doing.' 'Well, man.' I said, 'All right. Go ahead and play your best. Now when you were there, that was your best. . . .'

"So I got along with musicians. I'd say now, 'You're a stronger saxophone player than I am—on this one.' I'm making a joke out of it. Then: 'Seriously, now, when you come in on the 36th bar, don't just jump in. Just come in smoothly.' " Keeping things running smoothly, musically, emotionally, was important to him.

Kirk didn't check to see if the guys in his band all had matching socks, the way, for example, bandleader Jimmie Lunceford (whom he refers to as "a good businessman") did. He wanted his band to have a happy, comfortable feeling to it. Not marred with tension. Some musicians might have needed a tougher disciplinarian, but he did not want to assume such a role. He liked doing things diplomatically. "Running a group is a job. But if you have a personality to get along with people, to understand them—not 'you understand me' but 'let me understand you'— you're together. I was never anyone that said [and now he speaks in a harsh tone], 'Hey, what's the matter with you, man?' That's not me." He tried to make suggestions, rather than demands, in dealing with his arrangers, too, he says. "I would probably say, 'What do you think about the 32nd paragraph there? The reason

I'm asking is, I noticed how beautifully you came in, when we were going in to the rest of the band before. Let them come in smoothly, so when the band hits, you'll be all together.' 'Oh yeah, man.' We'd talk together."

Kirk's knack for diplomacy came in handy, too, when the band had to tour down south, where its records were quite popular. He met his share of bigots, he notes, but adds that they rarely posed any serious problems for him. He knew how to handle them. He explains with a smile and a knowing look: "As long as they can be giving orders, they're going to be doing what I suggest, see? As long as they are giving the orders, they're happy. So I'd say something about, 'I want it to be according to what your orders are, where we can. . . .' I think you have to use your head. You don't have to be the biggest guy in there. After everything is toned down, developed to this point, we all have no problems. I got along with people. I might say, 'I thought maybe you might like this thing; I want you to listen.' I didn't say, 'I want you to hear this.' Then, after we played it, I'm going to ask them what they thought of it. 'Beautiful, man.' Whether it was or not. But they would say it, they were happy, you know."

If Kirk's bands never made it to the top rung musically or commercially, they worked steadily enough, playing dances and theaters and recording, for about 20 years. He made a good living playing the music he liked without getting or giving any ulcers in the process. "Oh boy. I really enjoyed those days," he says. Eventually, he was forced to enlarge his band to stay competitive (the 12 and 13 musicians grew to 15, 16 and 17 by the mid 1940s); he didn't really favor the brassier sound, but he bowed to what he believed the public wanted. Among the jazz artists who played in his band at one time or another were Ben Webster, Don Byas, Shorty Baker, Kenny Kersey, Hank Jones, and Fats Navarro.

Kirk led small groups in the 1950s and '60s, occasionally fronting big bands for specific occasions. But times were changing and there wasn't always a demand even for his small groups. (He believes the musicians' union should have done something, like making the 52nd Street clubs change attractions more often to spread the work around more.) Gradually, interests other than leading groups, such as his religion (he's been a Jehovah's Witness since Denver days) and working in the union office, came to absorb more of his energies, although he still led groups when opportunities arose.

Kirk doesn't get out a lot these days. What does he enjoy doing? One answer comes readily: visiting with disc jockey-jazz historian-impresario Phil Schaap. "I don't know anybody I like any better in the music business than Phil Schaap. That cat is something. He's got a good memory and he's got a good heart. Oh, we have a lot of fun together. I call up Phil Schaap. And we get together. And if we have a glass of wine, that might make me feel a little stronger."

Kirk does not consider himself completely retired from the music business, even today. If somebody wants music for a wedding or a party, he says he can still help them out. "If it's a small room, we use a small group. Musicians are so friendly, it's easy to put together a group for anything that they want. If they want me to put a group together, well, I'm very anxious to put it together. I know all the other musicians. I say, 'Who can I have on tenor saxophone, who am I going to have lead on alto?' And I could put it together," he says. "I haven't done it in, I don't know—it's been a good length—but I always think about it," he says.

"Oh boy, this world is something. I've enjoyed this. I'm 90 years old now. I really do look back and I appreciate it, you know. I had no idea I was going to live to be 90. I'm reaching out for 100. I can still walk. And if necessary"—he laughs—"I can run."

1988

"Beat Me, Daddy. . ."

Of all the drummers that I've seen "live," I can't think of any who have given me more pleasure than Ray McKinley. That is not to say that he's the greatest drummer, in terms of technical facility, that I've ever seen. In a single concert, I once saw Buddy Rich, Louie Bellson, and Sonny Igoe all playing much faster and stronger than I could ever imagine McKinley playing. Art Blakey is a much more emotional, uninhibited drummer than McKinley; Max Roach a more dramatic one; Elvin Jones plays far more complex rhythms. But I can't say that any of those greats, much as I appreciate their particular talents, has given me more pleasure than McKinley. What makes McKinley so memorable? It's not just a matter of getting a good beat and appealing, varied sounds from his drums and cymbals (which he does), it's the originality, playfulness, and wit he displays in his drumming. He has a confident sense of style—you see it even in the way he'll lift a single drumstick, sometimes suspending it for just a tad, creating suspense, as if he's waiting for exactly the right moment to hit exactly the right part of his drumset. I watched him enliven different little bands at the 1986 Conneaut Lake, Pennsylvania, Jazz Festival. I don't remember him ever getting much above a medium-fast tempo the whole three days—it was almost all a very easy, no-sweat kind of swing—but the drum breaks he took were filled with such personality, so many joyful little surprises, his playing was for me sheer magic.

Depending on your age and/or musical preferences, you may associate McKinley first with the Glenn Miller name—either from the Glenn Miller Band he led in the 1950s and '60s or the Glenn Miller Army Air Force Band in which he played and sang in World War Two (McKinley's links to Miller actually date back to the 1920s), or perhaps you'll think of McKinley's own bands of the 1940s, including the one he co-led with Will Bradley, or perhaps, earlier still, the bands of Jimmy Dorsey and the Dorsey Brothers in which he drummed. He's been on the scene a long time. And like many of the especially individualistic drum stylists in jazz, McKinley was self-taught.

Born June 18, 1910 in Fort Worth, Texas (his voice still has the relaxed cadences of his native state), he says he just "fell into drumming." He doubts he ever would have become a drummer at all, he adds, piquing my curiosity, if his mother had had better eyes. "You see," he explains, "my mother must have been a little near-sighted. At the local theater, where the vaudeville acts came through, she would sit very close and often in the front row—and that, when she took me, would put me right down where the drums were. A guy named Johnny Grimes was the pit drummer; he played for all the acts. And I was just fascinated with this guy. After all, in those days, a show drummer in a pit—he had everything that you could ever associate with drums, you know, from the essential bass drum, snare drum, tom-tom, and tympani; besides that, he had all kinds of sound-things like ratchets and cowbells and temple blocks and xylophones and everything you could think of. Well, that to a kid was like Christmas! So I fell in love with the drums. And I don't know where I got my sense of rhythm. I'm not from a musical family. But I've always had that.

"There was a fellow that lived across the street from us in Fort Worth who owned a great big old field snare drum. You know those things that are like Napoleon's army used to use. I'd beat on that and I could play it pretty well. So that was the start of the whole thing. I was about six, seven years old when I started, something like that—maybe sooner, I don't know."

RAY MCKINLEY

How did McKinley get into drumming professionally?

"Well, it's a natural process of any musician in a town. Sooner or later, somebody says there's a kid that plays drums here. You come out and they ask you if you want to play in their orchestra, and you come out. The first one I played in was five pieces—clarinet, a C-melody saxophone, a trombone, a piano, and myself—we didn't even have a trumpet. It was called the Jolly Jazz Bandits. I was about 10 or 11 years old, I guess. Short pants. The others were older. I don't know where they even heard about me, but they pulled up in a car one day and asked me if I wanted to play with them. And it took me the shortest time interval known to man to say yes. And then I went on to another local orchestra, which was a little bigger, a little better. In fact, there were two of them there in Fort Worth.

"And then, after a few years of that, a band came through Fort Worth called the Duncan-Marin Southern Entertainers. How 'bout that? There was a dash between the names. Marin was the booking agent and Duncan was the leader. He played alto sax, and he was a singer, too. They were on their way to Chicago, to do an engagement at the Moulin Rouge nightclub. So, what can I tell you? I fell into a car and we rode to Chicago. And did that job," McKinley says.

"And a little bit later I left that band when a certain trumpet player in El Paso, when I was with this Duncan-Marin Band, told me about a band in Nashville, Tennessee, called Beaseley Smith, and he wrote some letters and they wrote back and they hired me. Here I go, with all these drums; I looked like Barnum and Bailey Circus coming into town, I had so many drums. I'd just gotten a new set. I'd borrowed the money from my Daddy to send out to California, and got a big fancy set of drums from Roy Duncan, drum-maker. Up till then, I didn't have very good drums. And I went with this Beaseley Smith outfit for several years. Beaseley Smith, yeah, was quite famous in those days around Nashville, Tennessee. He had several orchestras and I was part of all of them. We'd go out the summer up to Lake Paw Paw in Michigan and come back to Nashville. We'd play in a little, local theater there. And then we played all the dances in Vanderbilt University . . . and the other Peabody schools around

Nashville. The first time I ever made any real money in my life. I think I was making about $60-$70 a week. Hey! Heh-heh. How old was I then? I can tell you exactly. I was 17, 18, and 19, those three years."

McKinley says he took lessons, briefly, from only one drummer in his career. "There was a very famous drummer with Paul Ash out at the Oriental Theater in Chicago, and his name was Art Layfield. He later played snare drum with the New York Philharmonic Symphony. Art was known as a good jazz drummer and a good man on the tympani, on the kettle drums. I used to ride in there from Lake Paw Paw once a week to take a tympani lesson from him. I even bought a set of tymps. I didn't play 'em in Smith's band; I just bought 'em, kept 'em in a little room and practiced on 'em, you know. Never got me anything. Never got me a single job or anything. But I had 'em anyway. That's all the studying I ever did," McKinley notes. "Then I joined a band in Pittsburgh, which was quite a larger band, called Tracy-Brown. Now again, we're into a name with two fellows. Tracy was the bass player and the boss and Brown was a violin player. Can you imagine one violin? I can't. But it was a larger orchestra. And they were very big in Pittsburgh. They had Pittsburgh sewed up. Oh boy! They had a winter home down in a place called the Plaza Cafe, and then in the summertime they'd go out to the Willows in Oak Mont, which is just a suburb of Pittsburgh. And I had a couple of very enjoyable years there.

"From there I went up to New York to join Milt Shaw's Detroiters, which was playing in the Roseland Ballroom. That was 1930. They had some pretty fair boys in there, for those days. A couple of them were good. And we played opposite Fletcher Henderson, who was on the other bandstand. They had two bands. Each band would play a half hour. And I was there for a couple of years with them."

McKinley remembers playing tangos and other popular dances of the day. Shaw's men didn't dream of cutting Henderson's when it came to hot jazz. As he puts it: "Shaw's band was playing the skim-milk stuff and Fletcher was playing all the good music, you know. I mean he had a great band there. Whee! Wow! He had Coleman Hawkins in that band and Rex Stewart, and

[Walter] Johnson on drums—a whole bunch of good players. And anyway, I learned a lot of things just listening to those guys. Especially how to play the hi-hat cymbals from Johnson. And Chick Webb came in later on that other stand there—two years with Fletcher and one with Chick Webb. And Chick was a great drummer, you know, so I learned a lot more."

Who were McKinley's earliest influences on the drums?

"Well, now that's a funny thing. The first guy that really had any influence on me was a fellow named Ray Rohle, who was a drummer with Don Bestor's Orchestra [and recorded with Bestor 1925–28], which came down to Dallas, Texas, to open a new hotel called the Baker Hotel and played for quite a number of months before they left. I got to hear him a lot. He was a good showman and a good drummer. And Ray had an influence on me. I guess the next drummer was Fletcher's drummer, [Walter] Johnson. I learned how to play the hi-hat from listening to him, because that's all he did. He stayed on that hi-hat all night long. He never hardly ever—he never played the top cymbal or never played the snare drum—all on the hi-hats. And in that band you didn't have to—they were all drummers, you know. And then who would be the next one? Oh, Chick! Chick Webb, of course, Chick. I had met Gene Krupa when we were kids, up at this Lake Paw Paw I mentioned earlier. He was with a band up the road about a half a mile, and I was down at this other place with Beaseley's Nashville orchestra. Strangely enough, though, I never got to hear Gene back then, because they were working the same hours we were working. But I got to meet him and know him, and become friends with him, and then later on, he came to New York about the same time I did, and I got to hear him; Gene was playing in a band that Benny Goodman had in a nightclub. It wasn't a very big band, but a fair size—about 12 guys, I guess. And I learned some things from Gene. From there on, it just boleroed into whoever you heard that was good, or did something you wished you could do and thought you could, and then you tried it and found you can do it, and if you can't do it, forget it. In those days, drummers were supposed to have everything, you know. You remember Sonny Greer with Duke? Good Lord! He had everything, including *chimes* in back of him.

Well, in those days, it was quite the thing—or we *thought* it was going to be this way, to have everything."

McKinley backtracks for a moment: "I forgot—one very important guy I left out as an influence, who was probably the greatest of all—Ben Pollack. Ben was, if not the best drummer of those days, he was one of the best. And he did some things that were just great. He had his own orchestra and he played in it, until he later on got out in front and became a front man instead of playing drums. But Ben Pollack, I think, had the biggest influence of anybody on me: So, I guess that's about it."

McKinley drummed at Roseland in the depths of the Depression, in the early 1930s. When he wasn't working there, he picked up jobs as he could. "I did a tour of New England with Red Nichols—a small band," he recalls. "But the only record I ever made with Red, I didn't play drums on it. They had Red McKenzie set up to do a vocal on a tune called 'Moan You Moaners.' I did the vocal. Why they ever asked me to do the vocal, I haven't the *faintest* idea," he insists. The Brian Rust discography credits McKinley with drumming as well as singing on Nichols' May 26, 1931 recording of "Moan You Moaners" (the other musicians are Glenn Miller, Jimmy Dorsey, Babe Russin, Jack Russin, Perry Botkin, Art Miller, and Charlie Teagarden), but McKinley has a very definite recollection that he only sang and that Gene Krupa handled the drumming on the session, which is certainly plausible (Krupa drummed on other Nichols sessions in this period and it would have been easier from a recording standpoint to have someone else drum while McKinley sang than to have McKinley do both).

"I made a couple of trips over to England on the old ship, the Leviathan, with Ben Bernie's brother, Dave, just to work. I just honked around there, doing this and doing that—not doing very well, to tell you the truth. Because work was scarce. And then I was playing with four or five pieces in a little basement in New York and nobody ever came in there. I don't even remember who was in the band—nobody who later made any noise.

"And then, one day I get a call from Glenn Miller. I had met Glenn when he was playing with the Pollack orchestra in 1926 in Chicago, when I was 16. And now he said that he was getting a band together for Smith Ballew. Smith Ballew was a great society favorite—the jet set favorite there in New York City for a couple of years. I had known him slightly in Texas because he was a Fort Worth, Texas, boy. But he was a lot older than I was, so I didn't really know him. I don't even know how Glenn Miller found me when he called me, but he did, and he asked me if I wanted to play with this new band he was getting together with Ballew. I said, 'Yeah, sure. Of course.' And he had some good guys in the band—Bunny Berigan on trumpet, and Sid Stoneburn on clarinet, Fidgy McGrath was the piano player, nice piano. And above all, there was Smith. Very handsome man. A big guy, about 6' 3", you know. Blond. And he sang a lot—all ballads. We went out on the road and then the Depression just got worse and worse and worse. We'd go out and play a job for a month at some hotel and then we'd break up for a month. And then we'd go out and play another hotel. And we'd always break up in between, because there wasn't that much work. But somehow we survived. This was just before Roosevelt was elected. The Ballew scene went on for about a year and a half, maybe two.

"Then this Ballew band did a job out in Denver. And out there, we picked up some local kids to play in the band—three boys and a girl singer. The girl singer was Kay Weber, the saxophone player was Skeets Herfurt, the trombone player was Don Matteson, and the guitar player was Roc Hillman," he says, mentioning names that would later become known as members of the Dorsey Brothers' Orchestra. In New York, the Dorseys were trying to put together their first organized big band.

"Glenn knew the brothers, Tommy and Jimmy. And Tommy wasn't about to hire a lot of New York guys, you know. He wouldn't have been able to yell at 'em, I guess; I don't know—guys that he'd been working with in New York. He wanted good musicians that were new and younger. So [in mid-1934] he hired the whole schmear—Glenn, myself, the three boys from Denver and the girl singer—we all became part of the first Dorsey Brothers' Orchestra. And that was the beginning of the transition up to what you might call wherever it is I am now."

While Glenn Miller played an important role in both the Smith Ballew and Dorsey Brothers bands, McKinley says that

Miller (despite suggestions to the contrary in print elsewhere) did not write many arrangements from scratch for those bands. "No. He was very good at taking stock orchestrations—you know, printed orchestrations—and cutting them up, making little deletions and assigning solos, and that sort of thing. He was always good at that. He did a lot more of that than he did any arranging. He only wrote three or four arrangements for us in the whole time we were together." (The Rust discography credits Miller with having arranged "Annie's Cousin Fannie," "Honeysuckle Rose," "Basin Street Blues," "Weary Blues," "Dese, Dem, Dose," and "Tomorrow's Another Day" for the Dorsey Brothers' Orchestra.)

Rollicking, inventive, McKinley was an excellent drummer for the light and happy Dixieland-oriented jazz the Dorsey brothers liked to feature. The band worked steadily. The only problem was the increasing tension between Jimmy and Tommy (who ultimately left the band to form his own). "We were out at Sands Point Casino with the Dorsey Brothers the first summer [1934]. We went from there down to the Palais Royale on Broadway. Then we went on a tour with several acts—a sort of a show, you know—all around the East. And came back into Glen Island Casino, where the brothers split up. We all stayed with Jimmy."

Why did McKinley decide to stay with Jimmy rather than going with Tommy?

"Don't ask me. Don't ask me. I don't think Tommy wanted any but a couple of us. And besides that, he wasn't soliciting men right there and then in the band. He just wanted to get out, and get away from Jimmy. Oh, that was a real bad scene there for a few days, a couple of weeks," McKinley recalls.

"And then after we finished the summer at this Glen Island Casino, the band went out to Hollywood, appearing with Bing Crosby on the Kraft Music Hall [radio show] for a couple of years." While out in Los Angeles, McKinley cut his first sides under his own name, including "New Orleans Parade" and "Shack in the Back" (March 31, 1936); except for pianist Joe Sullivan, the members of his recording sextet were all from the Jimmy Dorsey Band. Dorsey, meanwhile, had also begun featuring McKinley on occasional vocals. While Dorsey's regular vocalist, Bob Eberly, was superb on ballads, McKinley had a kind of downhome quality and natural feel for rhythm that made him much better suited for certain songs (usually with a bit of a bite and some humor), such as "Cowboy From Brooklyn," "The Love Bug Will Get You," and "Show Your Linen Miss Richardson." He got to join with the Andrews Sisters on "(Where Have You Been) Billy Boy." He didn't have a great voice by legitimate standards, but (like fellow Texan Jack Teagarden's) it was warm, open, and personable.

He was a featured player in Jimmy Dorsey's Band. On portions of "Song of the Volga Boatman," he drummed under trombonist Bobby Byrne while the rest of the band stopped playing; there was also a point in "John Silver" when he and Jimmy Dorsey played in alternation while the rest of the band stopped. The only really extended drum solo McKinley recorded with Jimmy Dorsey's Band was the popular "Dusk in Upper Sandusky." He recalls he also had a long drum solo on "Old Man Harlem," a popular feature in the Dorsey library, but the Jimmy Dorsey Band never recorded that number (no doubt because the Dorsey Brothers had recorded it with a studio group in 1933). George T. Simon reported in the January 1937 *Metronome*: "In 'Old Man Harlem' there's a coda which calls for a break repeated every other two measures. One night, they say, Mac played 23 different breaks in succession, each one screwier than the one before, and finally ended up by standing and whistling the last break through his teeth!"

Occasionally, rather than playing a break on drums in a given number, McKinley would shout out a brief rhythmic phrase in its place, emphasizing certain syllables the way a drummer might emphasize certain drumbeats. His climactic, staccato cry— " 'bout 15 men and on a dead man's chest"—in Jimmy Dorsey's hit "John Silver" is typical. His penchant for calling out such phrases would later give him the biggest hit of his career.

McKinley's rising prominence as a drummer and personality did not go unnoticed. In 1939, he recalls, band booker Willard Alexander came up with the idea of making him co-leader of a new big band band with Will Bradley, a trombonist of exceptional tone (rich, full-bodied, and penetrating) who had been working in the studios for the past four years (prior to that, he had worked with Ray Noble, Red Nichols, and Milt Shaw). McKinley liked the idea of having a big band of his own; he wasn't sure he liked the idea of sharing leadership with someone—particularly when he was told Bradley was to get top billing. He recalls: "I almost balked at the last minute. I had known Will, because we had both been in the Milt Shaw Orchestra. I said to Willard, 'What am I doing with this guy? Nobody knows him.' He said: 'They know you and they'll think that he's important.' In those days the only guy who could get by with being a drummer *and* a leader was Gene [Krupa], because he had a national reputation. Willard didn't think anybody else could. If I'd been a trombone player or something, I'd have been a natural. But Will was a trombone player and a very good one, and trombones were hot at the time; there was Tommy and there was Glenn, and a couple of others. So that's the way we went out, with that ridiculous title, 'Will Bradley and his Orchestra featuring Ray McKinley'—Holy Smokes! That was Willard's idea, too, that title." The band, informally known as the Will Bradley-Ray McKinley Orchestra, was pulled in different directions by its two leaders.

Bradley's remarkable tone was shown to best advantage on ballads; but if he'd call several ballads in a row, in the mood-setting way Tommy Dorsey had made work so well, McKinley would grow restless. On such numbers, McKinley hardly seemed needed—any society drummer could have provided the polite tempo-keeping required—or noticed. Bradley liked playing melodies taken from classical music (in later years, he would get increasingly involved in composing serious music); among the other swing bands, he liked the refined, forward-looking charts being crafted for Benny Goodman by Eddie Sauter. McKinley liked his jazz a little earthier, a little more downhome and rollicking. But on the rhythm numbers that showed his drumming and singing to best advantage, you barely needed (or noticed) Bradley. McKinley was all for getting into boogie woogie, the old eight-to-a-bar blues-based music that (like McKinley) had come from the southwest. Pianists such as Meade Lux Lewis, Albert Ammons, and Pete Johnson had revived interest in the form. Now McKinley, pianist Freddy Slack (whom McKinley had pulled into the band from Jimmy Dorsey's), and arranger Leonard Whitney began experimenting with big band boogie woogie numbers. One night at the Famous Door, while playing a boogie woogie number, McKinley, rather than taking a break on drums, shouted out: "Oh beat me, daddy, eight to the bar!" Two songwriters in the audience, Don Raye and Hughie Prince, asked McKinley if they could work up a song based on that break. McKinley collaborated with them. The number the three recorded, with McKinley on vocal and drums, became the best selling record the Will Bradley-Ray McKinley Band ever had. It was a felicitous bit of material for McKinley; his drawl worked perfectly as he sang of a pianist in a mythical Texas bar with the best beat by far. The band churned out follow-ups in that vein: "Fry Me Cookie, With a Can of Lard," "Bounce Me Brother, With a Solid Four," "Scrub Me Mama, With a Boogie Beat," and so on—none of which left Bradley with much to do. (They helped cast enough attention on pianist Slack, however, for him to split off and form his own big band.)

And even when the band wasn't playing boogie woogie, McKinley's high spirits and good humor seemed to color the material. The band had a hit with "Celery Stalks at Midnight"—which probably owed its success not just to the suspense-building, carefully controlled dynamics of the musicians, but to McKinley's high-pitched rhythmic vocal break near the end—"Celery stalks along the *high*-way!" McKinley still professes to be baffled by the popularity of his vocal breaks.

"I don't know why people remember those things. Isn't that weird?" he says. "Gee whiz, that 'Celery Stalks at Midnight'—you know where I yell that thing out? When I had the new Glenn Miller Orchestra, I would have the whole band yell that, because we played in a lot of big places and one guy hollering it back from the drums didn't always get across. So one night a fellow requested the number and afterwards, he came back to me and he was furious. He said: 'Why did you have the band yell that? On the record, you did the vocal alone.' He called it a *vocal*! Two bars! And in a falsetto. And I still get requests for that number. I have a chart on it. I play it." (In similar fashion, the vocal break McKinley originated in the Jimmy Dorsey Band's 1938 recording of "John Silver" was shouted out by the entire Jimmy Dorsey Band, under the direction of Lee Castle, in its concert appearances.)

Will Bradley grew uncomfortable with the direction the band was taking. McKinley notes: "Our band didn't last long. Because two leaders—it just doesn't work. The Dorsey Brothers found that out. So Will Bradley and I parted company and I got my own band. There were a lot of reasons. Will wanted to get a band that sounded like Goodman. And I thought we ought to stick with the boogie woogie stuff because we had that market cornered, you know—even though all of those tunes were nothing but the blues. We were going good in that department. I didn't see any reason to change. So we squabbled a bit, decided to separate. It was friendly. He got a band and I got a band." In his book *The Big Bands*, George T. Simon recalled the new McKinley band as "a swinging outfit, featuring Mahlon Clark, the brilliant clarinetist who had followed Ray from Will's band, a fine seventeen-year-old trumpeter named Dick Cathcart, a swinging young pianist named Lou Stein, a very pretty and very good singer named Imogene Lynn, and two veterans: trombonist Brad Gowans and tuba player Joe Parks, who, instead of burping with the rhythm section, played right along with the brass, to which he added an unusually full, rich, sound." The band emphasized swinging numbers. McKinley acknowledged it couldn't play ballads well. "It only lasted about eight months, because the war was on—you know, fellows became drafted," McKinley notes. "We tried to enlist as a unit in the marines, out in California, but it didn't work out.

"Glenn [Miller] had told me—when I had seen him in Boston, just before he enlisted in the army—'If you get drafted, get in touch with me.' And he gave me a number. So when I became drafted, I called him. I said, 'I'm in.' He said, 'Good, send me your serial number.' I sent him my serial number. The next thing I know, I'm on a train going to Atlantic City to take basic training, and the beginning of that great AAF Band was started there in Atlantic City. That would be in the end of 1942 and the first few months of '43—around that anyway. The Air Force had taken over Atlantic City. They didn't have quarters for all these men.

Ray McKinley in 1942 (top photo), and in 1986. (Author's collection.)

Ray McKinley (front row, far right) played drums in the Dorsey Brothers' Orchestra of 1934, which also included, in addition to Tommy Dorsey (back row, third from left) and Jimmy Dorsey (back row, third from right), Glenn Miller (back row, second from right). (Courtesy of Duncan P. Schiedt.)

Ray McKinley (waving) and his Orchestra, including such featured soloists as clarinetist Mahlon Clark (front row, second from left) and trumpeter Lee Castle (front row, third from left), prepare to board a plane in 1942, when air travel by musicians (who usually went by bus) was something of a novelty. (Courtesy of Mahlon Clark.)

Sergeant Ray McKinley fronted the Glenn Miller Army Air Force Band following the disappearance of Miller in December 1944. McKinley subsequently led the re-formed Glenn Miller Band for nearly 10 years, beginning in 1956. (Author's collection.)

And so they took over all those hotels that are on the boardwalk. There was nobody in those hotels but soldiers, thousands of them. We were playing in little groups. And there was one band of the standard size (four trumpets, four trombones, five reeds and a rhythm section) that Zeke Zarchy was leading. Then all of a sudden we were shifted up to New Haven. And that's where we really started to get the best guys, because Glenn could get anybody he wanted. He had a friend, a General Weaver, who was the commanding general of the technical training command of the Air Force. New Haven was an officers' candidate school. Just like West Point. All the guys'd graduate—90-day-wonders, they called them—they were there three months and they'd come out as second lieutenants. That's where we built the band, there, before we went overseas," McKinley recalls.

The accomplishments of the legendary Glenn Miller Army Air Force Band have been documented with exceptional thoroughness by Edward F. Polic in his book, *The Glenn Miller Army Air Force Band: Sustineo Alas / I Sustain the Wings* (Scarecrow Press), and there is no need to repeat that history here. Suffice it to say that Miller assembled an all-star orchestra whose members included alumni not only of Miller's civilian band (such as trumpeter Zeke Zarchy, arranger Jerry Gray, bassist Trigger Alpert, and trombonist Jim Priddy), but also alumni of Artie Shaw's (trumpeter Bernie Privin and saxist Hank Freeman), Benny Goodman's (pianist/arranger Mel Powell and trumpeter Steve Steck), Tommy Dorsey's (guitarist Carmen Mastren), Harry James' (saxist Chuck Gentry), Vaughn Monroe's (trumpeter Bobby Nichols), and so on. They played the best-known numbers created by various big bands in recent years, as well as coming up with a few new ones of their own—including the memorable "Blues in the Night March" and "St. Louis Blues March," both of which featured McKinley's swinging march drums.

McKinley played a vital role in the Glenn Miller Army Air Force Band. He drummed, he sang, he even led it when Miller himself could not. He notes: "Well, I was the only one in that band, I think, that had ever led a band. And as clumsy as it was to have a drummer-leader, the point was—somebody had to get out there in front that could talk, you know, to audiences. One night in England, for some reason, we played a base for a lot of big brass and a lot of GIs and Glenn couldn't show up. I think he was sick or something, I don't know. So for the first time, I fronted the band down there and I did a good job. It was easy to do a good job with that band. And from then on, then after Glenn was lost [in December 1944]—we were in Paris and we didn't know about it until we'd been over there about 10 days or so—they put me up in front of the band permanently.

"The band was so well organized in all departments: arrangers, copyists, instrument-repair man, and everything. We just had everything. Because Glenn was a great organizer—I mean truly great, and all in capital letters. He foresaw a lot of problems that we would encounter over there, which other bands didn't foresee. For instance, the United States Army Band was over there and when we got there, those guys were crying because they didn't have any pads for the saxophones, springs for the trumpets; they didn't have manuscript paper, they didn't have reeds for the reed instruments. So we loaned the United States Army Band this fellow who Glenn had the foresight to attach to our outfit—Vido Pascucci—and he had all this stuff. He could fix any instrument.

"We were stationed there in Paris for the remainder of the war, and then we came back home. We did one broadcast after we came back home. And you know, once a year, the President (Harry Truman in this instance) has what's called a Press Club Dinner in Washington; all the press guys from all over are there, and a whole lot of other people. Well, at this one, they really had some dignitaries, starting with the President and General Eisenhower and General Arnold, and the Canadian Prime Minister I think was there, right on down. And so we went there and did a show for them. And it was at that show that Eddie Cantor got up and read a eulogy about Glenn, and how much the band meant, and how he'd gone in when he didn't have to—he was overage—and gave up his money and fame in the States. And when he finished with that—it was kind of a tearful situation— General Arnold turned to some aide there and said, 'Let them out; they've done their share.' So the band was discharged as a unit. I'd gotten out about a month earlier."

The Glenn Miller estate, McKinley recalls, asked him to become the leader of a re-organized Glenn Miller Orchestra. "But, you know, I was young; I wanted my own band. If I'd taken it, I would have been under the thumb of the Miller estate, and I didn't have any idea what that would mean. And besides, as much as I loved that band, when you play some of those old chestnuts as many times as we did, you're kind of tired of them. Ironically, I had to do that all over again ten years later! Heh-heh."

In 1946, the Miller estate named Tex Beneke leader of the new Glenn Miller Orchestra, but by 1948 he and the estate had a parting of ways. He stopped using the Miller name, although he continued playing some Miller hits (as well as plenty of new things) leading what was billed simply as the Tex Beneke Orchestra. From 1948 to 1956, there was no Glenn Miller Orchestra.

After the war, McKinley recalls, "I formed a new big band. I got Eddie Sauter to write the arrangements, and I got the best guys I could get. And believe me, we had some good ones in that band [including clarinetist Peanuts Hucko, trombonist Vern Friley, and trumpeter Nick Travis]. What a pity recording techniques were so primitive in those days. What we played was great, but what got on that wax was not so good until some years later. We were still recording on those old wax masters, you know. My band went with Majestic Records, which was a newcomer. That was a mistake, too." The band's instrumentals, such as "Hangover Square," "Sandstorm," and "Borderline," were more popular with musicians than with the public. "I had to break the band up. The big bands just started to go downhill. There was no market for them—especially this one of mine. It was so good, it was over everybody's head; it was a little too progressive. Not that we couldn't play good dance music, but I guess we didn't play it simply enough. Some places we were a big hit. Like in New Orleans, the Roosevelt Hotel; we went for a month and stayed four or five. We had some simple things we'd play. But we'd play a dance, and then we'd pull out a few of these other things that we liked to play, you know—and everybody was caught with their left foot up in the air, see. It was just a bit too good."

McKinley's most commercially successful numbers were not

the carefully composed and arranged pieces the band played with such pride, but more casually created things. " 'You've Come a Long Way from St. Louis' was with the big band—but that was a last-minute thought on a date. I've had three records that were big and all three of them were that way. What happened was, we had a certain assignment for however many tunes we would do on a date, usually four tunes in a three-hour date, with maybe a little overtime. And in every instance the arrangers wouldn't come up with the fourth number. So, we'd get together and make a little head arrangement. Artie Malvin, who was one of the Crew Chiefs [vocal group] in the Glenn Miller Army Air Force Band, he came in with a little sheet music; a guy had written 'You've Come a Long Way from St. Louis.' So we went in the back room and cooked up a little routine on it, with piano and finger drums (timbales) and a guitar, and made the record. And that was the biggest hit of that session. That's how those things happen. I do that song every now and then." He still gets requests to do numbers such as "Hard Hearted Hannah" and "Down the Road Apiece," too.

"After I broke up this good band, I did some things on TV, play a little role and everything. I was everything on TV—I was a weatherman, I was the disc jockey on radio. I was playing with small bands, guest shots, and with big bands." He recorded a sextet album for Grand Award in 1955. In the meantime, the release of the film *The Glenn Miller Story* in 1954, with James Stewart portraying Miller, had revived interest in Miller's music. In 1956, the Miller estate asked McKinley to reorganize the Glenn Miller Band. He had his work cut out for him. "See, when they split with Tex [in 1948], the library was taken out to a warehouse in Long Island and locked up. It was Willard Alexander who thought it would be a good idea to rejuvenate the band, because the name was so big—Glenn Miller. So he got with their attorney and they talked to Helen [Glenn's widow] and she okayed me as the leader. And I started and got this old library. Now you should have seen it. Oh boy, was it a mess! Parts missing and tunes missing. Oh yeah, we had to have quite a lot of stuff copied off of records. It was a terrible time in that respect. And we finally got it and kicked off, and I had nine years and seven months of it. It was a good band," he recalls.

He had an arranger who, while not particularly creative, could write arrangements of new songs that sounded exactly like arrangements of the original Glenn Miller Orchestra. The Miller name still proved a potent box office draw. And McKinley, who had not been able to keep his own big band afloat economically, now found he was working constantly. The band even had a TV show of its own one summer, "Glenn Miller Time." He was pleased with the band he led. (He does not believe the current Miller Band has the caliber of players he had.)

In 1966, he stepped down as leader of the Miller Band. "They wore me out," he says. "I couldn't take that much work. We hardly ever had a night off. Oh boy! I got so I couldn't sleep in a bed, I could only sleep in a bus." (The Miller Band has continued working steadily to this day, under the successive leadership of such musicians as Buddy DeFranco, Peanuts Hucko, Buddy Morrow, Jimmy Henderson, Larry O'Brien, and Dick Gerhart.) Since 1966, McKinley's worked intermittently with big bands and small groups. He's appeared a couple of times on PBS-TV specials recalling music of the big band years. In recent years, he says, he's taken things easy: "Guest shots here and there—they didn't mean anything except a little money, you know. Playing around with orchestras—I'd take my library and work with them. Well, for instance, now I go out to Disneyland once a year for a week. A fellow out there, Art DePew, gets me a *real* good band— not a great big band: three trumpets, two trombones, five reeds and three rhythm. And I take my library, which is a good dance library. And we go out there and we swing for a week. And get along fine. I've been there a lot of years now, in a row. This is my own library, not Glenn Miller's. I play a few of the Miller chestnuts, but not many. And the rest of them are just things that I like—good swingin' dance numbers."

1986

From Long Island to South Rampart Street

The Bob Crosby Band, unique among the big bands in its depth of commitment to exuberant New Orleans-style jazz, came into existence because the key members of the Ben Pollack Band wanted to stay together after they had given up on Pollack as a leader in 1934. The following year, they got Crosby to front for them. Every important musician in the new Crosby Band had formerly been a member of the Pollack Band, with one exception: bassist/arranger Bob Haggart. He was just 21 and had never before worked for a big name band. And yet Haggart, as much as any member of the Crosby band, wound up helping to define its character. He arranged and composed or co-composed many of the band's best-remembered numbers, including "What's New?," "The Big Noise from Winnetka," "My Inspiration," "Dogtown Blues," "I'm Prayin' Humble," and "South Rampart Street Parade"—the last-named being about as widely recognized a New Orleans number as has ever been penned (not a bad credit for a Long Island lad).

Haggart has become permanently linked with the music he played and helped create during his seven years in the Crosby Band. More than a half century later, he's still playing numbers he played back then, in very much the same kind of spirit, and usually in the company of at least one other former Crosby star, pungent trumpeter Yank Lawson.

I caught up with Haggart at the 1986 Conneaut Lake, Pennsylvania, Jazz Festival. He was right at home with both the repertoire and the personnel, which included such fellow former Crosby-ites as tenor saxist Eddie Miller and trumpeter Billy Butterfield, and other musicians with whom Haggart had been friends for more than 50 years, such as tenor saxist Bud Freeman, guitarist George Van Eps, and drummer Ray McKinley.

As we relaxed in front of the Hotel Conneaut one afternoon, Haggart recounted his development as a musician.

Born March 13, 1914, Haggart grew up in Douglaston, Long Island, where, he recalls, a rather musical family in the neighborhood, the Petries, introduced him to the records of "Red Nichols and the Five Pennies. That meant, in the beginning Miff Mole and Pee Wee Russell—all those funny names—Arthur Schutt on the piano [about 1927–28]. I listened to all the early Five Pennies things. And then little by little, it got more modern. They got Jack Teagarden and Gene Krupa and Benny Goodman and Joe Sullivan in the Pennies [1929–30]. I loved all that stuff." Red Nichols' Five Pennies were the most popular white jazz recording band of that period.

"And then I suddenly discovered Louis Armstrong," Haggart says. "And see, living in New York, as a kid I was able to go into places like Roseland and the Savoy Ballroom, to hear those big bands, you know. Fletcher Henderson and Luis Russell. All the good ones that played Roseland. There were two bandstands at Roseland, and they'd have two bands. Sometimes both black bands. McKinney's Cotton Pickers, for instance." Haggart heard these pioneering black bands which were anticipating the direction leading white swing bands were to take later in the decade.

In the meantime, Haggart was learning how to play a variety of instruments, at first in the neighborhood, and then at public school, and finally at prep school, before he finally settled on the string bass as his instrument. "I got started with the Petrie family when I was around 11, playing ukelele, and banjo uke, and banjo guitar, in that order. I never even considered a bass at that time," he notes.

"Summers, my family would take a cottage up at Lake George, at Hewlitt's Landing. And they always brought a New York band in the hotel there. I would hang around that band with my mouth open, watching them and listening to every note, and hanging on everything. When I was about 14 years old, I took guitar lessons from the guitar player in the band.

"And then I went to high school, and I played the tuba in high school. Marching band, you know. I didn't enjoy that too much, lugging that damned Sousaphone around. Then I went away to camp in 1929. It was a music camp, in that they had a real good camp band and you got a scholarship—you paid much less tuition if you played an instrument. They supplied a nice upright tuba for me. An older man conducted and we played concerts around New Hampshire and Maine. That summer I started fooling around with a bugle, too, and became the bugler for the month of August. Then I bought a cornet in a pawn-shop—a Czechoslovakian cornet that cost $12.50 (the valves never did work right). And I started playing cornet.

"I went away to the Salisbury School in Connecticut, and played cornet in a five-piece band there. I went home one winter on the Christmas break and got a nice, brand-new trumpet with a couple of mutes and everything—I traded in the Czechoslovakian cornet—and I was in business; I loved that. I would have played the guitar in the band, except they already had a guitar player and they needed a trumpet.

"I had a roommate who was a drummer and he had a collection of Ellington records. And I had started collecting Louis Armstrong, the ones that were just coming out at that time, like 'I Can't Give You Anything but Love' [recorded March 5, 1929], all those things that he recorded with the Luis Russell Band. That was with [J. C.] Higginbotham on trombone. This was in 1929–30. The strange part is, I had never heard the Hot Five or the Hot Seven, the early Louis things. I only latched on to Louis Armstrong when he was just starting to play the high notes and do all that good stuff. I think he really hit his peak about 1931–32." Armstrong's Hot Five and Hot Seven records, made between 1925 and 1928, which now are well known to jazz buffs (indeed they include a couple of the most celebrated performances in jazz), were initially marketed mostly to black record buyers; when they were first released, they were not as well known to white record buyers as the recordings of Nichols or

Bix Beiderbecke. It is not surprising that Haggart really only became aware of Armstrong's records beginning around 1929; at that point Armstrong was starting to record popular songs rather than the hot stomps he had favored earlier. Promoted as the world's greatest trumpeter, he was then developing a rapidly expanding, increasingly broad following. Hot jazz aficionados (such as Haggart) who became great Armstrong admirers in this period often then sought out his earlier recordings. And one hot jazz devotee spread the word to the next to check out the authentic jazz on the brilliant, passionate (and rather rough-sounding, to those used to dance bands) Hot Fives and Hot Sevens.

Armstrong was of interest to any aspiring hot jazz musician, but he was of particular interest to Haggart then because Haggart played trumpet. Haggart remembers happily what was perhaps the high point of his short-lived career as a trumpeter: "One year when I was at Salisbury and playing the trumpet, the Yale Collegians played our spring dance, in June. And I sat in and played trumpet with them, which was a big thrill for me. And they were cheering me! I'd play a little [he hums]—a Teagarden lick. 'Yay!' They were clapping. It was a big night for me." But he soon reached the conclusion: "I wasn't very good on trumpet. I didn't have very good chops and I couldn't get above a Concert F much." He built up his skills on guitar.

"I took guitar lessons from George Van Eps, who was playing in Smith Ballew's Band [around 1929 or '30]. George, at that time, played a four-string guitar; he was just switching over to six-string. I'd go in every Saturday and have my session with George; I picked up a lot of stuff from him. We played a lot of duets together. I went to Roseland a lot and Ray McKinley was playing drums with Milt Shaw's Detroiters at Roseland. As a guitar player, I got to know Ray. (Here we all are today—full circle—playing together.) And sometimes I'd have little sessions with him and Will Bradley and Stew Pletcher, a trumpet player who later went with Norvo; he was with the Yale Collegians.

"Shortly after that I was visiting a school chum from the Salisbury School, and his family had a summer place out in Westhampton, out in Long Island. And they took us to dinner at the Quogue Inn. There was a Meyer Davis five-piece band

and Artie Bernstein was playing bass. I heard him up close. Our table was right next to the band and I could hear this nice, big chomping sound coming out of that bass. And I said, 'Man! I could do that. That's for me!' " Thus is a bass player born.

"And in school, they had a bass sitting in the corner. And so I started fooling around with that. I was 16 maybe. I started playing jobs right away on the string bass. I gave up the trumpet and the guitar. From then on, I was strictly the bass. My first good bass was from Charlie Barber, who was with Milt Shaw's Detroiters. He was selling his bass and I bought it—a nice old Italian bass," Haggart recalls. He wasn't out of high school long before he fell into his first good job. "I'm walking down Broadway one day and I ran into this musician from New Jersey, who had played at Hewlitt's Landing one summer. And this fellow, who knew me as a guitar player, says, 'Gee, how you been?'

"I say, 'I'm playing the bass now.'

"He says, 'You're playing the bass? We're looking for a bass player. How would you like to go down to Nassau? We're leaving for a 10-week season.'

"I said, 'Where the hell is that?'

" 'You know, in the Bahamas.'

"I said, 'Well, I'll ask my mother.' I was with them for three years—Bob Sperling's Band. They were from Somerville, New Jersey, most of those guys. Plainfield, Somerville. I played in Nassau three winters: 1933, '34, and '35.

"The third year I was with them, I got a telegram from Tommy Dorsey; he wanted to know if I wanted to join the Dorsey Brothers' Band. That was through Ray McKinley, who was then with the Dorsey Brothers. Their bass player, Delmar Kaplan, was leaving; he was going back to Pittsburgh. And he was a symphony player. He was not really a swinging bass player. He got a beautiful sound and all that—he played all the right notes—but he was not a swinger.

"But I turned Tommy Dorsey down. I got his cable. I sent a cable back: 'I'm sorry. I can't make it at this time because we're out on an island here and there's no one to take my place. I can't leave these guys right now.'

"Actually, I was scared. You know, I wasn't quite ready for

the big time. So we got through that third year, and we went back to this Blue Hills Plantation, which is where we worked in New Jersey." By the time the next invitation to join a big time group came, though, Bob Haggart felt he was ready.

"I got a phone call from Gil Rodin. He says: 'I've been looking all over for you. Finally located you. I'd like to have you come in and audition for our band. This is the Ben Pollack Band.' " They had left Pollack and they were just hanging around New York, rehearsing new arrangements. Matty Matlock, the clarinetist, kept on writing them. And they were getting arrangements from all different arrangers around New York, building up a library, and looking for a leader. They wanted Teagarden, but they couldn't get Jack away from Paul Whiteman (he had a contract with Whiteman). And so they decided on Bob Crosby.

"A lot of the guys in the band worked in Red Nichols' radio program for Kellogg's: Eddie [Miller] and Matty [Matlock], and Gil [Rodin] from the sax section, and Glenn Miller. But they wanted to go on the road; the reason I was pulled in was because the bass player they were using didn't want to go on the road. They were looking for another bass player. And that's where I came in. I was 21. Bob Crosby and I came into the band at the same time. He fronted it, but the band was a cooperative."

Gil Rodin, who had helped run Pollack's Band, played second tenor in the Crosby Band (no solos) and served as president of the band corporation. He was the organizer of, and set the musical policy for, the Crosby Band. Crosby, who had sung with the Dorsey Brothers' Orchestra and Anson Weeks' Orchestra, was made vice president of the band corporation. Crosby realized he had not been chosen to front this band because any of the musicians imagined him to be an outstanding singer. He had a pleasant enough baritone to give the band some commercial appeal, he was personable, and, most important, as a brother of the nation's most popular singer, Bing Crosby, he would help get the band publicity. (When I asked trumpeter Billy Butterfield what Crosby contributed to the band, Butterfield answered succinctly: "Well . . . he contributed the name.") The other founding members of the band were all shareholders in the band corporation. They, along with the band's booking agency, Rockwell-O'Keefe, would divide whatever profits the band made. (Several other Swing Era bands—the Casa Loma Band, the Mitchell Ayres Band, and the Woody Herman Band—were likewise initially organized as cooperatives.)

The Crosby Band did not, at first, have a female vocalist; one reason the musicians had left Pollack was because they felt he was focusing too much attention on his band's female vocalist, Doris Robbins (who became Mrs. Ben Pollack), at the expense of the superb instrumentalists in the band. Bob Crosby, naturally, would have his share of vocal numbers now, as would another singer, tenor Frank Tennille, but Rodin would make sure the band played plenty of instrumentals—and that even on the vocal numbers there'd be space for the musicians to blow. This was a band in which the musicians would be a prime attraction. They wouldn't play *only* Dixieland, of course—there'd be plenty of current pop and show tunes as well (the band's theme was the Gershwins' "Summertime," featuring a languorous Eddie Miller sax solo), for Rodin knew you couldn't get choice hotel jobs playing only hot jazz, but it would be the emphasis on Dixieland that would give the band its identity. The musicians were of one mind about that; they had a good collective feel for such two-beat oldies as "Panama," "Fidgety Feet," "Royal Garden Blues," and the like. Their focus might cost them a few fans—for Dixieland wasn't everyone's cup of tea (it wouldn't woo those who wanted primarily sweet sounds nor would it please certain "hep" young swing fans who wrote off all Dixieland as old-fashioned)—but they knew that could play that particular kind of music better than any big band around.

The Crosby Band caught on right away, Haggart recalls. "We did our first record date at Decca [June 1, 1935, according to the Brian Rust discography] before we did any one-nighters. Our first job—a break-in job—was June 4th, 1935, at Roseland. And that was a wonderful night. Because you know, the Pollack band had a lot of head arrangements, things that they had memorized; there was no music written. So I just had to keep my ears open and fake it, do a lot of faking, you know. But it was great, because I had heard Wingy Manone records with Ray Bauduc

and Eddie Miller, Matty—all those guys were on them. And
Eddie Miller I was crazy about. And I had heard Deane Kincaide's
arrangements with Benny Goodman on that 'Let's Dance' program from 1934–35, like 'Did You Ever Hear the Story of the
Dixieland Band,' with Helen Ward doing the vocal. And I heard
Kincaide's arrangements and I said, 'I never heard anything like
that in my life. Marvelous.' So the fact that they called and said,
'We want you to join the Pollack band'—I couldn't believe it, you
know. God! How lucky can you get?" Kincaide was arranging for
the Crosby Band, as well as playing tenor sax in it; in fact, one
of the numbers they recorded at their first session was Kincaide's
arrangement of "The Dixieland Band." The band recorded
"Beale Street Blues" (the type of thing for which the Crosby Band
is fondly remembered today) at its first session, too. But the side
from that first session that actually sold the best—a reminder of
public preferences—was a sweet number with Crosby on vocal,
"In a Gypsy Tea Room."

"We were booked right away—never out of work," Haggart
recalls. "We landed a job at the Hitz hotel chain. Ralph Hitz
owned these hotels. A string of hotels like the New Yorker and
the Hotel Lexington in New York, the Adolphus in Dallas, the
Nicollette in Minneapolis, the Roosevelt in New Orleans. . .So
we'd go right from one hotel to the other. And with one-nighters
in between, you know, driving our own cars.

"I didn't start arranging for the Crosby Band right away.
They didn't know I arranged. Finally I did one arrangement of
'Heebie Jeebies'—that's Louis' thing, taken right from his [1926
Hot Five] record. The way they did it, the end of the arrangement
they had a dance, where three guys came down from the stand
and did the shim-sham, which was a dance all guys did in those
days. So that's the way the arrangement ended, with a shim-sham
[he laughs]. The three that did the shim-sham were Ray Bauduc,
the drummer (he's a good dancer); Eddie Miller, tenor sax (he
learned the shim-sham); and Frank Tennille, who was the singer.
They had a tenor singer, besides Bob Crosby, back then—big,
tall good-looking blond guy; he had a high voice. He happens to
be Tony Tennille's father. They changed the pronunciation,
though. In those days it was Ten'l. Frank's mother owned a big

119

furniture company in Montgomery, Alabama. He didn't need the money; he just went along for the ride." (The band eventually decided it did not need to carry a second male vocalist and took on a female vocalist instead, which most fans expected a big band to have.) The Crosby Band never recorded Haggart's arrangement of "Heebie Jeebies." But it recorded plenty of others. Haggart had a hand in creating some of the band's greatest numbers.

He recalls: " 'South Rampart Street Parade' [recorded November 16, 1937] came about when we were at the New Yorker Hotel. Ray Bauduc and I were sitting at a table at intermission and he says, 'Hey, I got an idea for a march'—or the way they say it from New Orleans, 'a *mawch*.' He says, 'Write this down.' And he's beating on his leg like this, just like the way he plays the drums. And he's doing a parade beat. 'Da-da-ta-dadum, bum ba ta tadum,' and so forth [he scats the opening to "South Rampart Street Parade"]. I put ledger lines on the table cloth and wrote that out. I didn't happen to have any manuscript with me. Besides, the bandstand was way up there, and we were down there, so. And then [Haggart scats more of the tune], the beginning, I wrote that out, [he scats a few more bars], then that. And I took the tablecloth and took it home, made the arrangement."

The number, a thrilling evocation of a street parade in New Orleans, was initially named "Bulls on Parade"—after a New Orleans social club with a band that Bauduc remembered; the title was subsequently changed to the more easily understood "South Rampart Street Parade."

"It was a big hit," Haggart notes. "The first time we ran it down in rehearsal, the guys in the band fell out when they heard it. It was hard on the trumpets. Andy Ferretti [the lead trumpeter] griped like hell, because it was hard on him. It stays up high all the way through the last part.

"It was longer than most of the arrangements were back then. We went to the studio and made a 12-inch record of it (the standard record was 10 inches). On the other side was a thing I wrote called 'Dogtown Blues.' That was long, too. In fact, we had to cut both of them, just to get them on 12 inches. They were longer than that. But we had to cut it down to get it on the record. And then they had to cut them down again to get a regular 10-

inch record. They had to cut out the Bob Cat chorus on 'South Rampart.' " (Decca released both 10- and 12-inch versions.) The number became a classic of its kind, played by everyone from New Orleans bands to college football bands to Guy Lombardo's Orchestra, although no one ever stole the thunder of the originators.

The band was turning out some mighty fine records; *Metronome* picked its "Muskrat Ramble" and "Dixieland Shuffle" as among the best recorded sides of 1936, and its "Sugar Foot Strut" and "Between the Devil and the Deep Blue Sea" as among the best of 1937. When *Down Beat* conducted its first readers' poll in 1937, the Crosby Band was voted second most popular (Goodman was the overwhelming favorite), beating out Tommy Dorsey's Band by three votes.

The band was riding high in 1938. During an extended stay at the Blackhawk Restaurant in Chicago, they turned out one successful recording after another. Haggart has good memories of the Blackhawk period. "We weren't traveling now—we had done plenty of one-nighters before—and I had a good chance to get a lot more work done, writing for the band. We were on the radio two or three times a night. And we were recording a lot. And so, everything I wrote was played immediately. That was a marvelous incentive to write. No matter what I wrote, it was done."

Did he prefer writing or playing?

"Well, I don't know. It goes hand in hand," he notes. "I had a compulsion to write. I'd think of something and it'd wake me up in the middle of the night. And I'd have to get up and start writing it, you know. Very compulsive with writing. I had an idea and I had to do it. And I was always at the piano at the Blackhawk between sets. That's how I thought of some of those tunes—just fooling around on the piano, quietly. I never played so anybody could hear me. There was quite a lot of noise in there, clattering plates and everything. And every intermission I'd sit down and look for things on the piano, in my fumbling way. I could never play a tune straight through, or anything like that. I was strictly an arranger-type piano player, you know."

Clarinetist Irving Fazola (who, like Miller, Bauduc, and guitarist Nappy Lamare, was a New Orleans native—Barry Ulanov wrote he had "perhaps the most polished concept of the New Orleans reed tradition") proved a fine addition to the band in 1938. "Fazola replaced Matty Matlock, who had quit playing and just wrote arrangements, because we needed a lot of arrangements. Because we were on the air so much, we needed to do a lot of new tunes. And I was doing a lot of originals. Things like 'I'm Praying Humble' and 'Dixieland Shuffle,' and 'Dogtown Blues.' A lot of those things."

The Crosby Band offered arranged, big band Dixieland with its full complement of 13 players (three trumpets, two trombones, four reeds, and four rhythm), and looser, sometimes hotter-sounding jazz from its eight-man band-within-the-band, the Bob Cats (consisting of such players as Lawson, Haggart, Miller, Fazola, Bauduc, Lamare, trombonist Warren Smith, and pianist Bob Zurke; the exact personnel, of course, changed over the years). The Bob Cats made records of their own, including such memorable ones as "Jazz Me Blues," "March of the Bob Cats" (a thinly disguised reworking of "Maryland, My Maryland"), and their oft-requested "Big Crash from China." They developed an enthusiastic following.

Haggart recalls: "Sunday afternoons at the Blackhawk, we had what they called the Bob Cat Club. Kids would join up to be in the Bob Cat Club. And we (the Bob Cats) would do a little show for them. We had a special upright piano we'd pull down on the dance floor, and then a set of drums we'd slide in on a dolly. And the Bob Cats would come down out of the big band and stand between the drums and the bass, and we'd play five or six tunes for the kids. Usually ending up with 'Big Crash from China.' That was a Ray Bauduc number, in which he did like a machine-gun: rup-a-bup-bup-bup. He had a big crash, a Chinese crash cymbal. *Crash.* And then went into the tune. It was a long drum solo and he broke it up; he's a good showman, you know. Great to watch him play. A very original style of playing the drums. A little like Baby Dodds, Zutty Singleton. That style. A New Orleans style. He had wooden rims, and he got a sound from the drums that no one else got, a nice, soft, mellow sound to the drums. A little like Ray McKinley. They're very much alike—Ray McKinley and Ray Bauduc. Except McKinley keeps much better time. Bauduc was uneven, up-and-down, rushing and dragging."

One of the most celebrated numbers to come out of the Crosby Band—probably second only to "South Rampart Street Parade" in popularity—was "The Big Noise From Winnetka," an infectious bass and drum duet which featured Haggart's whistling (he had been inspired by the way a waiter used to whistle through his teeth while spinning a tray on one finger), exceptionally deft plucking of the strings using alternate hands, and some wackily playful drumming on Haggart's bass strings by Bauduc. The record credits Haggart and Bauduc as having been the number's composers. But nothing was ever written out; it was purely a spontaneous creation which developed at one of the Bob Cat Club sessions.

Haggart recalls: "One Sunday afternoon we were supposed to be on the air at five o'clock. Well, we'd pull in around 4:30. We did five or six numbers, finishing with 'The Big Crash from China.' And so Bob Crosby said, 'We're going on the radio at five o'clock and we have about five minutes to kill. So here's Bobby and Ray Bauduc doing 'The Big Noise from Winnetka.' Because the kids were all from Winnetka [Illinois]. They went, 'Yaaay!' So we went into it. There was nothing written. I started whistling. We just fooled around until it was five o'clock.

"So the next week, we were in the studio to record this album, and we tried to remember what the hell we did. We made the record [October 14, 1938]. God knows what we did originally, but it wound up the way it is, you know. Stick to the record!" The record sold so well that Haggart and Bauduc were called upon to play it on countless occasions just as they had done on the record. In the past half century, Haggart has done the number with countless different drummers. (It's also become a staple in Crosby's repertoire; Crosby had to learn how to simulate Haggart's whistling, so he could do the number in later years on gigs without Haggart.)

"We did a lot of things on that album, like a tune called 'I'm Free,' which featured Billy Butterfield [it later became 'What's New?' after Johnny Burke added lyrics to Haggart's melody].

And then, 'My Inspiration'—Fazola's solo. That caused a lot of talk. All the clarinet players in the country fell in love with Fazola's sound right away, you know. It was beautiful. I actually wrote that number with Billy in mind. And then they said, 'Well, Billy's going to do "I'm Free." Why don't you give Faz "My Inspiration"?' So they switched it around, put Faz in. And Zurke did a lot of things on that album. Of course, he was quite a sensation. Piano players all around the country wanted to play like Bob Zurke.

"At that time an article came out in *Colliers* magazine by Paul Whiteman, supposedly, picking his all-American band. And out of that, you got me, Ray Bauduc, Eddie Miller and Bob Zurke (among many others, you know). And so we called ourselves 'The All-American Four.' And we did a couple of tunes, too." Haggart's comments understate his own importance to the Bob Crosby Band. George T. Simon summed up Haggart in the September 1939 *Metronome* with these words: "To many, the musical brains behind the band, his arrangements setting a merry pace." Haggart won the *Metronome* poll as best bassist in 1937 and 1939–44, and the *Down Beat* poll 1937–42 and 1944. Gunther Schuller observes that Haggart was not only one of the first consistently fine jazz bass soloists, he was "probably the first white player to successfully 'walk' bass lines in the manner of Walter Page."

The Crosby band reached its musical peak in the late 1930s. *Metronome's* listing of best recorded sides of 1938 included seven recordings by Bob Crosby's Band ("At the Jazz Band Ball," "Dogtown Blues," "Panama," "Royal Garden Blues," "South Rampart Street Parade," and "Squeeze Me") and two more by Bob Crosby's Bob Cats ("Can't We Be Friends" and "You're Driving Me Crazy")—nine in all, far more than by any other band (the closest runner-up was Artie Shaw with four sides). Duke Ellington had the most records on *Metronome's* list for both 1939 (in which the Crosbyites were represented by four sides: "Big Noise From Winnetka," "I Hear You Talkin'," "What's New," and "Smokey Mary"), and 1940 (in which the Bob Cats' version of "Spain" was the only Crosby release chosen).

What contribution, in Haggart's view, did Bob Crosby make? What was his role in the band?

BOB HAGGART

Bob Haggart, at a recent recording session (photo by Zack Cullens), and mugging in a 1930s snapshot (courtesy of the Institute of Jazz Studies).

Bob Crosby's Bob Cats serenade an actual bobcat, 1939. Crosby and clarinetist Irving Fazola are in the foreground. In the rear, from left to right, are drummer Ray Bauduc, guitarist Nappy Lamare, tenor saxist Eddie Miller, bassist Bob Haggart, pianist Jess Stacy, trumpeter Billy Butterfield, and trombonist Warren Smith. (Courtesy of Duncan P. Schiedt.)

Bob Haggart with drummers Ray Bauduc (top photo, courtesy of Duncan P. Schiedt), and Ray McKinley (photo by Chip Deffaa). A highlight of any appearance by Haggart is "The Big Noise from Winnetka," the infectious bass-and-drums feature that he and Bauduc introduced in 1938.

One of the most enduring partnerships in jazz: Bob Haggart and Yank Lawson, chatting during a 1950s recording session. Their association dates back to 1936 when they were charter members of the Bob Crosby Band. Fifty-five years later, they co-lead their Lawson-Haggart Jazz Band at festivals and on recordings for the Audiophile label. (Courtesy of the Institute of Jazz Studies.)

"To talk about the guys in the band," Haggart replies. "Tell stories about 'em. Introduce 'em and tell everybody where they're from, and funny little things about each guy. So it was really quite a build-up that everybody got. Because that was a band where, you know, there were at least six guys that everybody still remembers the names: Matty Matlock, Nappy Lamare, Ray Bauduc, Eddie Miller, Yank Lawson, Bob Haggart, Fazola. And they've had guys like Jess Stacy and Joe Sullivan (he was there before Zurke but got sick; later he got well and came back). A lot of names passed through the band, you know."

Crosby did not hire the musicians nor set the band's general musical course. "He left that all to Gil Rodin. Gil Rodin was really the brains behind it that made all the decisions," Haggart says.

Haggart adds that Crosby struck him in those days as acting "like a spoiled brat. He was always getting into trouble with playing the horses. And his brother Everett would have to come and bail him out. And he owed money."

Haggart and others in the band often wondered if they were getting all of the money to which they were entitled. "See, there was a corporation in the band. But we never really divided much money up. It was just a lot of talk. We made four movies. You get pretty good bread for that. And we were always working. There was some leakage someplace, I'm sure of it. I can't prove any of it. I'm not saying that Gil Rodin *stole*, or that Bob Crosby *stole*; it just wasn't managed very well. Of course the guys in the band should have done better." The musicians even changed booking agencies to see if they'd wind up with more money in their pockets, but still no one seemed to be making much money, considering the renown of the band.

When Tommy Dorsey offered three key members of the Crosby aggregation—trumpeters Yank Lawson and Charlie Spivak, and arranger Deane Kincaide—substantially more money to go with him, they did, weakening the Crosby Band in terms of both music and *esprit de corps*. In 1939, the Crosby Band was honored by being chosen to succeed the Benny Goodman Band on the popular "Camel Caravan" radio show. (Airchecks from the series have recently been reissued by Legend Records: *The Summer of '39: Bob Crosby's Camel Caravan*.) Getting the radio show, however, seemed to be something of a mixed blessing as it nudged the band into an increasingly commercial direction.

The band was not too successful in producing the really big commercial record hits. Haggart notes: "The Crosby Band didn't have many tunes of the day, you know, like, say, Glenn Miller had all those dozens of hits, and Artie Shaw had, and Jimmy Dorsey and Tommy Dorsey had. Look at all the big, big records they had. The Crosby Band didn't have any big records like that. And, too, the vocal department was kind of weak. Those other bands had strong vocal departments; you know, Jimmy had Bob Eberly and Helen O'Connell, Tommy had Frank Sinatra and the Pied Pipers, and before that was Edythe Wright and Jack Leonard, and Glenn Miller had the Modernaires and Ray Eberle and Marion Hutton." Bob Crosby was never as popular a singer as those others were (he also suffered by being inevitably compared with his brother Bing).

Aiming to woo a larger following, in 1940 Gil Rodin changed the band's musical direction. "Gil decided that we were barking up the wrong tree by playing Dixieland. And he brought in some arrangers, like Phil Moore, who did Ellington-style-type arrangements. I liked him, but they just didn't sound convincing. It was not what the band was known for. I thought it was kind of a mistake to change horses in midstream like that. We wound up doing 'One O'Clock Jump' with the three sliding trombones and playing 'Tuxedo Junction' and Lunceford things—trying to be doing what everybody else did. Chickening out. I thought they should stick to their guns and do what they had always done," Haggart says.

"They got Paul Weston—or Wetstein as we called him in those days—and he was doing sort of just middle-of-the-road ballads and hit tunes of the day. And a lot of sentimental kind of things. And we had a quartet, the Bob-O-Links. And Johnny Desmond was singing with them. We had Doris Day for a while. And different girl singers."

The personnel, which had been rather stable for the band's first few years, fluctuated a good bit. Billy Butterfield left to join Artie Shaw's Band. Muggsy Spanier came in for a bit. Floyd O'Brien, then Buddy Morrow, soloed on trombone. The band

had its ups and downs (Yank Lawson's return proved an important "up"). In the early '40s, it didn't receive the kind of public
attention that the bands of say, Miller, Goodman, James, Shaw,
or the Dorseys received. Haggart stayed until the band finally
broke up.

"Yeah, I was there all seven and a half years," he notes.
"Then Crosby went into the Marines. And I went back to New
York with Yank. We both expected to go into the service. And
neither one of us went in, because we had kids and we didn't
need to go. Eddie Miller and Nappy and all of them went back
to California. Eddie went in the service. Ray Bauduc went in. Gil
Rodin went in. So there wasn't any band. And when Crosby came
back out, he stayed in California, and he got an afternoon radio
program. He's been in California ever since," Haggart notes.

"When the Crosby Band split up, I moved to Jackson
Heights, New York. I put the bass in the barn and I was just
arranging for all different people. You know, Sammy Kaye, Abe
Lyman, the NBC house band with Bobby Hackett (Irving Miller
was the leader), Jerry Jerome. I was arranging for everybody,"
he recalls. He did arrangements for albums Bob Crosby recorded
in the 1950s, too.

Haggart formed a firm to produce "jingles"—commercials
for radio and, later, TV. He started playing the bass again, job-
bing on a variety of radio shows from "The Hit Parade" on down.
"I played on, I don't know, a dozen or so shows every week. And
recorded for all the record companies. I was very busy. I'd be
jumping in one cab—eating sandwiches in the cab, you know—
and going to the next show.

"Decca used me for Louis Armstrong, some of Louis' things,
and Bing Crosby, Evelyn Knight, Ella Fitzgerald—all different
backgrounds. I'd do the arrangements and call the musicians. I'd
use Billy [Butterfield] whenever I could. Or Yank [Lawson]. Or
both of them," Haggart recalls. Haggart arranged and conducted
the definitive versions of such famed Billie Holiday classics as
"Don't Explain," "Solitude," and "Good Morning Heartache."
Haggart and Sy Oliver divided arranging responsibilities for
Armstrong's magnificent four-album collection, *Satchmo: A Musi-*

cal Autobiography (1957), in which Armstrong recapitulated his Hot Five, Hot Seven, and early big band successes.

Occasionally Haggart got together with Bob Crosby and other musicians from the old Crosby Band for reunions. In 1951, Decca suggested that Haggart and Lawson organize a recording band, in the tradition of the old Bob Cats, to do an album of music by Jelly Roll Morton, to be called *Jelly Roll's Jazz*. The album sold well enough to justify more by "The Lawson-Haggart Jazzband," as the group became known. "We flipped a coin to see whether it would be Haggart-Lawson or Lawson-Haggart. He won the toss, so it was the Lawson-Haggart Jazzband," Haggart recalls. "We used Bill Stegmeyer, a clarinet player who's really good (he had been playing with Billy Butterfield's big band), Billy Butterfield, Lou McGarity [trombone], Lou Stein [piano], Cliff Leeman [drums], George Barnes [guitar], Cutty Cutshall [trombone], Bud Freeman [tenor sax]. See, sometimes we were up to nine men. But we started with six. We started with just Yank, Stegmeyer and McGarity—three horns—and Lou Stein and Cliff and myself. Then, the third or fourth album, they added George Barnes and Cutty and Billy Butterfield and Bud Freeman. As we needed it, we added more men. Some of them are, you know, 10 pieces. But they're really good."

The Lawson-Haggart Jazzband was a kind of spiritual descendant of the Bob Cats and a precursor of the World's Greatest Jazzband, but it only existed in the recording studio. Most of the work Haggart, Lawson, Butterfield, and the others did to earn their livings in the 1950s and '60s was anonymous—playing written parts at sessions for records or commercials or network shows (which Lawson once told Nat Hentoff was "like going to a business office. It doesn't have much to do with music as I like it.").

In the 1960s, Dick Gibson, a wealthy enthusiast of traditional jazz, began inviting musicians he liked to play at annual jazz parties in Aspen, Colorado. As Haggart recalls it, Gibson had started with just two bands the first year, 1963. "The second year he brought us in—he wanted the Lawson-Haggart guys. And the third year, '65, he brought some West Coast players: Van Eps, Venuti, Red Norvo, Charlie Teagarden, Stan Wrightsman, Nick

Fatool. In 1966, he had still more musicians. His party kept building. He's still doing it."

Besides having them play at his annual jazz party, Gibson presented Lawson, Haggart, Butterfield and others, billed as "The Eight Greats of Jazz," in the summer at Elitch Gardens. By the fourth year, 1969, the band had grown to 10 men: Haggart, Lawson, Butterfield, Freeman, McGarity, Bob Wilber (clarinet and soprano sax), Carl Fontana (trombone), Ralph Sutton (piano), Morey Feld (drums), and Clancy Hayes (banjo and vocals).

And because the guys had a gig—they weren't just getting together to jam at a party—Haggart began writing new arrangements for them. The challenge of playing new charts, rather than just winging everything, appealed more to the musicians than to their audience, Haggart recalls: "We had music stands. And all those people, they had never seen us with music, you know. All these libraries, and all the parts spreading out, and musicians putting on their glasses, and calling out the numbers. Everybody says, 'What the hell?!' They're yelling: 'Get rid of the sheet music!' They liked it—but not that much. No. They didn't love it. They love it when we just break it up, do what we always do—just play 'Wolverine Blues,' you know, just fake it."

Meanwhile, the band was recording its summer get-togethers, and those records were beginning to catch the attention of different people. "We were in Denver and Joe Venuti and Teddy Wilson were saying that they heard some of our records and they said, 'Jeez, you guys should be terrific in Europe. You ought to take this band to Europe. Play some of those things and you'll break it up.' So we called a guy named Ernie Anderson, who had been Eddie Condon's manager. He'd been in Europe for years. He was in Vienna or someplace. And he said he'd work on it.

"Then Yank got a call from a fellow named Tony Cabot, who was booking the Riverboat, at the Empire State Building in New York City. And he says, 'Let you guys come and be the house jazzband—seven men.' As soon as we got this offer to go into the Riverboat, Yank and I called Gibson, to see if anything had happened about our European tour. He said, 'No, take the job. As a matter of fact, I'll pay for the extras if you'll put in all

10 men. And if you bring in the whole band then we'll call it the World's Greatest Jazzband.'

"I said, 'Call it *what?*' He says, 'Well, we'll call it the World's Greatest Jazzband, because it is.'

"We hated that name. Hated it. He says, 'First you've got to get their attention.' I said, 'That's going to be terrible in England.' You know, it's understatement over there.

"But jeez, we were booked right away. So we were off to the races. We played the White House several times. We went to Rio, we went to Hawaii, and Anchorage.

"In 1970, the Roosevelt Grill was our base. That had been dark for three or four years. It had been Guy Lombardo's hangout. So they opened it up (we actually started in the fall of 1969). Gibson talked them into it. He got some kind of a deal where he'd work on a percentage basis," Haggart recalls. Gibson's earnings were based on the number of patrons who showed up, but he paid the members of the band a fixed salary each week, whether or not what he took in covered their salaries. Gibson said his only goal was to break even; he was willing to subsidize the band at the Roosevelt Grill until it got established. The musicians were glad to be working together every night. Lawson said frankly that he felt Gibson had rescued him from oblivion.

When the World's Greatest Jazzband of Yank Lawson and Bob Haggart eventually left for a Las Vegas engagement, "Gibson put in another band, with Zoot and Roy Eldridge and Al Cohn, a bunch of good players, to take our place. Then he always had two bands. He'd have like Teddy Wilson's group, or George Van Eps' group, or Joe Venuti, something like that—alternating with the big band," Haggart recalls.

The WGJB (as the World's Greatest Jazzband became known to followers) used Haggart's "My Inspiration" as its theme and often played other numbers he had written for the Bob Crosby Band as well. As new members joined the band, they enlarged the library with their originals. (Check out, for example, drummer Gus Johnson Jr.'s sentimental "Under the Moonlight Starlight Blue" and trombonist Vic Dickenson's appealingly gruff and warm "Constantly," both of which are on the album *The World's Greatest Jazzband of Yank Lawson and Bob Haggart Live,* recently reissued by Atlantic.) Haggart also had the idea of arranging contemporary music for the band. He gave, for example, "Mrs. Robinson" a "South Rampart Street Parade" feel, and let Bud Freeman go spinning off on it. He had Billy Butterfield on trumpet answer Carl Fontana's statements on trombone on "Ode to Billy Joe." (Butterfield told me that playing the new tunes was what he liked best about the World's Greatest Jazzband; he preferred that to simply rehashing things he'd played a thousand times.) Playing new music, of course, was only possible because the WGJB was an organized band. Working together night after night gave the players time to learn, break in, and develop new material. Not all fans—and not all critics, either, for that matter, were entranced by the band's playing of contemporary tunes. Nat Hentoff suggested in *The New York Times* (March 8, 1970): "Those new charts are an attempt to entice the young, but most of the young are irretrievably gone into rock, and I hope the World's Greatest Jazzband ceases to make concessions. Their value, after all, is in who they are and what they learned on the way." I enjoyed a number of their newer things, but must admit I sometimes found it jarring for the band to go from classic jazz to something by Blood, Sweat, and Tears and then back to the sort of material they seemed more comfortable with.

Gibson spoke of establishing other such all-star bands as ongoing entities, but it never came to be. There seemed to be enough of an audience for such bands to get them a certain number of bookings at festivals, concerts, and in hotel or club type situations, but not enough to keep them operating full-time. Gibson had hoped the Roosevelt Grill would become the band's permanent base; the band lasted there, however, less than one year. Gibson was not interested in subsidizing the gig indefinitely. (His pockets were not quite as deep as some of the musicians had supposed.) And there were personnel changes.

"The first guy to leave, I think, was Lou McGarity. He'd been on 'The Arthur Godfrey Show' for so many years. Our band was doing more and more traveling and he couldn't take off. So we got Vic Dickenson. Carl Fontana went back to Las Vegas; he could make more money there, without traveling, and we got Eddie Hubble. Billy and Yank hung in. And so did Bud and Bob Wilber and Ralph and Gus Johnson and myself. Clancy Hayes left—he got sick. He died shortly after. And Morey Feld died—burned up in a fire. We kept Gus Johnson and he did a fine job.

"Then Dick Gibson bowed out," Haggart remembers. There was a limit to just how much money he was willing or able to invest in keeping the World's Greatest Jazzband afloat. "Well, everybody thought he was a millionaire but he wasn't. He let people think so. He didn't deny it. All the articles came out about him: 'Denver millionaire.' Denver salesman he was. Well, he did make a lot of money from the Water Pic. Then he invested it unwisely." The band had about five years operating at full strength. It recorded quite a bit in that period, too.

"In 1974, a lot of the key guys left. Ralph Sutton left, Bob Wilber left, Bud Freeman stayed in England. Then we got George Masso. We got other clarinet players, other tenor men: Al Klink, Eddie Miller. Bill and Yank still hung in. And Ralph now and then. Other piano players in between," he notes.

Haggart and Lawson stuck together. In 1985, they headed back to California to help Bob Crosby celebrate the 50th anniversary of the founding of the Bob Crosby Orchestra. (Haggart and his wife decided they liked southern California so much, they bought a home in San Diego on that trip.) Haggart and Lawson celebrated the 20th anniversary of their own World's Greatest Jazzband while playing in England in 1989. They've continued to record and take bookings as they came, sometimes billed as the World's Greatest, at other times simply as the Lawson-Haggart Jazzband. In recent years, they've often used such players as George Masso (trombone), Johnny Mince or Al Klink (reeds), Bucky Pizzarelli (guitar), and Nick Fatool (drums).

"We cut down to seven men, from nine," Haggart notes. "And we quit using charts. Because we didn't have two trumpets and two trombones, and the charts didn't sound right. So we quit using the library. And it gradually petered out to just a jazzband."

1986

"Twentieth Century Gabriel"

Billed as "the Twentieth Century Gabriel," Erskine Hawkins first gained attention for his daunting, flamboyant, high-altitude trumpeting—the sort of thing that pleased the crowds and annoyed certain critics who fretted about "grandstanding." Unlike most musicians accused of grandstanding, however, Hawkins was always generous about giving others in his band opportunities to shine. Hawkins' most celebrated recordings, in fact—the bluesy, oft-imitated "After Hours," the irresistibly buoyant "Tippin' In," and his laid-back, infectious theme (which he helped compose), "Tuxedo Junction"—displayed the talents of other members of his band much more than his own. And those who danced to Hawkins' band at the Savoy, its base for many years, are apt to tell you they remember the band for its warm ensemble sounds and eminently danceable tempos—it knew how to get into a comfortable groove for dancers and stay there—as much as for Hawkins' own florid soloing.

Born July 26, 1914, in Birmingham, Alabama, Hawkins notes he didn't initially plan on being a trumpeter. "I started off on drums, then went to other instruments, like alto horn, baritone sax, trombone—I have played all of them. When I was in school, in Birmingham, musicians used to play out in Tuxedo Park, just outside of Birmingham. You'd have to get off [the

streetcar] at Tuxedo Junction and walk across the street to Tuxedo Park. I used to play there every summer when I was eight,
nine, ten, eleven, twelve, you know, whatever; I'd play in this
four- or five-piece band. When I was in high school, my teacher
was a trumpet player; they called him High-C Foster. And when
I got to be 16, he moved me over on trumpet," Hawkins recalls.

Was there any trumpeter Hawkins particularly admired?

"Sure," he says. "After I left Birmingham and went to Alabama State Teachers' College in Montgomery, Louis Armstrong
was my guy. Louis used to broadcast out of New Orleans till
11:00 at night. I used to listen to him. Then I got a chance to get
some of his records. I just took the records and copied the solos,
before I knew anything about getting my own style of jazz."

Are there any Armstrong records that stand out in his memory as ones that particularly impressed him?

"Louis' record of 'When You're Smiling' [recorded September 11, 1929]—I used to play that a lot. And 'Chinatown, My
Chinatown' [November 3, 1931]. And 'Shine' [March 9, 1931].
Those are some ones that stand out. I used to copy those. Then
after I got to New York, I just went for myself," he says.

Hawkins was inspired by the Armstrong of the early 1930s—
not the pure-jazz Armstrong of the 1920s small-group sides, but
the Armstrong who, with big band backing, seemed to revel
in showing off his technical prowess: the inevitable high-note
endings to pop tunes, the extravagant, multiple-high-note displays in concert performances that dazzled fans. Hawkins may
not have been able to imitate Armstrong's rich, majestic tone or
genius for phrasing, but he could, like Armstrong, carry listeners
upwards with him on trumpet. And while a student at Alabama
State Teachers' College (1930–34), he earned a regional following for his stratospheric playing. "They used to call me 'Iron
Lung' when I was in school," he recalls. "I fixed my own mouthpiece; I'm still playing that now, the mouthpiece that I cut out to
fit my lip. I was copying after [Armstrong] because he used to
hit high notes all the time, like C above high C. And so I was
doing the same thing that he was doing. "When I first got to
college, I played in the second band at the college, the 'Bama
State Revelers. I was in that band, Heywood Henry was in that

band, Dud Bascomb was in that band, Bob Range, Edward Sims, and a few others," he says, naming musicians who would later be members of the Erskine Hawkins Band. "So after we were there for so many weeks, they moved me up to the 'Bama State Collegians, which was the number one band. And then the other fellows moved up, too. A fellow by the name of J. B. Sims fronted the band then. I was the leader—they called it the 'Bama State Collegians featuring Erskine Hawkins—but initially sat in the trumpet section. Sims was a singer. He also could play the sax and things, but all he did was direct and make announcements.

"During my last year there, the band had a tour as far up as Asbury Park, doing one-night stands. When we got to Asbury Park, some of the musicians from New York came over to get a listen at us; John Hammond and Benny Carter came over to hear. It was the talk of the town: this young boy comes from the South—and they were talking about me—hitting all those high notes. So they wanted to come and see what it was all about. And Frank Schiffman, the owner of the Apollo Theater and the Harlem Opera House, came over to hear us. So he booked us in to the Harlem Opera House. When we got there, we did such a nice job—the place was packed, we did five, six, seven shows a day."

Hawkins awed audiences with his version of one of Louis Armstrong's displays of virtuosity. "When I played at the Harlem Opera House, I'd hit out high C's—up to 100 of them—and the band would count them out behind me. Then I'd hit an F above it, to end it up. (That's the reason why down south they had called me Iron Lungs.) I was doing that like five or six shows a day for a whole week. And then after I played that number, people used to ask me for an encore and I used to do 'Star Dust' right behind it, and then play it above the staff. And then hit altissimo B flat on the end. But then I did that whatever amount of shows they had. And before I got to do all of that, I used to have to play in the pit. I had to play the show—playing first trumpet—for the acts in front of me. And then we would close the show and I did all that. It didn't bother me. I guess I'd turned 20 years or 21. I was kind of young," he says.

The idea originally had been for the band to do the tour

and then return to school. It was then somewhat ragged and unprofessional compared to the top New York name bands, and hadn't yet formed an identity of its own. (It played some music of the top bands of the day, such as Ellington's and Calloway's.) It would take the band a couple of years to get fully seasoned. But Hawkins' technically impressive trumpeting got the band some offers of bookings right away.

"The others in the band said, 'Hawk, if you can get us work, we'll stay with you.' See, they were supposed to go back to school then. So a fellow came up there by the name of Feet Edson and he talked me into staying, you know," Hawkins says. Edson became the band's manager.

"And it was kind of rough, then, you know, trying to keep us moving around, because we couldn't stay on one job all the time, on account of we didn't belong to the New York local. But finally, we got to know someone in the New York local and they fixed it so we could join. And after a few weeks, moving around here and there, we got a regular job at the Ubangi Club and stayed there for a few years. John Hammond and a lot of other critics used to come see us up at the Ubangi a lot." Hawkins refutes the notion, which has appeared in some write-ups about him, that his band played mostly to black audiences. "The Ubangi Club was in Harlem but it was mostly white. Mostly people from downtown would come uptown, like the Cotton Club and, you know. . . . And we played school dances, a lot of white school dances, after we hit New York. If we'd played a dance down south it had to be either whites by themselves or blacks by themselves, during that era. But when we got here, that's when we started venturing out to, you know, everybody.

"Within the first or second year," Hawkins remembers, "I sent back for Sam Lowe, so he'd sit in my [lead trumpet] chair, and I got in front of the band. Sam Lowe, who also arranged for us, was from Alabama but he'd gone to Tennessee State. His older brother went to Alabama State. (I still see them. They bring me to Birmingham every year—like to Tuxedo Junction, because they always celebrate my birthday there in July.) We had to give back the 'Bama State Collegians name—that was a school name,

to be used for the school's band. We weren't in the school anymore, so we had to call the band Erskine Hawkins' Band." (The
band's early recordings, for Vocalion, from 1936 to 1938, bore
the billing "Erskine Hawkins and his 'Bama State Collegians.'")

"We'd play in and out of the Ubangi, because we had a
regular spot we could go in. And then finally in 1935 or '36—
I'm not sure of the year, during that time—we got an offer at
the Savoy Ballroom. We went in there for a week, alternated with
Chick Webb. Then later on, I got in there regular. Moe Gale, who
owned the Savoy, asked me about being my personal manager. I
could see that we'd be working all the time by him being my
personal manager, so I agreed. Moe Gale got me the contract
with RCA Victor. I was down there for better than 20 years,
recording." The band began recording for RCA Victor's Bluebird label in September 1938.

"The Savoy was sort of like a home for me. I played there,
off-and-on, from 1935 until they closed in the 1950s. I used to
go in there and stay like six months out of the year. Then I
traveled at the end of that, to break it up every year. Sometimes
I stayed at the Savoy longer than that, until my tours were already
built up," he recalls. The band became much more popular after
it began working at the Savoy and recording for RCA.

The band played varied fare to please a broad spectrum
of listeners—everything from rather square oldies such as "I
Love You Truly" and "Song of the Wanderer" (saxist Jimmy
Mitchelle doubled as a barely adequate vocalist on such numbers)
to contemporary swing/riff things bearing titles like "Riff Time,"
"Strictly Swing," and "Swingin' on Lenox Avenue." Hawkins did
some of his own arranging; most came from other band members. Hawkins liked things in a medium-fast groove. "I had a
certain tempo, knowing what the people liked to dance to; I liked
to play danceable tempos. Seeing how the people at the Savoy
was dancing by. . . . Yeah, danceable tempos. We used to get big
crowds!

"We used to broadcast from the Savoy Ballroom on NBC
once a week, like four in the afternoon. One time, as I was going
into my theme—at that time it was 'Swing Out'—the announcer

happened to say: 'And now, the 20th Century Gabriel. . . .' Moe Gale heard it and said: 'Keep it in, keep it in.' So that's how we got that." The billing began appearing on his records in 1938.

Some critics and jazz purists may have disliked Hawkins' showing off of his ability to hit high notes. But I must admit I've never been bothered by the notion of grandstanding. If you've got it, why not flaunt it? What's wrong with occasionally adding some excitement via high notes? What *does* bother me about Hawkins' playing—and I have this complaint with the popular trumpeter/bandleader Charlie Spivak as well—is the (to my ears) excessive vibrato on his ballad playing; he tends to get too schmaltzy for my tastes, and without any great beauty of tone that might make me overlook the vibrato.

But Hawkins didn't hog the solo space on his band's records. He not only let audiences hear from the likes of reedmen Paul Bascomb, Julian Dash, and Heywood Henry, and pianist Avery Parrish, he also let them hear plenty of trumpeter Wilbur "Dud" Bascomb. It was highly unusual for a leader to feature another soloist who played the same instrument he did. (Can one imagine Harry James building up another trumpet soloist in his band?) Hawkins handled the ballads and the high-note work on trumpet; he let Dud Bascomb supply most of the lively jazz improvisations.

Hawkins says of Bascomb: "We didn't live too far from each other in Birmingham. And then when we went to 'Bama State, he and I were roommates. And we came up here, we were just like brothers; we were very close. So being the trumpet player that he was, you know, I wouldn't take his chair; we loved each other. I didn't take nothing from anybody in the band; I liked to share. People go in to see everybody that can be seen. That's the way I felt. I still feel the same way today. I didn't try to hold up anybody. I liked that; that's the way I felt about it." And somehow that collective, generous feeling comes across in the music the band made. There's a certain down-home friendliness to many of their recordings.

Several of the Hawkins band's most popular recordings actually came about almost as flukes, Hawkins notes. "I recorded 'Tuxedo Junction' down at RCA Victor in 1939. See, I needed one more tune to record at that session. I told them, 'Give me

Erskine Hawkins, trumpeting—and stopping midday traffic—in front of Macy's Department Store, New York City, in the summer of 1938. Hawkins was playing on the sidewalk because he had lost a bet to fellow bandleader Ben Bernie—or so a publicist claimed. (Author's collection.)

Erskine Hawkins and his Orchestra, with Avery Parrish on piano. (Courtesy of Duncan P. Schiedt.)

about a half hour.' So I went in to tune up, along with [alto saxist and arranger] Bill Johnson, and I took the rhythm section and they put it together. The band recorded it. Then they said, 'What are you going to name it?' I asked for suggestions from everybody. My valet thought, 'Why don't you call it "Tuxedo Junction"? That's where you're from.' And that's how it got its name." The number, which Hawkins recorded July 18, 1939, is credited to alto saxist William Johnson, tenor saxist Julian Dash, and Hawkins. The memorable second trumpet solo, which many people mistakenly assumed was by Hawkins, was played by Dud Bascomb, as he has always been careful to acknowledge.

"And then after we recorded 'Tuxedo Junction' and it started doing a little good, then I gave Buddy Feyne, the lyric writer, the story of what Tuxedo Junction was and what happened there. I told him the story and he put the lyrics together: 'Way down south in Birmingham, way down south in Alabam, a place where people go to dance the night away. . . .' I paid him straight out, no royalties. Then the tune got big, so I had to put his name on it. He's from up here. I was introduced to him by the publisher."

Glenn Miller also recorded "Tuxedo Junction." In fact, his record eventually sold better (and is better remembered today) than Hawkins' own. Hawkins notes: "Back then, a lot of people thought that Glenn Miller had taken my number, stolen it. But there was no truth in that. You see, Glenn Miller recorded for RCA Victor, too. I had met Glenn up in Boston when he was getting his band together. He was the regular at a ballroom up there, and I went in there as guest band for a one-night stand.

"Then I recorded 'Tuxedo Junction' in '39 and the Glenn Miller Band got big. It played the Pennsylvania Hotel here in New York. Glenn was broadcasting. And I was at the Savoy, broadcasting. Then Glenn came in as guest band at the Savoy; he and I alternated on a Sunday afternoon. So when we finished, Glenn said, 'Hawk, I want to talk to you.' We went into the manager's office, sat down, and he told me he wanted to record 'Tuxedo Junction' but RCA Victor said he had to see me, on account of two bands couldn't make the same tune on the same label. So he gave me his idea. He said, 'You try to make it your theme, so that people know that it's still your number. And then I'll play it as a regular number and you'll still have it as your theme.' And that's what I did. I switched it over, and I gave the OK for him to record it. I had already sold over a million records, so my records had begun to go down, you know. I let Glenn Miller record it in order to keep the thing going big. Glenn also said, 'Don't you let nobody else record it within six months.' I said OK. Then his record got *big*. It outsold mine. I said, 'My goodness!' And that's how he happened to get it, by my okaying it. But I get all the [composer] royalties, see what I mean? I feel good about his record becoming so well known. Every six months I hear from 'Tuxedo Junction'—I get a [royalties] statement. After six months, then Gene Krupa made it. My goodness, I've heard so many different versions of it. Later people sang it. Lately I've been hearing so many different versions. I heard Ted Heath's arrangement out of England—good. Manhattan Transfer sings it; I've got that record. And then I didn't know Ella Fitzgerald had made it. I happened to be listening to the radio one day, and she had a terrific arrangement on it. And Cab Calloway told me he's got a record of 'Tuxedo Junction' by Quincy Jones I should hear. Maybe if I didn't let Glenn Miller do it, at that time, the tune wouldn't be where it was today. Down in Tuxedo Junction itself, they've got a big plaque up there about me. They've also got a park right on the side: Erskine Hawkins Park, right there in Tuxedo Junction. . . . I go down there every year for my birthday party. They have a parade and stuff out to Tuxedo Junction in the afternoon. And then I can go right into Birmingham, which is about a five or ten minutes drive from there, to the middle of the city, where we have a party there with a birthday cake. Every year."

Like "Tuxedo Junction," Hawkins says, "After Hours" [recorded June 10, 1940] essentially came about in the recording studio. "I had to record a tune by the name of 'Fine and Mellow' with the Lois Brown Singers. On the arrangement, Avery Parrish, our pianist, had to play about four or five choruses at the beginning of the tune, before the vocal would come in. I got ready to record it but the tune was too long; I had to cut out something. So I had to take all those choruses out that Avery used to play, except one chorus, then record it. Finally, they asked me, 'Hawk, what are you going to do for your sixth number?' I said, 'Give me a half hour.' So I take Avery and the rest of the rhythm section, and we go on and put those choruses together. I say 'Avery, you know all those choruses I took out?' He said, 'Yeah.' I said: 'Play them.' So we lined them choruses up, the ones that had been before the vocal part. We got that part straight, then I called the whole band together, and then we faked an out-chorus behind that, and then we played it." The number, a piano show-case for Parrish, became an enormous juke-box hit and was copied by pianists, both amateurs and pros, all across the country. It's still a number any journeyman pianist might keep in his repertoire in case he gets a request for something bluesy. (It's ironic that that blues also became the one piece with which Avery Parrish, who was not fundamentally a blues player, would always be associated.)

Hawkins reveals one not-generally-known tidbit about the recording session. "On 'After Hours,' I played drums," he says. Neither the Brian Rust discography nor the liner notes to the latest Erskine Hawkins CD, *Erskine Hawkins—The Original Tuxedo Junction* (RCA), credit him as drumming on the recording. He explains: "I didn't have nothing to play in it [on trumpet] because of the piano. So I told the drummer, 'Big Jack, you get up in front, you direct. I'm going to play the drums. When the red light comes on, I'm going to bow to you when you should bring your hand down.' And I did that, then I played the drums. And after we got through playing that, I said, 'Give me suggestions about the name of it.' Everybody was giving me names. I had a hat with a lot of names in it. So, you know who named it? The people in the control room at RCA Victor. They'd put in 'After Hours.'

"A lot of times, I didn't know what I was going to record, unless it was something sent to me special to record, like RCA may have said, 'Make an arrangement and record this.' I used to keep around a thousand tunes in my book and call them by numbers. So, I'd take the whole book down. And boy, he'd say, 'Hawk, why do you take the whole book?' So I get down there, and I'd say to take out whatever number I had in mind—like

'Cherry' was number 13. I liked that, on account of I'd go by what the public liked when I played on the dance floor. If I see you come back and ask me to play that tune . . . that's how I used to pick my recording tunes."

"Cherry" became a bigger success for Harry James than for Hawkins. Hawkins comments: "Harry James and all them, we was good friends, too. When I used to play the theaters there, Harry James, Ziggy Elman and Chris Griffin used to come there and get right up the first two or three rows in front of me, catch my whole show, all the time. And then when he got his band, Harry made 'Cherry' later. . . . Yeah, we were good friends. He wrote or called his mother and father in Beaumont, Texas—he told them to go see my band. And when I got to Beaumont, and they had a front table and they made themselves known to me.

"Bobby Smith, the first alto player in our band, put 'Tippin' In' together when we were in California [in 1945]. Bobby named the tune after a little dog he had. I think he called him Tippin so he made the whole thing 'Tippin' In.' Bobby made the arrangement so good and he started playing it, and every time we played it, I liked it more and more. We headed back to New York, traveling by train. We'd get off at whatever city where we were going to stop, do a one-night stand, and then get back on the train. Well, some people started asking at the theaters for 'Tippin' In.' " The number, a wonderful showcase for Smith's confident, beckoning sax, which Hawkins had not yet recorded, was already winning a following. "When I got to Chicago, I called the manager, Moe Gale, and I said, 'Set me up a recording date in Chicago. I've got some tunes I want to record.' He made RCA Victor set it up. We went up, recorded 'Tippin' In.' I was afraid. I didn't want nobody to hear the melody [and record it] before we had a chance to record it. That was the reason." Hawkins was a bit gun-shy about others recording his numbers and scoring bigger successes with them than he had.

"A lot of musicians, when they got through at one a.m., they used to come up to the Savoy, and listen in; I played until three. I used to let some of them sit in. Les Paul, he would come up many times. He was down there with Fred Waring. He came up, he wanted to play jazz. He sounded good. And Jimmy Dorsey used to come up to see me a lot. He liked my little girl vocalist at that time, Ida James. Ida was with me about nine or ten years." Indeed the whole personnel of the Hawkins Band remained rather stable. "We were like a family," he says. "That's the reason, I guess, I stayed in the business so long.

"I outlasted a lot of the bands until, you know, it got hard for the big band places. Then, somewhere in the '50s, I had to break my band down. I brought it down to about seven pieces, then five. I kept that a long time when I went into certain places, then I used a quartet plus a girl vocalist. I started playing clubs because the places weren't big enough to hold big bands. I used to play a lot of places with the small group like it was a big band playing them.

"I have some of my old arrangements. But I lost a good book of arrangements in a fire. When the Savoy closed, I had a valet across the street, he would rent a place and take care of my music when I was out on the road. The place caught on fire one night and that's how I lost my music. I had a lot of it rewritten; Sam Lowe took a lot of it from the records. I've got quite a bit, where I can go out and do concerts and different things."

Hawkins played frequently in the 1970s and '80s with a small group at the Concord Hotel, a resort in the Catskills. He has made some appearances at jazz festivals. Occasionally he gets to play at a concert or on a cruise ship with a big band, playing music from his heyday. Mostly, though, he works these days with small groups. He still plays swing, he says.

"I didn't change my style of playing. I didn't like to go like bebop or rhythm-and-blues. The same style I was playing with the big band, I'm still doing that now with my small group. People can understand what I'm playing," he comments. And he likes that. He adds: "I don't got nothing against what young people are doing, but I figured: Why should I change my style to theirs? Why should we try to take theirs away from them?"

1989

BILL · DILLARD

Versatility Served Him Well

"I don't know what it is, being old. I don't know," muses trumpeter Bill Dillard, who is 79. "I see people who are 10, maybe 15 years younger than me and they really look like older people. But I look in the mirror and I don't seem to feel that I'm old."

We're chatting backstage at New York's Village Gate where, for eight performances a week, Dillard plays in the band—and also has one featured number, playing, singing, and dancing—in the show, *Further Mo'*, which is set in 1927 and includes some numbers Dillard actually played in that period.

Dillard continues: "I belong to five senior citizen centers. When I retired, supposedly, at 65—actually I never retired—I said, 'I'll join some of the centers.' And sure enough, they sit around and they nod and they look at television, and then they go to lunch and they sit around. The women sew or the men shoot pool or something. I think they believe what our culture says: when you reach a certain age, you're old. But the mind doesn't get old if it's healthy. So I never thought I was old. I don't know how it feels to be old. I'm still doing the same thing. I get up 6:30, 7:30, 8:00—I only need six, maybe seven hours sleep. The whole day I'm going—and I do the show, too. This show, every night it's like reliving my life again. I'm playing the same growling stuff that I did in the '20s and '30s."

150

BILL DILLARD

Born July 20, 1911, in Philadelphia, Dillard was 11 when he got his first horn. He recalls: "A fellow living two doors from my house used to parade with Marcus Garvey, playing the bugle. Then Garvey ran into some problems with the FBI and the Internal Revenue and his 'Back to Africa' movement was disbanded. Well, the last day this man paraded, he came home and I happened to be sitting on my doorstep. He said, 'Billy, you want a bugle?' And I said, 'Yes, Mr. Hardy.' So he gave me his bugle in a little black bag. I blew it and I couldn't get any sound, and the other two fellows I was with, they couldn't get any sound. But every day when I came home from school, I would take it in the back yard of the house and I would start huffing. One day, I got a sound. Then I began to realize it's the vibration of the lips that makes the sound. And pretty soon I was able to play the bugle calls that I'd heard the soldiers play."

Dillard's father was so impressed by the way his son had taught himself to play that neighbor's old bugle, he decided to buy him a new cornet for his 12th birthday. "We went down to the store," Dillard remembers. "And I picked up a cornet and started playing. The dealer said, 'Wait, wait a minute, wait!' And he goes under the counter and takes out the case and puts the mouthpiece in the cornet. And I put that up to my lips and I got a better sound. You see, I had learned to play it without the mouthpiece!" Dillard occasionally gives talks and performances at public schools, he adds as an aside, and when he relates this tale, he removes the mouthpiece from his trumpet. "I hold the mouthpiece. I pick the horn up. And I play the same chords. I can still do that."

Dillard's father found him a teacher—a man from their family's church—who taught him to play the cornet properly. Much of his real education came, however, simply from observing other musicians. "I used to go to a theater in Philadelphia called the Standard Theater. It was part of the black theater circuit, the 'Toby' circuit we used to call it. By then, I had become very, very attracted to cornets—mostly cornet, they didn't play trumpets much in those days. So I used to go to this theater every Saturday matinee time and I'd sit in the front row, right next to the cornet player in the pit orchestra."

151

He was fascinated with the whole world of show business, not just music. It took a while before his own interests focused mostly on making music. "I went to every Saturday performance for years. I saw Bessie, I saw Mamie Smith, Clara Smith. I didn't see Ma Rainey; I was a little too late for her. But all of the famous black vaudeville shows I saw."

Who were some of his favorite performers?

"I sort of liked the comedians a lot. As a matter of fact, I do comedy, too, if I have to," he says. "Of course, I admired Ethel Waters when she was young. She was tall and slender and had a short haircut that was stylish in those days—like a mannish haircut, you know, with the sideburns. I saw so many of the great performers of that era, and continued into the '40s and the '50s. But I always had a great attraction to the theater—not necessarily as a trumpet player but as an actor. Because when I was a young fellow, maybe 14 and 15, I had a dance partner and we used to dance and do shows in the schools, too, in our junior high and in our high school. He was my buddy, we grew up together—Fats Atkins was his name.

"And I used to go to the movies, of course, in those days. And some of the boys that I grew up with, we'd come home, and after we had dinner at nights we'd come out for a while. And we would impersonate what we had seen in the movies, especially the cowboy things. William S. Hart was my favorite cowboy in those days. We used to impersonate those fellows.

"And when I was 16, 17, I boxed amateur. It was a little hard on my lips so I said I'd better stop. But I'd been going to the gym two or three times a week. So I started lifting weights. And I became a physique model 50 years ago. I used to compete. Being into physical culture and boxing and swimming and going to the gym, I didn't drink or smoke. I didn't hang out much, either, because it didn't go along with what my real plan was. So now I think it's paying off—because a lot of people don't think I'm that old."

In his upper teens, Dillard began concentrating more on playing cornet. He learned the names of different musicians he'd see in Philadelphia theaters and dance halls. He remembers admiring the De Paris brothers, Sidney (cornet) and Wilbur (trombone). "And I guess I saw most of the big black traveling bands of that time. In 1927, Fletcher Henderson's Band came to the Strand Ballroom, one of the main ballrooms in Philadelphia. And that's the first time I met Benny Carter, who was playing in that band then. And I met Pops Smith, the first trumpet player, and his brother, Joe Smith. I met Rex Stewart, Buster Bailey. Fletcher's Band was like the top band in those days. And that was really a thrill for me. I'll never forget when their bus drove up and they came into the ballroom. Another band was playing until they showed up. They came in the ballroom with long raccoon coats and I had never seen a coat like that—you know, they were really big time!"

Dillard worked around Philadelphia with leaders including Linwood Johnson, Josh Saddler, and Barney Alexander. "Barney Alexander had been Jelly Roll Morton's banjo player [recording with Morton in 1929]. Then he left Jelly's band and moved to Philadelphia and organized a five-piece band. By then I was pretty well known in Philadelphia and I started working with his band," Dillard recalls. But he left town for a bit when he got an opportunity to work in New York.

"In the meantime, Jelly Roll Morton had been traveling and he came through Philadelphia. He was looking for a trumpet player and Barney Alexander recommended me to him. Jelly came to my house looking for me, but I had gone to New York to replace a trumpet player in one of the dancing schools—one of those dime-a-dance places called the Diana, on the second floor at the corner of Fourteenth Street and Third Avenue. That was the first dancing school I worked in and I was supposed to stay just two weeks—but I never came back to Philadelphia.

"When Jelly came to New York several months later, he got in touch with me and I started playing with his band. I think I recorded twice with him. People have the records. I don't have hardly any of the records I made. Well, I never even knew I was going to be around this long, do you know what I mean? It was just a job. Because we didn't make much money. I didn't know anything about royalties. So we just got the $35 or $50, which was good money then, for the session, and that was it." (Although the Brian Rust discography, *Jazz Records, 1897–1942,* does not identify Dillard as being present on any of Morton's records, it notes the presence of a second trumpeter, identity unknown, on two of Morton's 1930 recording sessions. It's possible Dillard played on those sessions.)

Dillard notes: "Jelly Roll used to make arrangements. That's one thing about Jelly—most of the things I recorded with him, he more or less wrote the arrangements, which was a little unusual for the average band, because we used to make head arrangements back then. Some of the best arrangements I recall with Teddy Hill's Band [in the 1930s] were head arrangements— like 'Christopher Columbus,' we put that together at one of our rehearsals.

"Jelly was a real musician. He must have been, to write some of those early songs that made him very popular. When I was 15 and 16, I used to go up to my cousin's house in a suburb of Philadelphia. She had an Orthophonic Victrola—it was a new kind of a sound—and I remember just loving the kind of songs he wrote and sang."

It was a thrill for Dillard—not yet even 20—to be working with a musician whose records he had long appreciated. "And it was quite exciting to later work with Sidney De Paris and Wilbur De Paris and Ethel Waters and Bessie Smith, who I had seen when I was a young boy, you know. When I came to New York, I played all the theaters with the Toby circuit, yeah, many times. I played the Standard Theater with the bands that I used to go to when I was a young fellow, you see. I had the pleasure of working with those fellows that I admired then."

Dillard got a job working in a dancing school in a band led by sax player Bingie Madison. On October 31, 1930, Dillard got to make a recording date with the renowned Clarence Williams (composer of such numbers as "Sugar Blues" and "Royal Garden Blues"); he was in Williams' band when it recorded "Papa De-Da-Da," "Hot Lovin'," and "Baby Won't You Please Come Home" (which six decades later Dillard would be playing in *Further Mo'*).

"King Oliver was going to make another record session, so he got Bingie Madison to put the band together for him. That's how I got to play and record with King Oliver. And we went over to the studio in Camden. Bingie used to make arrangements, small arrangements. King Oliver still played all right." The Oliver session, which used most of the same musicians who had played on the Clarence Williams session, yielded recordings of "Papa De-Da-Da," "Who's Blue," and "Stop Crying."

Dillard played in the big bands of Luis Russell (1931–32) and Benny Carter. He was in Carter's band when it recorded such numbers as "Swing It" and "Six Bells Stampede" (March 14, 1933), and "Lonesome Nights" and "Symphony in Riffs" (October 16, 1933). He also made record dates for sides under the nominal leadership of Spike Hughes (the band was essentially Benny Carter's), including "Someone Stole Gabriel's Horn," "Pastorale," and "Bugle Call Rag" (April 18, 1933).

That same year, 1933, was when Dillard first met an unknown singer by the name of Billie Holiday. He recalls: "John Hammond used to go hear her sing in a club up in Harlem, the Hot-Cha Bar and Grill, a little club at 134th Street at Second. At that time, I was with Benny Carter's Band and we were doing the vaudeville theaters. So John Hammond persuaded Benny to try Billie Holiday out. A theater in Long Island City. She sang there three days and I think we went to a theater in the Bronx for the other four days. But she was fat, ungroomed, country-looking. Very excited about being with this big band on the stage and everything. Then the next time [around 1940]—see, by then she was with Louis Armstrong when I was with his band. We played the Paramount with her then. But then she had become Lady Day and Tallulah Bankhead and some of the other people were hanging out with her. She was on drugs then. But I can say I knew her when she was happy."

From about June to October 1933, Dillard played in Europe. "I went with Lucky Millinder's Band. See, by that time, they had started hiring a show person, someone that could announce the acts and wave a baton and do something—stand in front of the band. Lucky Millinder was a dancer and he was hired to lead a band which was called Lucky Millinder's Band, comprised of some Harlem musicians. We went to Monte Carlo in 1933 to open the gambling casino on the beach called the Sporting Club.

That was quite exciting, for me to go to Europe in 1933. It took a whole week to get from here to Europe, so, after the first day we would start rehearsing.

"I have wonderful memories of that particular trip in Monte Carlo. And the show was a big hit there. It happened to be a Broadway show that had closed. The director, a Frenchman named Fifi Ferry, hired the whole show to come and they called it the *Midnight Follies of Monte Carlo*." Included in the cast were Buddy Ebsen (known to a later generation as television's Barnaby Jones) and his sister/partner, Vilma, who were then dancers. Dillard still has an autographed photo Ebsen gave him back then and has followed Ebsen's subsequent career with great interest.

Another performer whom Dillard first came to know back in the mid '30s as a dancer was Pearl Bailey. "I knew her when she was 16, 17; she had a dance act with a girl partner we called Chocolate," Dillard says. "Pearl was maybe 17 when the doctor discovered she had a heart murmur so she had to stop dancing. So she told me she was going to start singing. So she did. And the fact that she did something funny one time, and the way she used her hands, singing, you know—that made her.

"I knew a lot of people—Lena Horne, I knew her when she was just a show girl, she didn't even sing or nothing, she just looked pretty—wore the costumes and walked around the stage in dresses. After awhile, she started dancing and then she started learning to sing," recalls Dillard of the singer who started as an unknown at the Cotton Club in 1933.

In the fall of 1934, Dillard joined saxist Teddy Hill's Band. He stayed until 1938, playing first trumpet on such recordings as "(Lookie Lookie Lookie) Here Comes Cookie" (February 26, 1935), "Passionette" (May 4, 1936), "The Harlem Twister" (March 26, 1937), "Twilight in Turkey" (April 23, 1937), "King Porter Stomp" and "Blue Rhythm Fantasy" (May 17, 1937). (Featured trumpet soloists in the band during Dillard's tenure included, at first, Roy Eldridge, then later Frankie Newton, Shad Collins and Dizzy Gillespie). Dillard also found time while with Hill to play on record dates under the leadership of singer Bob Howard, such as "Lulu's Back in Town" (July 10, 1935) and "In a Little Gypsy Tea Room" (July 18, 1935). Dillard also got to make some records, on which he was featured as both a trumpeter and vocalist, with a septet billed as the "Little Ramblers": "The Music Goes Round and Round," "I'm Building Up to an Awful Letdown," "I'm Shooting High," and "I've Got My Fingers Crossed" (December 27, 1935).

Dillard recalls his years with Hill fondly: "We were one of the three main bands who called the Savoy Ballroom home. They had two bandstands, you know, so you'd do a set, then another band would do a set. And we also made a lot of records for the music publishers. In those days, they used to go around and they would go to the nightclubs and sing their music during breaks. That's how they'd plug their songs; the songwriters would come themselves. We made records of a lot of those new songs and I sang in many of them. When we got to the recording studio, they passed out the music for us, stock arrangements that we used to get free in the Brill Building. They gave them to us because that would advertise the music." Dillard sang on such Teddy Hill recordings as "Big Boy Blue" and "Where Is the Sun" (March 26, 1937), "I Know Now," "The Lady Who Couldn't Be Kissed," and "The You and Me That Used to Be" (April 23, 1937), "Yours and Mine" and "I'm Feeling Like a Million" (May 17, 1937).

"I worked with Teddy Hill in most of the Toby theaters in the New York or Washington or Baltimore area. We had a little circuit of theaters out of New York. It was the Lafayette Theater before it was the Apollo in New York; we would go to the Howard in Washington, then we'd go, I think it was the Penn Theater in Baltimore. We used to call it, 'Well, we're going around the world.' That meant you were going to do the three or four weeks of that circuit. So I did that with Teddy Hill's Band.

"Then they sent a show to Europe, the *Cotton Club Revue,* in 1937 and Teddy Hill's Band was hired to play. Now Frankie Newton, a wonderful trumpet player in the band, had organized a little quintet and gotten a job in the Village. He didn't want to disband that to go to Europe, so we had to replace Frankie in a week or so. By then, Dizzy [Gillespie], who was quite a young guy, had been coming up to the Savoy, asking Chick Webb, Benny Carter or Teddy to let him sit in with the band, which usually they did. He used to sit in a lot with Teddy's band so when we had to replace Frankie Newton, Teddy hired Dizzy and we sailed away with him. It was, I guess, maybe the first big band he had ever played with. He was a good musician then. But he'd be playing section things, you know.

"Did you read what he said about me in his book, *To Be or Not to Bop*? He talks about how I helped him more than anybody in the business. We liked him a lot. It was my job to keep the brass section together, phrasing and attacking, all of these things. Because I usually played first trumpet, even though I did solos, too.

"Our band went to Europe. We had a wonderful time in Monte Carlo. It was such an education, really. We didn't live in the big hotels, they didn't have that many on the beach then, you see. We lived in a section overlooking the beach up in the mountains, a little village called Beaujolais. It was Italian and French people living there because it's so close to Italy. So we ate in their restaurants, spent time with the girls, we swam and sailed in their ships with the fellows, you know. We really hung out with them because we couldn't hang out with the money people at that time. You really came to Monte Carlo if you had money to gamble.

"So I used to get very dark. Usually, I would spend a lot of time on the beach when I was free to do that. So the girls were very friendly with us. And having been brought up in a segregated kind of environment, it was enlightening, very enlightening. That's the thing about going to Europe, if you're a black person who hasn't thought too much about the situation—you know what I mean? At that time, we didn't have any civil rights movements and all of that thing; you just accepted what the situation was. But, for instance, one time I was sitting on a raft anchored out about 50 feet from the beach. We used to swim out there and lay on it with the girls and the boys from up in Beaujolais. So I was sitting on the raft and I had long curly hair then. And one girl did that to my hair [touching and stroking it]. And when she did, the other girl—they pushed my hair, they wanted to feel my hair, you know. And said, '*Ooh, très bien, bon, bon,*' you know. I said, 'Oh, what the—we're supposed to have nappy hair but they say it's nice.' And then they [stroking his arm] say, 'This

Bill Dillard. (Photo by Martha Swope Associates/Carol Rosegg, courtesy of the Jacksina Company.)

The New Orleans Blues Serenaders—Bill Dillard (trumpet), Orange Kellin (clarinet), Emme Kemp (piano), Joseph Daley (tuba), and Kenneth Sara (drums)—as featured in the 1990 musical production Further Mo' at New York's Village Gate. (Photo by Martha Swope Associates/Carol Rosegg, courtesy of the Jacksina Company.)

is nice, too. Brown, ohh.' So I said, 'Gee.' It made me start thinking—you see what I mean? It made me find out more about who I am, not necessarily what I had been more or less accustomed to here.

"That's the thing that still exists in Europe. When a black artist goes to Europe, you are treated like an artist; you're not just a horn blower, you're an artist. And people seem to appreciate your contribution to the world, the happiness and the joy that has evolved from a situation that came up that wasn't too good. But out of it came something that's brought happiness and joy and pleasure all over the world. They seem to appreciate that more, so consequently a lot of men go there and they never come back here any more. But traveling is wonderful for everybody, not only for that reason—to go and see what's going on in the world.

"Now Dizzy was a young, wild sort of a guy who loved life. It was very exciting for him to come, you know, suddenly into that environment, and he really had a wonderful time. Shad Collins was playing solos mostly with us, and Dizzy would play solos as well. Sometimes, Dizzy would be playing a solo and he'd be playing fast—you know how he plays his modern jazz—and very high, and he'd make a wrong note; he would stop playing and laugh! We thought that was so strange, but I enjoyed working with him; he was a wonderful guy.

"We went to the Palladium [in July 1937], had a nice trip there. Hugues Panassie [the French critic and record producer], who had printed the *Hot Club of France* magazine a few months prior to that, came over to the Palladium Theater to see us. And he wanted Dicky Wells, our trombonist, to get a group together when we went to the Moulin Rouge in Paris, to record with him over there. Hugues had stayed in London several days and he didn't like Dizzy's playing, he didn't want to use Dizzy. He wanted to use Bill Coleman, who had gone to Europe prior to that, in the group Dicky put together." Among the sides recorded by Dicky Wells' group in Paris were "Bugle Call Rag," "I Got Rhythm," and "Hangin' Around Boudon" (July 7, 1937) and "Hot Club Blues," "I've Found a New Baby," and "Dinah" (July 1, 1937). "Then after I came back from Europe, I stayed with Teddy Hill for quite a while," Dillard recalls.

161

"I worked in Coleman Hawkins' Band [for a short period in 1939]. We worked in Kelly's Stable on 52nd Street. And we played the Savoy. We had two battles with Count Basie's Band. They had the two stages, Basie here and Hawk here. And that's when Lester [Young] was really wailing, you see. And it was so interesting and exciting to see the two tenor styles competing. And of course up at the Savoy, the audience determined who was who. But Lester was cute and he was spry and he had a stylized kind of playing and his attitude, you know [Dillard's voice takes on a certain hipness, and with his hands he suggests Lester's way of holding and playing the sax at an angle—he is sort of becoming Young as he recalls him] but Hawk [his voice deepens] was old, we called him old Bean, you know, he played—it was so exciting and wonderful." Young and Hawkins were the two leading tenor sax stylists of that time; Hawkins had a heavier sound, with more of a vibrato; Young opted for a lighter, sleeker approach.

Whose band did the audience favor?

"Well, generally speaking they favored Hawk, but musically speaking I think they favored Basie. The band Hawk had, he had a drummer, Arthur Herbert—very few people have even ever heard of him—who had a good beat, like a shuffle kind of a thing, that the Lindy Hoppers could relate to very well. In those days the drummers didn't play all the solo stuff—they just kept that rhythm section together. As a matter of fact, the rhythm section used to rehearse by itself, just to get that right feeling.

"I had first met Hawk in 1927 with Fletcher and for me to be working with him was a thrill. He was very calm and cool. He had a attitude that implied he's made a contribution to the progress that [jazz] has made, and he sort of carried that around. He was a quiet sort of a guy. Very businesslike and almost shy. I liked the way he would tell a story with his horn. Paint a musical picture with his instrument. That's all jazz is, anyhow. It's like surrealist painting; it's an improvisation."

From January to November of 1940, Dillard played in Louis Armstrong's big band. "Actually, I worked with Louis Armstrong on three different occasions in my career. The first time, it was with Luis Russell's Band, in the early '30s. I joined the band and we worked in a club across from the Savoy Ballroom in the basement, called the Saratoga Club. And it was run by a black man, Casper Holstein. He was like a politician in Harlem in those days. We had shows and we had this New Orleans band—Red Allen, Higginbotham, Pops Foster.

"Well, Joe Glaser, who managed Louis Armstrong, hired Luis Russell's band to back Louis Armstrong. The heading was Louis Armstrong's Band but it was actually Luis Russell's Band. And we toured the big theaters, toured the vaudeville houses. See, he carried a show as well. So when we did the theaters [in 1940], he had Sonny Woods, he had Midge Williams, the two singers, he had sometimes [dancer] Peg Leg Bates or somebody that traveled, too."

An incident that occurred while Dillard was touring with Armstrong prompted him to redirect his life. He recalls: "When my little son, the third boy, was born, I had to go to California with Louis Armstrong. He was doing about a week or so, two weeks, but it was Depression time and I had to go. So we left for California—worked all the way to Oklahoma City. Beyond Oklahoma City there was nothing but desert so we used to take a bus sometimes or we'd hook our own railroad car on the back of a freight that was going out and that's how we'd train. It took a whole day or so to get there from Oklahoma City. Well, I got back home three months later and I go to pick up my little new son and he pushes me, 'waaah.' When I had left, he had been just about to be born. And he didn't know who I was. He was almost three months old then. And I said, 'Oh, gee whiz.' It made a little change in me. It made me realize, if you're a big superstar, the agent's got to make some money from your talent so he's going to book you here and there and you've *got* to do those dates. It made me decide that I'm not going to—I'm going to do what *I* want to do, as long as I can. It was mostly from that particular incident. Ever since then—I only do what I want to do. See, I don't have no chain, no ring. All that's material—I don't need that. But I've been satisfied because I only do what I want to do."

Dillard found ways to make a decent living—sometimes by playing music, sometimes by doing other things in the performing arts—without having to travel far from his family. He played with Red Norvo's Band at Kelly's Stable. Then in 1943, he made his debut as a stage actor, with a small part in *Carmen Jones*.

"I happened to get a part in *Carmen Jones* because when Billy Rose and Oscar Hammerstein were casting it, John Hammond, who had been pretty active bringing talent into New York, persuaded the producers to give me an audition for the part of Pancho, the Panther from Brazil, the Brazilian prizefighter. Well, I looked Latin. I had curly long hair in those days. And I was still in athletics—I was a bodybuilder—so when I went down to audition for Rose and Hammerstein, they just took one look at me and said, 'Oh yeah, you'll be fine.' I didn't do anything. That part was more or less a walk-on."

It wound up leading to a good deal of stage work for Dillard, though, including acting roles in such shows as *Anna Lucasta* (1945), *Memphis Bound* and *Beggar's Holiday* (1946), *Lost in the Stars* (1950), *Green Pastures* and *My Darling Aida* (1952).

"I really like acting. After *Carmen Jones*, I studied acting with two different people in New York. I said, 'Well, this is nice, isn't it, to work two hours or a little more and get dressed up nice and they want your autograph.' And that encouraged me to go into the theater more seriously. I did maybe seven, eight Broadway shows in which I acted. In three shows, I had a spot to play on the trumpet, on stage with the trumpet as I do in this show. I also had a running part on a soap opera, 'Love of Life,' for almost four years. I worked maybe two, sometimes three times a month. I was the bartender in the Steeplechase Room that was run by the leading lady in the show, played by June McBride.

"I was still a musician. I never stopped playing. When I was in Broadway shows I always kept my horn available and I practiced. So when the show closed, I went back into music again." For a while, he was a staff musician at NBC.

Did he prefer acting or playing?

"It's both the same. This number that I'm doing in *Further Mo'* ["Pretty Doll"], when I came to the rehearsal the first day, [musical director] Orange Kellin said, 'We want you to do this number.' So I looked at it: 'You're so pretty, oh so pretty, you're some pretty doll.' I mean, what can you do with that? So, with my theatrical training and background, I figured, 'I'll sort of camp it up a little.' And dance a bit. Sure I dance! I don't feel anything because I took care of myself all my life. Physical culture has helped a lot. I studied dancing, too—modern dance at the Dunham School. This was all after *Carmen Jones.*

"And I studied legitimate singing. Because we didn't have mikes then. Today some of the performers are being cheated, because of the devices they have available now. [He croons real softly:] 'What a difference a day makes, 24 little hours'—bring it up [he booms:] 'What a difference a day makes. . . .' They can't do that. They don't breathe from the diaphragm. Sometimes I coach singers if I see they're willing to listen. They get hoarse, they're singing up here. You say you should sing from the diaphragm; they don't know what it is, singing from the diaphragm. Even in this show, I've spoken to some of the girls about breathing in the diaphragm. They don't know that. And I show them how to breathe."

Dillard's versatility served him well. The fact that he had other options besides playing trumpet helped him when most big bands folded after the Second World War. He had never made a big name for himself as a musician. He had played— mostly section parts, not solos—in bands that were good but not the very best. He had never played for Ellington or Basie or Lunceford or Henderson. He would have found the going rough had he sought to get by just as a trumpet player.

"After the war, when we didn't have any more ballrooms and nightclubs, the concert maestro from *Carmen Jones* taught me some Yiddish songs. I put an act together so I could play the Catskills. For 12–15 years, I survived, when we didn't have the nightclubs, the ballrooms—everything had closed up. [Dillard starts singing in Yiddish.] I learned all that stuff. And the new Israeli stuff I do.

"I used to open up [he sings in a deep, legitimate baritone:] 'I Feel a Song Coming On'—as a legitimate singer, you know. Then from there, 'That Old Black Magic.' I used to do *Porgy and Bess*—'I Got Plenty o' Nuttin.' Then I would go off. But when I came back for the encore, I'd bring my trumpet. Usually I'd say,

'I'd like to do a trumpet solo of Hoagy Carmichael's "Stardust,"' and I'd put my Harmon mute in, play the verse, so right away they'd say, 'Oh gee.' Because quite a few guys who were dancers used the trumpet just as a gimmick. Then I would do 'Basin Street Blues.' And I used to do 'Birth of the Blues.'

"When I started doing the Catskills, I met some of the band-leaders who played in the hotels. So when the summer was over, I saw them again in New York and they'd say, 'Come on, I got a bar mitzvah' or whatever. That's how I got into the bar mitzvah business, too, in the rest of the year.

"I've done shows in public schools. And I'm a member of the Forest Hills Community Center. Any time they need music for installations or whatever it is, usually I play if I'm available. . . . I'll go there with a piano player and I'll sing Yiddish, or I'll sing 'Old Man River.'"

In the early 1980s, Dillard was featured in touring companies of *One Mo' Time*, playing in Canada, Europe and Australia. He sang and played "Sugar Blues" for his featured number. He also played Australia with a group of his own in 1983. He's frequently toured with Sandra Reaves-Philips in her one-woman salute to Bessie Smith, Billie Holiday and other "Late, Great Ladies of the Blues." He played trumpet in the original Paris production of *Black and Blue* (1985–86).

Now, each night in *Further Mo'*, he gets to play such oldtime numbers as "Shake It and Break It," "Salty Dog," "Trouble in Mind," "Boogie Woogie," "Alabamy Bound," "Don't Advertise Your Man," and "Hot Time in the Old Town Tonight." His style is simple, direct. His sound is still clear, unwavering. And he gives every indication of enjoying his one number in the spotlight, "Pretty Doll."

Did he ever wish, I wonder, that he had done more trumpeting as a soloist in his career?

"No, I never really aspired to be any particular star," Bill Dillard maintains. "I don't want to be controlled by nobody. I just want to be myself."

1990

"I Fell in Love with that Clarinet . . ."

The only reason he became a a clarinetist, Johnny Mince says, is because a friend of his father's from work happened to have a clarinet he wanted to sell. It was 1924 and John Henry Muenzenberger (Mince's real name) of Chicago Heights, Illinois, was 12 years old. "My father came home from the Hamilton piano factory where he worked and asked me, 'Johnny, do you want to get the clarinet?' And I said, 'Oh dad, I sure do!' He said, 'Well, you're going to have to earn it.' And so I went to the golf grounds—I was a caddy—as much as I could. In those days, people paid a dollar per 18 holes, and you were lucky if you got a dime tip. When I finally came up with the money—$15—he got me the clarinet. And boy! I was so anxious to get at that thing. We figured out how to put it together, and what to do with the reed.

"My father said, 'I'll bet I can play it before you do, Johnny.' And I said, 'Well, go ahead.' So he tried to play it and all that came out were squeaks. We didn't know at that time that a reed won't play unless it's wetted up a little while. And by the time he gave it to me, it was wetted up a little bit. I noticed the clarinet had the six holes, just like my little tin whistle I was playing on at home. And so sure enough—daa de da da—I played the whole 'Silent Night' on that clarinet, the first time I tried to play it! My mother looked at me and said, 'Johnny, how can you do that?' I said, 'I don't know.' It was a natural talent I found out that I had. I took that clarinet to bed with me! I fell in love with it.

"I played it for two years before I ever had a lesson. We had a record at home called 'The Poet and Peasant Overture.' I used to play along with it, with the phonograph. By the time I was 14, my folks realized that I was getting pretty good; I'd better have some lessons. And my mother took me to this man who taught all the instruments. We were very poor people. And the first thing she asks the man was, 'Well how much money can Johnny make playing clarinet?' He said, 'Oh, as much as $40 a week.' So she said: 'By golly, Johnny! You're going to play clarinet!' You know, like that was an order. I studied with him for awhile. And I found out that some of the fingerings that I was playing by ear were not the correct fingerings, but I still made them work somehow.

"And finally, after my parents realized that I was going to become a musician—that that's what I wanted to be—my father brought me this catalog from the Hamilton piano factory, which also had a subsidiary with a French clarinet company and he said, 'Pick out a clarinet.' They were half-price to him. I picked out the most expensive one. It was only about $80 at that time, around 1924 or '25! And it was the best clarinet I've ever had. I've never had one as good as that ever since. (Years later, when I was out with a band, it was stolen out of a locked car.)"

Was there one clarinetist who especially influenced or inspired Mince in his youth?

"Well, at first I copied, I had a record of Pee Wee Russell. And I thought that he was the end, you know. And he did a thing on 'Ida,' I think it was—beautiful solo. But then I heard Benny Goodman play, and I thought to myself: 'By golly, that's the way to play.' And so, Benny became my idol at that time, you know. And then later on, Jimmy Dorsey, also, and another guy by the name of [Frank] Teschemacher, a great clarinet player out of Chicago. And that's about it. People didn't know about Benny Goodman back then, when I first got interested in his playing. But I had a musician friend, who worked at the music store. And he would bring out these kind of records; he knew that I was interested in jazz. So he brought out Bix Beiderbecke, you know, after I'd been used to listening to Red Nichols—that was where I'd heard Pee Wee Russell [who'd played on Red Nichols and the Five Pennies' best-selling 1927 record of "Ida"]. And so they introduced me to Bix Beiderbecke and Trumbauer and all that stuff. *Wonderful.* So I got to playing like Bix Beiderbecke on my clarinet, more or less. Because he played with such beauty. . . . Gorgeous. Gorgeous. . . . But of course, Louis Armstrong was the king in his own right, you know.

"I started working professionally when I was 17 years old. I wasn't doing well in high school, because I was playing in a band in Chicago, and we were playing very late hours. And I was trying to get my studies in school, but I was really asleep in school.

"I had to do an audition for Joe Haymes' Band. Joe Haymes was the arranger for the Ted Weems Band. In fact, [in 1929] Ted Weems made a hit record of his arrangement of 'Piccolo Pete.' Back then the kids were all buying tin whistles; then they'd play the break from that record. [He scats it.]

"I left high school to go with Joe Haymes' Band and we had a job at the Mayo Hotel in Tulsa. We started out, incidentally, with $40 a week, and I thought I was right on top of the world. I was tickled to death to get this job—I wasn't making it in high school, anyway. And my family was tickled, too, because I was able, out of that money, to send $25 a week home to help support the family. I had five sisters, and my uncle lived with us also. That's a lot of people they had to support." Mince's financial assistance helped keep his family from losing their house during the Depression.

"Dick Clark, a good tenor man, was in the band then," Mince recalls. Pee Wee Erwin eventually came into the band on trumpet, rooming for a while with Mince. In his autobiography, *This Horn for Hire* (written with Warren Vaché Sr.), Erwin recalled: "Johnny lugged along a phonograph and records wherever we went. This was my first real introduction to the wonderful world of records, especially those of Louis Armstrong. It was thanks to Johnny and his phonograph that I became aware of what was going on in music. Since I had played all the way through school, I seldom got a chance to hear other bands, even on records, and Johnny's records were a revelation. Among the records we played in Tulsa were Jimmy Dorsey's solo record of 'Beebe' and lots of Louis' classics. It was a new world to me."

Haymes is probably best remembered in music history for forming good bands which other leaders with bigger names then took over. (Tommy Dorsey's first big band, for example, was a Haymes band.) Mince recalls: "M.C.A. used to book Joe Haymes' band. And when it was slow-going for us, they'd tell Joe, 'Well, Buddy Rogers needs a band. . . . ' " M.C.A. would then book the band, with actor-singer Rogers fronting it, as "The Buddy Rogers Band." Mince recalls working in the band, under Rogers' nominal leadership, at the Paradise Restaurant in New York, on a bill with strip-tease artist Sally Rand. "We played for Sally Rand, who was doing a bubble dance at the time. She had great big rubber balloons. Real strong. Because they should never break, you know—that wouldn't be nice. Heh!"

"Zez Confrey also took over the band for a while," Mince recalls. "He's the guy that wrote 'Kitten on the Keys'—that's way back—and we went through the worst week that I ever spent in the music business. We were on the road in the middle of the winter—a miserable winter. And we drove our cars; that's how we got to the jobs. The only lucky guys that made any money at those times were the guys that had cars; they would get three cents a mile and we traveled so much. And they had to get their money because we wouldn't get to the next job otherwise. Well, we spent a week where we'd spell each other at the wheel, driving in this miserable cold winter of slush—a whole week without getting to bed. We'd sleep in the car, as the other guy was driving. It was dangerous. We ran into a ditch when a buddy of mine, Pee Wee Erwin, Paul Mitchell, and myself, we all fell asleep—the three of us and the driver. All of a sudden we woke up—crash!—and I found myself outside of the car on my hands and my knees. Pee Wee Erwin was upside-down. His feet were in the car and his head was down on the running board. But we were OK. We weren't hurt badly at all—thank God for that!" Car accidents were an occupational hazard for musicians in the Swing Era who frequently had to drive great distances between jobs, whether or not they were rested.

"Buddy Rogers broke up the band in Chicago. We were playing at this College Inn, and J. Arthur Rank offered him a film to make in England. So that's what he did. So he let the band go. We had a wonderful band. We had Toots Mondello in it, Gene Krupa was in that band, Pee Wee Erwin. A hell of a band! And he let it go. He didn't know that he had something very valuable there. Later he came back to see me one time. By then, I was in Tommy Dorsey's Band, and so was Pee Wee Erwin. And Gene Krupa was in Benny Goodman's Band, making a big name for himself. And he told me: 'Boy, I didn't know what I had there. I could have been the number one band.' He had a great band before Benny Goodman and Artie Shaw and all these guys. God, he had a great band! But he wasn't about to make a hit with it, exactly. The people weren't ready for that kind of a band when he had it. Benny Goodman had the kind of a band—and he made it. And he made that whole Swing Era get going! And thank goodness he did. And Artie Shaw and people like that, that came along later. But Benny really started something. He didn't realize he was even doing it, either. He went out to Denver and he played at Elitch's Gardens and the people weren't paying much attention to him. So he figured then, well, we're not really making it, so let's just play some things that we like to play. So they played jazz. And people woke up and all of a sudden, 'Yeah, that's a wonderful way to play.' And that started it! That started it!

"When Buddy Rogers' Band broke up, I came to New York to look for work. And I was rehearsing with a band led by Eddy Peabody, the great banjo player. I happened to run across Tommy Dorsey, in the street, right in front of the place where he was working with the Dorsey Brothers' Band. And he says, 'Johnny, what are you doing here?' I said, 'I've been looking for work and I'm rehearsing with Eddy Peabody's Band.' He said, 'What are you doing tonight?' I said, 'Nothing.' He said, 'You're taking Jimmy's place *tonight*. It's five o'clock now. Have you got a tuxedo?' 'No.' He said, 'Well, get one! We start at eight o'clock.' I was thrilled to death because Jimmy was one of my idols. That was a wonderful opportunity for me.

"Tommy and Jimmy Dorsey were having fights, you know,

171

disagreements—they didn't get along well at all. So Jimmy would leave once in a while and come back maybe the next night and everything would be patched up.

"I went home to my hotel and told my roommate, Walt Yoder (who later became manager of Woody Herman's Band), 'Do you know what? I'm taking Jimmy Dorsey's place tonight. Gee, I've got to get a tuxedo right now.' " Yoder traded Mince one of his tuxedos for a pair of dress shoes Mince had recently bought. Mince adds: "And Walt was a big tall guy. The sleeves of the tux came way over my hands, and I was slobbing along on the sidewalks; the pants were too long. But I didn't care! I was taking Jimmy Dorsey's place!"

Mince replaced Dorsey—then one of the best-known, most highly respected clarinetists and alto saxists in the business—for two weeks in late 1934. Jimmy had numbers in the book that showcased his technical virtuosity as a reed player. "And the strange thing is, Tommy was trying to find out how good I really was, and he pulled out some very difficult saxophone things of Jimmy's, like 'Oodles of Noodles' and 'Fingerbuster' and things like that. He gave me this music, and I said, 'Oh well, yeah. . .' [with a worried tone]. It called for double-tonguing, a special kind of a thing, where you have to go 'Tucka-tucka-tucka-tucka,' and then for triple-tonguing—that's 'tucketa-tucketa-tucketa-tucketa.' You can hear the triplets: da-da-da, one-two-three, one-two-three. But I didn't know how to do that. In fact, every time I tried, it sounded terrible. It'd come out 'tuck-KUH, tuck-KUH, tuck-KUH'—it sounded like a wild animal of some kind.

"But I thought going back and forth across the reed with my tongue would work. It gave you the same sound, but it wore out the reed real quick and you got a sore tongue from it. Well, it happened that Tommy hit just the right tempo for me to play it at, because I could only do it about one speed, just like you just heard, 'duddle-uddle-uddle-uddle-uddle-uddle,' about like that. So he hit the right tempo and I thought: 'Oh! I can't believe it. I'm not going to tell him the truth, that if he'd have counted out a little bit faster or a little bit slower, it would have been horrible.' But I happened to hit it right on. So they thought, *'Wow!'* " Mince laughs. "I wasn't as good as they thought I was." But Tommy

JOHNNY MINCE

Dorsey, and the other players in the band, were amazed to find this relative unknown playing Jimmy's parts so well.

After about two weeks, Jimmy had cooled down enough to reclaim his chair as co-leader of the Dorsey Brothers' Band. "I said to Glenn Miller, who was playing trombone and arranging in the Dorsey Brothers' Band then: 'Gee, I haven't got anything to do now.' He says, 'Sure you have!' And he showed me this list. Ray Noble, the British bandleader, had been in touch with Glenn to get him the best band he could get—New York musicians. So Glenn picked me; he liked the way I played. So that put me, in 1935, in the Ray Noble Band with Glenn Miller, who was the trombone player and arranger. So that was a bit of luck!"

Mince, according to the Brian Rust discography, recorded with Ray Noble on sessions from February 9, 1935 through May 25, 1936. Occasionally, although not enough to satisfy some of the jazzmen in the band, the Noble band played moderately hot numbers (one fine sample of Mince with the Noble Band in this vein is "Chinatown, My Chinatown," June 10, 1935) but the emphasis was on superbly played sweet music. "We made some beautiful things, really," Mince notes. "But I think Ray Noble's English band sounded better on records. We were always looking for different places to record, where they had just the kind of right acoustics that were equal to the English acoustics. We never found it. We went to churches and big halls and different things, to try to get that sound, but we never were that successful. It was a good band and everything. My God! In that band, we had Glenn Miller, Claude Thornhill, Pee Wee Erwin, Bud Freeman, Will Bradley—just a whole bunch that ultimately became bandleaders. Not me—but they all did. I never wanted to be a bandleader and still don't want to be. (I've now got a couple of jobs in Boca Raton where I'm the leader, but I have to do it because the money's good and it's important to keep that experience going—even at this late age.)"

Mince left Noble in 1936 to play with Bob Crosby's Band; actually, Mince and Matty Matlock simply switched places with the consent of both bandleaders. The Noble Band was playing in New York, where Matlock's wife was; Matlock was eager to get off the road and be with his wife. Mince, who was single and didn't feel a need to be tied to New York, knew he'd get to play more free-wheeling jazz in the Crosby Band than in the Noble Band. After three months, however, Noble offered Mince a raise if he'd return to the band, and he did.

Glenn Miller was the musical brains behind Noble's American Band. Mention of Miller's name prompts several recollections from Mince. "One night as we were playing with Ray Noble's Band at the Rainbow Room, before we went on the stand, Glenn came in with a piece of music. A few of us were still in the back room and he asked us: 'Would you guys mind running over this tune of mine? It's a lesson for Joseph Schillinger, my teacher.' So we said, 'Sure.' And we went over that tune, and it went: 'Daa, da-da-daa, da-de-da da-de-da da-da-da-da. . .' [Mince hums the theme now universally known as "Moonlight Serenade."] And we thought, 'My God! What a beautiful tune.' I thought, 'It's unbelievable.' With our enthusiasm, when he heard this thing and how good it sounded, he asked us if we'd do him a favor and go down to Broadway and 49th Street; there was a little place there where you could record your voice for a quarter. So we go down there the next night before going to work and about four of us—we had a violin, a saxophone, and George Van Eps on guitar. So we made this record, this little plastic disc for a quarter. I wonder how much that little disc would be worth today, to somebody that saves Glenn Miller records. My God! It would be a fortune. And I don't know if it's still around somewhere or was just thrown away. Who knows?"

Mince notes he also participated in the birth of what was to become the famous "Miller sound." Miller had arranged some music for the Noble Band in which Erwin was to blow lead on trumpet, playing an octave higher than the saxes who were to blend with him. But Erwin couldn't make the rehearsal and Miller asked Mince to play Erwin's parts on clarinet; the clarinet and saxes, shimmering together, created a far more romantic sound than the trumpet and saxes had. Miller would later build his whole band around that sound.

Mince notes that when Miller left Noble's band in 1937 to try forming his own band, he invited both Mince and Erwin to go with him, but they weren't about to leave Noble's successful (and high-paying) band to go with Miller, who was then, as far as the general public was concerned, an unknown. (Mince had actually played at Miller's first recording session, April 25, 1935, cutting such soon-forgotten sides as "Solo Hop" and "In a Little Spanish Town.") By the end of 1939, Miller would be leading the most popular band in America, but in 1937, Mince and Erwin had no way of predicting that.

"I stayed in Ray Noble's Band for about two and a half years. Then when we were in Washington, Tommy Dorsey called me up. Ray Noble was supposed to take the band to the Coast soon; we were going to do Earl Carroll's Vanities. But Tommy says, 'I've got it on good authority that Ray's not going to take you to the Coast.' Tommy said we were going to get our notice. We didn't believe it; we thought he was giving us a line to get us to join his band," Mince remembers. After all, the married members of the Noble band had just given up their New York apartments; their wives were traveling with the band for the relocation to the West Coast. "But sure enough, the next day we got our three weeks' notice," Mince adds. A lot of uprooted musicians were suddenly left scrambling for jobs.

"Pee Wee Erwin and I said to Tommy: 'We'll join your band if we can also take Mike Doty with us. He's our good first alto sax leader.' So Tommy said, 'Come on, all three of you!' So that's the way we started with Tommy. We didn't lose one day's work. We went from Canada to the Commodore Hotel and worked the next night, right away, with Tommy," Mince says. Erwin, Mince, and Doty made their first recording session with the Dorsey Band on March 10, 1937, taking chairs that had been occupied on Dorsey's last session by Bunny Berigan, Slats Long, and Clyde Rounds.

"That was a wonderful band to play with. They had a good rhythm section with Davey Tough and Howard Smith and Gene Traxler and Carmen Mastren. And a good band to play with. And so was Ray Noble—a beautiful band. I was very lucky. I just came along at the right time and was able to do the job everywhere I went," Mince comments.

Between 1937 and 1941, Mince's clarinet was heard on plenty of strong-selling Dorsey records. "Panama" (July 11,

1938), "Milenberg Joys" (January 19, 1939), and any number of "Clambake Seven" small-group sides show Mince fit in well with the Dixieland-oriented sound that Dorsey initially favored. And Mince proved himself equally adept at playing the smoother brand of swing Dorsey came to favor in the early '40s (for an example listen to the June 1, 1940 aircheck of "Hallelujah" on the album *That Sentimental Gentleman*). Not all of Dorsey's 1930s sidemen could make that transition. Mince was a clear improvement over his predecessors on clarinet in the Tommy Dorsey Band.

But although Mince contributed to the high quality of many Dorsey recordings, as a sideman he didn't reap great benefits financially. He notes: "We got $30 for making a whole record date. For 'Boogie Woogie' and 'I'll Never Smile Again' and many of those hits of his, $30 was the union scale and that's what we got. We got nothing in royalties. *Nothing!* It's the biggest gyp in the world. What the union has done to musicians is just unreal and unforgivable. People are still buying so many of those records; they're put out and sold on television and whatnot."

Aside from some resentment over not getting any royalties, Mince feels: "Tommy was pretty good for me. I was with him four and a half years. He had a very bad temper. You better play your part right! He ruled with an iron hand, no doubt about that. But if you played your part and you played good solos, he had no complaints. He was just very nice."

Mince recalls Dorsey as something of a practical joker. "We were playing at the Paramount Theater one time. Well, he came in when we were in the pit, before we went on—it was April Fools' Day—with a box of candy. He's passing around this box of candy and I'm thinking to myself, 'Oh-oh. This is going to be a joke.' So he comes to me and he says, 'Johnny, take this one.' And I thought to myself, 'OK, Tommy, I got it.' And so when he was out of sight, I cut the candy in half and it had a garlic in it! So I thought, 'Let's see—what am I going to do to get Tommy, now?' I found his trombone and I took that garlic and rubbed it all over the mouthpiece but good! So then we went up, with the stage that went up. And in the blackened theater—except for this big blue light that shone on his phosphorized trombone

In this late 1930s photo, Tommy Dorsey conducts his band, while (from bottom) Mike Doty, Skeets Herfurt, and Johnny Mince play clarinet. (Courtesy of Duncan P. Schiedt.)

Johnny Mince and Bud Freeman, who had played together in the 1930s in the bands of both Ray Noble and Tommy Dorsey, are re-united at the 1986 Conneaut Lake Jazz Festival. (Photo by Chip Deffaa.)

A mid 1980s edition of the Lawson-Haggart Jazz Band. From left to right: Johnny Mince (clarinet), Lou Stein (piano), Bob Haggart (bass), Zack Cullens (not a band member, but a friend of the musicians), Yank Lawson (trumpet), Billy Butterfield (trumpet), George Masso (trombone), Nick Fatool (drums), and Eddie Miller (tenor sax). (Courtesy of Zack Cullens.)

Johnny Mince. (Photo by Zack Cullens.)

(that's all the people could see)—he's playing 'da-da-dee-da-daa
. . .' [Dorsey's theme: "I'm Getting Sentimental Over You"]. Then
he turns around with a downbeat and we start the first number,
right. Then the light comes on. And when that light comes on,
I was making off like I was sick, because I wanted to make him
think I ate that garlic. And I'm spitting out and not playing. And
he can't stand it! He's dying laughing. He's looking at me. And
you can tell that I really got him, but good! He thinks he got me.
But I got him right back. He couldn't have missed the garlic I
rubbed on his trombone. But he never let me know that anything
was wrong. He didn't like to have jokes pulled on him."

Dorsey liked having things his way. One time, after Mince
played a solo that elicited a lot of applause, Dorsey jabbed a finger
in his chest and told him not to forget who was the leader of the
band. Another time when Bunny Berigan failed to show up one
day, Mince recalls, "we were on the air playing 'Marie' and when it
came to Bunny Berigan's chorus, Tommy said, 'Take it Johnny!'
Take the chorus, you know. So I played some jazz on it—my jazz.
And after that program, Tommy said, 'Johnny, why didn't you
play Bunny's chorus?' I said, 'I don't play anybody else's chorus
when I play jazz.' He thought it would have been right for me to
play Bunny's chorus on the clarinet. I think that would have been
ridiculous. I never thought of playing somebody else's chorus
like that."

Mince particularly enjoyed it when Dorsey would present
his "band within the band," the Clambake Seven, which afforded
him greater opportunities for self-expression. He added lots of
brisk excitement to Dorsey's Clambake Seven recordings. "I liked
the small stuff. There were also good things about the big band—
blending with a good saxophone section was a nice feeling, and
I liked the occasional little jazz clarinet solos I got to play. But
there was more leisure, more time to play what you really wanted
to play, jazzwise, in a little Dixieland-type band like that than in
the big band."

Mince said he could have left Dorsey's Band and made more
money as a studio musician. "But I wasn't interested in that. I
was single and I *loved* playing with Tommy's band. I wasn't that
much of a businessman." He only left Dorsey's Band when he

got drafted into the Army. He performed in the show *This Is the Army,* in the U.S. and abroad. He also made the motion picture version of the show. After he was discharged from the Army in 1945, Dorsey offered him his old job back, but by now he had gotten married and he did not want to live on the road, separated for long stretches from his wife, Arline. (He probably would not have fit in the post-World War Two Dorsey band as well as his successor, Buddy De Franco, did anyway. Dorsey was moving towards increasingly clean, straightforward charts by Bill Finegan. Mince's playing was a bit busier than the younger, more modern De Franco's.)

Mince figured he could find work in radio and on record dates. "I was living at my mother-in-law's and father-in-law's house, 65 miles from New York in a little town of Blue Point, Long Island. I'd go into town every week, to the see if contractors at the different studios, CBS, ABC, NBC, could use me," Mince recalls. He finally got a job in a combo "playing five minutes warm-up, before 'The Phil Baker Show,' every Sunday. So I'd go 65 miles in to New York, play five minutes with a group of six jazz players, and go all the way back home. This went on for about three weeks.

"Then the contractor said, 'How would you like to do the Godfrey show?' And I said, 'What's the Godfrey show?' So he told me about Arthur Godfrey. By that time, though, I was starting to get record dates; people were starting to hear about me being available and I was getting kind of busy. So when I got home that night, I told my wife that I could go on the Godfrey show. She said, 'You go on that show! He's going to be the biggest thing on radio and television you ever heard of!' She just knew it, because she was that interested in it herself. So I went on Godfrey's show: Archie Bleyer and his Group—a trombone and clarinet front line, and a rhythm section. And that was the best thing that I ever did, money-wise! My God! We became the highest-paid sidemen in the business. Really. We were making so much money when we took the checks to the bank and cashed them, I always felt kind of guilty, like I had stolen the money, you know. Because it was the easiest job I ever had. But there was a lot of just waiting around, waiting around for Arthur to get ready to rehearse or whatever—you simply had to *be* there."

Mince particularly enjoyed the show when Godfrey had as a guest a musician he admired. "One time Benny Goodman came on the Godfrey show as a guest. There's a record out and I'm on it with Benny Goodman, exchanging choruses. It's right off the Godfrey program. You can hear Godfrey saying, 'OK, now you, Johnny. Now you, Benny.' It's a bootlegged thing—but I'm glad to have it anyway!"

Mince got used to the routine of doing the Godfrey show. "I was with Godfrey 20 years and I was able to raise my family on that show. Twenty years! From about 1945 or '46 to 1966. But when I got out of it, I had no connections with the music business other than that. None. I had done some outside record dates while doing the Godfrey show, but mostly just kind of fell back on the show. We thought we had a job for life, you know. That's the way it seemed. But things change," Mince notes.

He did gigs in the New York area, gave some music lessons. He was known to fellow Big Band Era musicians, but not to younger contractors in the business. He got some offers to go on the road, but he was in his mid 50s now and his wife was in poor health, due to diabetes. He really wanted to stay put.

When Buster Bailey died, April 12, 1967, Mince was invited to become the clarinetist in Louis Armstrong's All-Stars. He filled in for a week, but declined taking the job permanently; Armstrong was still doing plenty of one-nighters and Mince could not see himself living on a band bus at this stage of his life. He smiles as he recalls having to play "Mame" with Louis Armstrong's All Stars on the Grammy Awards show. "We're at the television studio to rehearse. And I didn't know the arrangement at all. So Louis's trying to explain it to me. He said [Mince imitates Satchmo's gravelly voice], 'Well listen, pops, man. I'll go, do do do, do to-do to-do *Mame*, and then you answer.' And I said, 'Well I can do that.' And he counts the thing off. It went along, and he comes to the place where he's singing, 'da da da da tada tada do, *Mame*.' And I sing, *'Mame,'* the same as he did. And he said, 'Stop! No, pops, man—you don't sing it, you play it!' Well, that was a joke on me. That stopped the whole thing, then we did it the right way."

In his later years, Mince has occasionally recorded as a leader (*The Summer of '79* for Monmouth Evergreen in 1979 and *The Master Comes Home* for Jazzology in 1983), played music of the Dorseys in special engagements with such bandleaders as Warren Covington and Lee Castle, and has performed at assorted jazz festivals and parties (including the Chicago Festival of Traditional Jazz, the Conneaut Lake, Pennsylvania, Jazz Party, and the Grande Parade du Jazz in Nice, France).

He moved to Florida in the early 1980s, after the death of his wife. "I just went down there to semi-retire. But it hasn't been working out that way; I've been pretty darned busy. And I've got a couple of steady jobs, one on Sunday and one on Wednesday. And then there's other things that come along and fill in." (Mary Lee Hester reported in the July 1989 *Mississippi Rag* that Mince has played in Florida in recent years with the Boca Raton Symphony Pops Orchestra, with Bob Crosby and his Orchestra, and was playing Wednesdays with Pepe Morreale's group at Chuck's and Harold's in Palm Beach, which she described as "a plush place with plushly dressed people in attendance," as well as other area rooms.)

"When I went to Australia about a year ago, I had to do 'Sing Sing Sing' again out on the radio and television station there. And that went over well," Mince notes. "Nowadays I'm getting good jobs of my own that they're giving me at the Boca Raton Hotel. It's a class place. They just want me to be there with a jazz band, and that's what I want to have, a jazz band. I play Dixieland or swing. And we have a lot of fun with it."

1986

Big Band Memories

The curtain rises to the familiar, ascending trombone strains of "I'm Getting Sentimental Over You"—Tommy Dorsey's theme, being played now not by Dorsey but by Buddy Morrow, who has been leading the Tommy Dorsey Orchestra for more than a dozen years. The band moves crisply, smartly through such Dorsey favorites as "Marie," with the trumpet choir exuberantly amplifying the famous solo that was played by Bunny Berigan on the original 1937 recording; "Well, Git It," with its still-dazzling high-register trumpet duel; and "Chicago," with an irresistibly offhand, loping feel that tells you you're listening to a Sy Oliver arrangement (Morrow himself joins in on the good-natured vocal on this one). The band executes with confidence and precision "Song of India," "Grenada," "Hallelujah," "Hawaiian War Chant," "On the Sunny Side of the Street," and "Opus One." On some ballads, an alto saxist rises to complement Morrow's warm trombone; Morrow mentions that the saxist would have been Jimmy Dorsey when these particular arrangements were first played by the band the Dorsey brothers jointly led in the 1950s. Morrow also comes up with driving swing charts from the early 1940s that TD had dropped from his repertoire by the 1950s, captivating pieces you'd never expected to hear again. Some of these arrangements had been lost or discarded many

185

years before Morrow took over the Dorsey Band in the late 1970s; he's such a believer in the validity of this music, he's had them transcribed from the original records.

Morrow has proven a worthy conservator of the Dorsey heritage, actually playing more varied and interesting programs in his appearances these days than Dorsey himself (judging from airchecks) played in his last years. (In the 1950s, Dorsey had to play a fair number of current pop tunes that did not turn out to have lasting value. Morrow picks and chooses carefully from among the best material played by Dorsey throughout his career.) Morrow has kept the Tommy Dorsey Band a sharp unit, with clean ensemble work and a good feel for the arrangements—not an easy task, considering that today's economics do not permit him to offer sidemen wages comparable to those Dorsey himself could offer in his heyday. The band's concerts leave you feeling good. If the individual soloists in the band today don't, by and large, have the brilliant originality of their Swing Era counterparts, they carry off their assignments with a good deal of polish and spirit. Under Morrow's guidance, this has been one of the best-maintained of the ghost bands. That professionalism is a reflection of Morrow's 55 years in the business, years that include serving as a sideman in big bands led by Tommy Dorsey, Jimmy Dorsey, Artie Shaw, Paul Whiteman, Vincent Lopez, Eddy Duchin, and Bob Crosby, studio work, leading his own big bands in the 1950s and '60s, and even for a short while leading the Glenn Miller Band, before accepting the leadership of the Dorsey Band in the late 1970s. Sometimes, after taking a chorus straight on trombone, playing it as much in the Dorsey tradition as possible, Morrow will add some zesty improvisations of his own—a reminder to listeners that he has got his own identity.

Buddy Morrow (real name Moe Zudekoff—he adopted his stage name in the late 1930s), who was born February 8, 1919 in New Haven, Connecticut, believes he inherited his gift for music. "When I was 12 years old, I started playing trombone," he recalls one afternoon in a Times Square hotel where he's staying while the band plays some dates in the New York area. "I was the one in our family who went at music all the way, but the whole family was very much musical, going way back. My brothers both played trumpet—they played professionally for a while, in Red Norvo's Band and a few other bands—and my oldest brother also played violin, cello and piano. My one sister played the violin; the other one played the piano. My dad played a little piano and my grand uncles played horn for the Czar's symphony orchestra in Russia. The musical genes were there." He mentions as an aside what a kick he got out of once meeting someone who'd known of the Zudekoff brothers as musicians back in Czarist Russia.

His own career started early and never really slowed down. "I played with the Yale Collegians when I was 15 years old. They needed a trombone player. I was just a ringer. I joined the union when I was 15, and said I was 16—big deal!" In 1936, one local bandleader who heard Morrow play knew Artie Shaw (who had also grown up in New Haven and was now in New York, preparing to make the switch from being a studio musician to a bandleader). "When Artie Shaw was forming his first band, this fellow had me come from New Haven to play for Artie. Artie heard me and I guess he was very impressed; he told all the various leaders that he knew around town that I was a talented, upcoming trombone player, and to listen to him. All they had to do was hear me play and I was in business. And in those days, my God, there was so much work it was ridiculous. In New York City alone, speaking of steady jobs, all the theaters had pit bands, they had stage bands; no matter where you turned around, all the hotels had big bands. You had the Arcadia Ballroom, you had the Roseland Ballroom, you had the Cinderella Ballroom. You had a ridiculous amount of work," Morrow recalls.

"I was just 17. I played in jam sessions with Bunny Berigan, and Babe Russin, and Harry James. I did Bunny Berigan's radio show when he had it, and also Benny Goodman's show. So those were marvelous times. But then again, when you are in that age where you're discovering everything, you're discovering life and man's relationship to woman, you know, you're discovering all these things, and you're hearing stuff like Ravel, Debussy, Delius, Schoenberg, the classic as well as the modern composers, you never forget it. It's a feeling—I guess it's like the first love affair, you know."

Morrow was freelancing. His first recording sessions were for singer Amanda Randolph (doing such numbers as "He May Be Your Man But He Comes to See Me Sometimes" and "Please Don't Talk About My Man" on October 8, 1936) and for trumpeter/singer Sharkey Bonano ("Mr. Brown Goes to Town" and "When You're Smiling," December 4, 1936). When his roommate, who was taking courses at Juilliard, suggested Morrow apply for a scholarship there, "I said, 'Sure,' you know, and I did it and forgot all about it. Then two or three weeks later I received a card suggesting I come up there and audition. I didn't bother bringing any books or anything—just took my horn and went up there and played for them. And they said, 'Where's your music?' I said, 'I don't have any. But I'd like to play for you.' So I played some of the legitimate literature, and some of the songs that I knew were part of the trombone repertoire, and I read some music for them. And two weeks later, I got a letter in the mail saying I had a complete scholarship on trombone from Juilliard! That was one of those things where poor kids who study hard and really beat their brains out looking for it—why, they have to sweat it out, but it just happened to me. Though I paid my dues; I practiced a lot, I can't say I did it all by pressing a button or something. And I was fortunate. I was in the right place at the right time—and could play like a demon! I did go to Juilliard—and my teacher told me there was nothing he could show me. This was the height of the Depression and there was nobody who could pay my expenses while I was going to school, and I had nobody to guide me. So I made my choice—I went on the road with bands instead."

Working for society bandleader Eddy Duchin, Morrow didn't get to play much jazz—the music was rather restrained—but Duchin paid his sidemen very well. "I left Duchin's band to go with Artie Shaw, because I owed him a lot. Shaw had gotten me to come to New York, and he had loaned me money, and advised me and stuff. When I worked with Shaw [1936–37], he hadn't made it yet. This was with his Dixieland band with the string quartet. Yeah, that was a beautiful band, just gorgeous. Tony Pastor was in that band, Jerry Gray, and Lee Castle [then Castaldo] and myself. Lee and I were roommates. All of us ultimately became leaders. So Artie knew talent and knew how to develop it. It just broke my heart when he had to break up that band. Then [in 1938] he offered me the job with his new band: a guarantee of a minimum of $40 a week, for up to four nights' work, with an additional $10 a night for each additional night that you worked in a week. So the maximum you could earn would be $70 a week. But by then I was back with Eddy Duchin and was making $187-something a week with him; I was not about to leave.

"Shaw was very good. And he knew how to organize a band. He predicted his own success, you know. I can still remember what Artie said to me: 'I'm going to have the best jazz band in the country.' He also told me: 'If you don't go with me, I think you ought to go with Benny Goodman.' But I had heard so many terrible stories about Benny Goodman, about the ray and how he's just unconscious of everything that was happening with other people that I turned him down. Today, of course, it's too late; my only regret, if I have any, is that I didn't try it. I have very few regrets. I don't think about them. But once in a while, you know, it does come to you—you say, 'Well, it would have been nice.' I did work with Benny later on, with the septet; I did some TV shows with him and things like that." But Morrow turned down both Shaw—whose 1938 band went on to become one of the most popular in the nation—and Goodman, who was then near or at his zenith, to continue playing with Duchin. Morrow may be heard on one of Duchin's very few jazzy records, "Between the Devil and the Deep Blue Sea," March 21, 1938.

In the meantime, Morrow was continuing to educate himself, musically. "Oh, I was buying records. Sure. I used to carry all that stuff with me on the road. I had several suitcases just packed with those old 78s. The porters would come to help me get on the train and they'd almost break their arms lifting my suitcases! Ravel and Delius. I was classically trained, you know, in the old stuff, and I still listen; I enjoy it very much."

Morrow left Duchin to become lead trombonist in Tommy Dorsey's Band. "I enjoyed Tommy," Morrow says. "He was tough. He was a bully. He'd have his favorites that he'd pick on. He was funny. He was like the loveable Irishman who would sometimes be so generous that you just wouldn't believe it and other times, he could be just a mean old son of a gun. But he was always nice to me.

"One time I asked him about certain things and he said, 'Look, you're sitting right next to me. Why don't you listen and watch.' So I said *ooops*. I was looking for a quick fix, you know— Do this and do that. No way! He just said, 'Listen and watch.' So I watched him and I listened. I did learn. I learned lots of things. And I also made up my mind that if I ever have a band, why, I'd be more consistent with my men than he was. But then again, he's a much better business person than I was. Much better. He was more demanding of his men. I try to instill pride in the people, so that they do what I want without my having to prod them with a hatchet or something. And Tommy was—well, let me put it this way: Look at the personality of Buddy Rich and Jackie Gleason and Frank Sinatra. Put them all together and you have Tommy Dorsey. He was that complicated. But there was nobody who could be as generous and as wonderful as Tommy— or as tough an enemy.

"He's the kind that if he was hacked at you, why, he'd get even if it meant spending a million dollars, you know. For example, when Glenn Miller hit it big, Tommy thought he was going to get part of the Miller Band [because he had loaned Miller money], and it just didn't happen that way. So Tommy invested a fortune in the Bob Chester Band to get it to sound like the Miller Band, hoping to steal the thunder from Glenn. He never did, of course. It's like Rembrandt; there are a lot of people who copy him, but the original is still the one they want. There were a lot of people who copied Miller, but the people still wanted Miller. Tommy was a tough one.

"One time we had a bunch of new men in the band, and Tommy was very unhappy with the way the band sounded. We were doing six or seven shows a day at the Paramount Theater then, we were working the New Yorker Hotel, we were rehearsing, we were doing 'The Raleigh-Kool Show' [on the radio], and we were recording—and that's seven days a week. The trumpet players' chops were just about gone. It was a bloodbath up there. We were doing a radio broadcast and Tommy, at the end, refused to play the theme. He was yelling at the announcer, 'Don't tell them whose band this is, don't tell them whose band this is!' "

Although Dorsey naturally took the trombone solos on records and radio broadcasts, leaving the other trombonists to do only section work, Morrow says, "I did all the solos on the stand. You see, at that period Tommy used to spend a lot of time with the music publishers. And outside of the radio shows and things like that, why, I was his favorite clone. If it wasn't me, it would have been somebody else who was playing lead trombone. But I got to play all the stuff, which was great experience. His confidence in his own playing was such that he didn't fear any competition. You know, when you create the style and the sound and the band, you don't worry about what the guy in the band is doing. He never criticized me. He never said, 'Hey, that sounded good' and he never said, 'Hey, that sounded bad.' He just expected you to play your best," Morrow says. "I imagine if he was mad he would have said something or he would have taken the solos away."

Morrow notes that Lee Castle, who has been the leader of the Jimmy Dorsey Band since 1957, also happened to be in Tommy Dorsey's Band during the period that Morrow was in it. (Both future bandleaders were present, playing section parts, on the Tommy Dorsey Band's recording session of December 30, 1938.) Morrow recalls: "Lee was sort of a hypochondriac. He always was. He used to wear a sweater underneath his shirt and stuff. He's a sweet guy, but he was always nervous and worried about catching a cold and this and that. I enjoyed Lee. He's a lot of fun to be around. He's a good trumpet player. He has a good ear. He's not Doc Severinsen; but then again, Doc doesn't have the background that Lee has, so, you know, it's six of one, a half dozen of another." It saddens Morrow to reflect on how few big bands are left. "The number of active big ghost bands today you can count on one hand. You have the Basie Band, the Miller Band, the Woody Herman Band, the Ellington Band works with Mercer, Buddy Rich's Band is a spasmodic situation." And working conditions for big bands have changed. "Today, we don't have the luxury of being in one spot 13 weeks, 15 weeks, or half a year. That was no big event years ago, but today, if you're in a place a week, it's like a vacation. You know, we're on one-nighters, strictly. We do our job and we do it very well. But that was an era I don't think we'll ever see again."

From Dorsey, Morrow moved on to Paul Whiteman's Orchestra, which also featured the great trombonist Miff Mole. Morrow was in the Whiteman band when it recorded such numbers as "Heat Wave" and "I've Found a New Baby," April 6, 1939. In 1940, Morrow became a CBS studio musician. "I left a good job [with Whiteman] to go to a low-paying one. When I went to CBS, we worked seven days a week for $90 a week. We were on the air from five in the morning until noon, doing various programs—I don't remember the names of them. I had met a girl that I was very much interested in, and I wanted to stay in New York. It was very simple." In 1941 and '42, Morrow was back on the big band scene, this time with Bob Crosby's Band, which was, he says, one of the two bands he most enjoyed being a member of (the other was Tommy Dorsey's). He played in the Crosby Band when it recorded such sides as "Black Zephyr," February 17, 1942, and "I'll Keep the Lovelight Burning," March 3, 1942. He comments: "I always liked the Bob Crosby Band— the old Dixieland band. I loved that band. And they were playing that old big band Dixieland when I was in it: the Deane Kincaide, Bob Haggart arrangements. Bob Crosby then had Eddie Miller, Matty Matlock, Nappy Lamare, Ray Bauduc—he had a hell of a good band! The guy who used to be president of the Los Angeles local, Maxie Herman, was lead trumpet and Lyman Vunk was the high-note guy. Elmer Smithers and Floyd O'Brien were the other trombones. Gil Rodin was the manager and second tenor. Bob Crosby didn't do much with the band. He just beat the tempos, that's all. The band did everything without Bob. Bob was a fair singer, you know. He was Bing Crosby's kid brother. That's about all I can say about him. In all fairness, Bob was a great front man. A wonderful storyteller. But his strength didn't lie in the singing department.

"Then the war broke out. My wife was pregnant at the time. I knew I had a low number and would be getting drafted any day. And I knew that I could always work in New York. So rather than be drafted from the West Coast, we moved back here to

New York. And sure enough, I went into the Navy. I didn't get out until just before the war was over. When I got out of the Navy, I went with Jimmy Dorsey [1945], in preparation for getting my own band. I led Jimmy's band for about three weeks in Chicago when Jimmy was sick. He went in for an operation. And that experience really solidified my thinking about having a band. And I had a band for two years."

The first big band Morrow led, in 1945–46, did not succeed, he notes. "It's the age-old thing with musicians: there are very few, outside of some arrangers, who know what kind of band they want, how they want it to sound. The only ones who really know how to create, as far as I can see, are those who are arrangers, who have a definite thing in mind. At that time, we had a certain number of instruments—and go find a new sound! We tried everything. We tried the symphonic instruments in the band, the bassoons, and the English horns—in my band. We did a lot of transcriptions for Langworth, and we were with Mercury Records. But I didn't know what the hell I wanted to do. I didn't know stylistically how I wanted to create it; I just wanted to play trombone. I had the band for about two years until I ran out of money. Oh, you get tired of living on popcorn and benzedrine! So I just gave up the business, that's all. I said, 'That's it! No more.' For the next four years, all I did was studio work. And I did very well as far as that goes.

"And then [in 1950] Tommy Dorsey and Sammy Kaye were having some trouble with the RCA Victor company, and they were leaving. I was doing all the recording in town for everyone, and RCA Victor said, 'Well, we made a band for Ralph Flanagan, let's try it for Buddy Morrow.' And I got a contract with them to record. Once again, I didn't know which way or how I wanted to go. So, we tried some beautiful things—which sold seven copies in New York alone! And then we tried the Artie Shaw style, with the melodic trombone. That didn't do too well. Artie couldn't sell it, so how could we sell it?" Big bands were fading in popularity generally. Nevertheless, Morrow became one of very few leaders who started a band in the 1950s that caught on.

The winning formula Morrow hit upon consisted of recording big band cover versions of R&B recordings that were regional hits. His manager helped find him breaking songs that he could record in a kind of compromise between the traditional, polished big band style of, say, a Tommy Dorsey (which Morrow would have preferred playing), and the rougher, earthier R&B that was foreshadowing rock 'n' roll. RCA Victor could provide the distribution and promotion the smaller labels recording R&B could not. And teens who, in the early 1950s, might not have accepted undiluted R&B, found Morrow's version of it highly acceptable. Morrow's music was gutsier than the fare played by conventional dance bands, but more refined than the pure R&B played by the originators of the music. The formula, black music filtered through a white sensibility, was the same that had worked for Benny Goodman (who rose to fame recording music of Fletcher Henderson) and would later work for Elvis Presley and any number of other rock 'n' rollers.

The number that made the Buddy Morrow Band was "Night Train." Morrow recalls: "We stumbled onto it. Ed McKenzie, a disc jockey in Detroit, was the man who first gave me 'Night Train.' Dick Rhodes, who was my arranger at the time, made an arrangement of it." (Although Morrow first became aware of "Night Train" as an R&B record that was popular in Detroit in the early 1950s, he adds he later learned that the "Night Train" melody had actually originated in an Ellington composition of the mid 1940s, "Happy Go Lucky Local," which had not been a hit.) "Night Train" became a hit for the Morrow Band, getting it plenty of bookings. It's a number Morrow still gets frequent requests to play. "My manager was astute enough to say, 'Ah! That's you.' I said, 'What do you mean?' And he started getting me all the rhythm-and-blues tunes," Morrow recalls. "At that time, the only records getting good distribution were those put out by the major recording labels. The small labels had no distribution at all. So they could have a local hit, but it would be a hit in one area, period. Well, we had great relationships throughout the country. So when we were ready to record, we would call—or my manager would call—all the various DJs that we knew personally, and we'd say, 'What's happening?' And the guy would say that 'Hey, Mrs. Jones' or 'One Mint Julip' was happening in his area. A lot of the things we recorded had been vocals but we

Buddy Morrow in the 1950s. (Courtesy of the Institute of Jazz Studies.)

Buddy Morrow in the late 1970s. (Author's collection.)

made instrumentals out of them. And they took off like wildfire. We sold umpteen records."

Morrow and the band had to produce bold, gutsy blats of sound in playing big band R&B. He notes: "It got so that I just couldn't take it physically. I was beating the hell out of my chops. My arranger, Howard Biggs, was one of the best around at the time for what we were doing. I asked him: 'Howard, how do you want this stuff played?' He said, 'Man, it's ignorant music. Play it that way.' It's like a painter; there are some who are known for their subtlety and use red sparingly to grab your eye. But we, doing our rhythm-and-blues stuff, we had to use splashes of red. Yeah. So my lip was red, let me put it that way. It was down to my navel every night. It would take me three quarters of an hour just to get so I could play. I finally said, 'This is ridiculous.'" And Morrow wasn't really crazy about rhythm-and-blues to begin with. He'd much rather have been playing songs like "I'm Getting Sentimental Over You." When rhythm-and-blues seemed to be losing popularity, Morrow recalls, "I said, 'Oh, thank God. Now I can have some decent music.'" He declined to record R&B songs he was being offered.

But popular music did not return to the older styles he would have preferred. Instead, he notes, "rhythm-and-blues became what is known as rock 'n' roll. By the time I recognized that I had been riding the crest of the wave and had gotten off the ride, it was too late—all these singers had gotten in. I turned down 'Sh-boom,' I turned down 'Tweedlee Dee,' I turned down a whole bunch of big records when they were still local hits and I still had the mass distribution. Our format was all set up. But, hey—you make mistakes," he says.

Morrow kept on with his big band until 1973, he says. "When my daughter was on her way to being born, I decided I wanted to spend more time with her and the family, so I restricted the amount of work I did with my band until finally, I decided to move to Florida in the '70s. Fifteen years ago, I moved down there. And after about a year of hardly doing anything, I was offered this thing [the Tommy Dorsey Band]. And I said, 'Well, I'll do it until you get somebody—no more than three weeks.' And after a couple weeks, I realized that this was what I had wanted all along. And I decided to stay with it. And here I am. I'm in my 12th or 13th year, I don't even remember any more. I have fun. The only thing I take seriously is the quality of what we're doing. Not the particular song—but how is it played, is the band together, is the pitch right, and do we get the feeling of the thing." The Tommy Dorsey Band is a road band. The same musicians perform together night after night, week after week. They'll tour for several months, take a month off, giving Morrow a chance to be with his wife, then go out for another three-month tour. The togetherness gives them a chance to get nuances right—such as subtle changes in emphasis and dynamics on "Boogie Woogie" that heighten the number's effectiveness, and that no pick-up band could master. Getting nuances right matters to Morrow. "It's easy to get to be an automaton, and you shoot off 15 cannons. But the whole thing is to make music. If you can make music all the time, or most of the time, you have an area where you can live with it," Morrow says. He's aware that some of the other ghost bands aren't living up to their heritage. He works with pride.

He's done a more conscientious job than some of his predecessors in terms of honoring the Dorsey legacy. The Tommy Dorsey ghost band has had a curious, off-and-on-again history, which makes Morrow's accomplishments all the more noteworthy. After Tommy Dorsey died in 1956, the musicians in the band he and Jimmy had been co-leading continued working as the Jimmy Dorsey Orchestra. Lee Castle assumed leadership of this band following Jimmy's death in 1957. The Tommy Dorsey estate authorized the formation of a new Tommy Dorsey Orchestra, fronted by Warren Covington, in 1958. Covington had enough success recording "Tea for Two Cha-Cha" and other new numbers to convince him that he didn't really need the Tommy Dorsey name. In 1961, he changed the name of the orchestra to the Warren Covington Orchestra; he still played some of the Tommy Dorsey things (but no longer had to give the Dorsey estate a cut). The Dorsey estate then made Sam Donahue the leader of a new Dorsey Band which toured in a package with Frank Sinatra Jr. singing songs his father had sung with Dorsey a generation before. In 1965, Donahue's band dropped the Dorsey name; the package continued touring that year as "The Frank Sinatra Jr. Show"; the band was soon cut back to an octet. In 1966, the Dorsey estate authorized Urbie Green to lead a new Dorsey Band, which proved short-lived. It appeared the Tommy Dorsey Orchestra had run its course. For the next eight years there was no Tommy Dorsey Orchestra. Lee Castle and the Jimmy Dorsey Orchestra kept some of the music alive by playing charts from the band the Dorseys had co-led in the '50s. In 1974, the Tommy Dorsey estate made still another attempt to establish a Tommy Dorsey Orchestra, this time under the leadership of trombonist Murray McEachern, who had most recently been playing in Duke Ellington's Orchestra. He led the band for two years before Morrow was chosen as leader. "Murray didn't play the Dorsey music as such. He played mostly Duke Ellington stuff," Morrow notes. The estate and Morrow both agree on the wisdom of playing mostly Dorsey music today.

The band offers a more varied program now than it did when Morrow first came on board. Morrow has revived some great charts from the 1940s, when the Dorsey Band was at its zenith, that had fallen by the wayside. "When I took the band over, I took over a set combination; that is, a set routine and everything else. And for protection, I also brought my library along, so that I could run what I considered a complete dance. It wasn't until I knew what was contained in the Dorsey book that I could make use of it all. Don't forget, I left the band back in late 1938 or '39, and there was quite a bit of development between then and the time of Tommy's demise. So, it took me a certain amount of time to gradually infuse the newer Dorsey charts into our program. Now, of course, I know what is there. We play a program that is about 70–75% Dorsey. The other 25% is re-lated—within the same scope, pretty much, treated primarily the same way. It includes some things that I've had that are relatively new, plus things that are of the Dorsey era that we didn't have readily at hand, so we had copies made of the records—from *Dorsey's* records. We don't use anybody else's music, in spite of the fact that it would solve a lot of problems; this is not a cha-cha band, it is not a Glenn Miller Orchestra, with all due respect to the band, it's not an Artie Shaw Band, it's the Tommy Dorsey

Band. People come to hear us, and we provide them with that particular escape mechanism."

Some ghost bands do offer hits of assorted other big bands, playing "In the Mood" one minute and "Woodchopper's Ball" the next. Morrow sees no need to play the music of other bands. And he's enjoyed reviving Sy Oliver charts, including some that weren't big commercial hits but hold up beautifully today. "Sy Oliver had his finger on the pulse and the beat. And to this day, somebody who wants to dance—I'm speaking of what I grew up knowing as dance music—why, you can't beat his charts. They're great," he says.

Morrow likes throwing in some of his own trombone licks. "I try to be my own person. And we try to keep the music fresh. Otherwise you go a little batty. Don't forget, when I had my own band, there was the element of new tunes every week. We'd have three to four tunes, and we always had at least eight out of the ten top tunes in the book. So we were constantly adding. Now if I were to add eight out of the ten top tunes, you wouldn't know what in the heck I was playing; it'd be a melange of who knows what. It wouldn't be the Dorsey Band. I'm sure Tommy would be very selective if he were alive today, just as I am."

One constraint Morrow faces is that he doesn't have the budget to work with that Tommy Dorsey had (and, of course, a cut from whatever the band grosses goes to the Dorsey estate before he and the sidemen get paid). Dorsey could afford to hire just about the best man available for any given chair. Even in his last years, he'd have, say, a Charlie Shavers on trumpet, a Buddy Rich or Louis Bellson on drums. Morrow can't afford to hire comparable big names today; he mostly has to use musicians recently out of school, willing to endure lots of traveling for not a lot of money. He has to try to discover new talent; he can't afford to buy established talent. Sometimes he lucks out, sometimes he doesn't. I was more impressed by the quality of the musicians I saw Morrow leading in the late 1970s and early 1980s than I have been in the most recent edition of the band that I've seen. Around 1980, '81, Morrow was featuring a fresh young clarinetist—nobody had ever heard of him then—he had discovered playing in a local band in Ohio. Morrow had such confidence in him that he'd even leave the stage to let the clarinetist soar on a feature of his own ("Oh, Lady Be Good") with rhythm section backing. That clarinetist who dazzled me in 1980 was Ken Peplowski—today one of the most promising younger mainstream clarinetists, recording regularly for Concord. After enhancing the Dorsey Band for a couple years (the only member of that particular band to make it big), he moved on with Morrow's blessings. Sometimes Morrow can find new stars; other times he has to make the best of competent but undistinguished players. Generally speaking, he's kept the spirit of the band strong, which is no small accomplishment. (I've attended mid-1980s concerts in which the Glenn Miller Band, directed by Dick Gerhart, played superb charts with minimal enthusiasm.)

The Tommy Dorsey Band gets plenty of work, Morrow notes. "We travel quite a bit, all over the country. And occasionally, we get to go to South America or Europe or Japan. Oh yeah, they like us in Japan. They go primarily for the myth and the stories, rather than the content, you know. See, when they want to have the Glenn Miller Band, they run *The Glenn Miller Story*. But that movie has great actors and actresses and everything else, doing a well-constructed story. So everyone leaves with tears and goes to see the great Miller Band perform. Well, the Dorseys played themselves in their own movie. And that's like a lawyer being his own defense counsel. Let's face it, the Dorseys were not consummate actors. So, there's a difference in the quality of the movie. Not the music, but anyway—we go to Japan about every couple of years."

The one thing Morrow wishes is that the Tommy Dorsey Band were recording. "But our problem is one that only Mrs. Dorsey [Tommy's widow, Jane] can solve. She will not let us record the music that the various companies want. They want new versions of the old stuff, so that they can put it on CD. And she will not allow us to do that. Anybody can put out an album of Dorsey music—anybody but us! It's weird. Mrs. Dorsey evidently is satisfied with the income that she is getting from the old stuff. Mrs. Dorsey gets a very nice income. We'd like to record.

We've had many opportunities. It looks like we're going to have a chance to record under my name—it wouldn't be called the Tommy Dorsey Band—which we'll do soon."

Does Buddy Morrow plan to stay with the Tommy Dorsey Band indefinitely?

"I don't know," he answers. "I have no idea what I'm going to do. At the moment, I'm slated to stay with this. I still have some time to go with the contract, and at this point I'm not about to junk it. So we'll see what happens."

1988

GEORGE · KELLY

From Florida to the Savoy

In his liner notes for Panama Francis and the Savoy Sultans' 1983 album, *Everything Swings,* John S. Wilson commented that "the most relaxed and persuasive swinger" in the band was tenor saxist George Kelly. And why shouldn't he have seemed persuasive? Kelly was a veteran of the original Savoy Sultans, back in the 1940s. And Kelly's association with Francis pre-dated that; when they were teens in Florida in the early 1930s, Francis was the drummer in Kelly's big band. These days, Kelly may be heard with the Harlem Blues and Jazz Band, or leading his own Jazz Sultans. He favors a medium-swing type of groove, the sort of thing that would have gone over very well with dancers at the Savoy Ballroom.

Kelly and I initially got together at a Times Square Howard Johnson's restaurant, where he reminisced over a pistachio milkshake and a burger. We later continued our conversations while driving through the city, the tape-recorder set on the seat between us.

Born in Miami, Florida, July 31, 1915, Kelly took his first music lessons—on piano, not saxophone—when he was nine. That was his grandmother's idea. "I never wanted to play piano," Kelly recalls. "I told my grandmother, 'I don't want to play piano, I want to play saxophone.' But she got me; she said: 'You prove

203

to me that you want to play the saxophone by learning to play the piano.' So I took piano lessons about six, seven years."

He got good enough to play piano in a senior citizens' band, but the saxophone always had a fascination for him. He remembers: "They were grown men in the band, and I was about 13. And when they had a break, they left me on the stand to watch the instruments. One man told me, 'Don't let nobody bother my sax.' I said, 'OK.' As soon as he got out of sight, I picked up his horn and took the mouthcap off, trying to see if I can just toot a note on it. So I toot a note on the horn and looked around to see if there's anybody looking. And put the cap back over, right quick. Man, I was just flabbergasted. I said, 'I'm going to enjoy this.' I went home and told my grandmother, 'I played Mr. McKenna's horn.' She said: 'You did? How could you play it if you don't know it?' I said, 'I only played one note.' " She wasn't yet persuaded of the need to buy him a saxophone.

He kept learning popular tunes; he could entertain, playing piano at parties. "During those days you could buy piano sheet music, and on the back of the song sheet they had like four or eight bars of another song that they were pushing. And I'd learn that. I wouldn't learn the songs that my grandmother bought, because when they got to the bridge—the middle part of the song, which they call the bridge—that didn't make sense to me. So I just kept on playing the first 16 bars. Never did get to play the bridge. So my grandmother—she called me Jack—said, 'Jack, there's more to a song than that.' I said, 'Well, that don't make sense, that part doesn't make sense to me at all.' So she said, 'Well, you're going to learn it.' So now I started playing the middle of the song.

"When I was about 14 or 15, my cousin Genevieve had a birthday party and she invited me. She told me to be sure and bring my sheet music. I had a lot of sheet music by then. And after the party, my cousin gave me a couple dollars. So I went home and showed it to my grandmother. She said: 'Where'd you get that?' I said, 'Cousin Genevieve gave it to me for playing the piano.' She said, 'Wonderful, wonderful.' I kept showing the two dollars; I was signifying to her that now that I had learned the piano, maybe now you'll buy me the saxophone.

"She said, '*Well?*'

"I said, 'You told me that when I learned to play the piano, you're going to buy me a saxophone.'

"She said, 'You and that damn horn again!'

"My uncle had an alto, but when he started trying to learn to play it he was a grown man, working as a doorman at a department store, so he couldn't really get the knack of it. My grandmother said to him, 'Willie, I want you to let this boy play your horn. And if I see where he's going to improve on it, I'll buy it.'

"But I said, 'I don't want *that* horn. I want a tenor!'

"She said, 'What's the difference? A saxophone is a saxophone.' I said, 'No, a tenor is a larger horn, it has a better sound to it—the sound I like.' " He finally persuaded his grandmother to buy him the sax he wanted from a friend of the family. He took lessons on sax from the same man who'd been giving him lessons on piano.

"This was around 1930. With the saxophone, it only took me about six months, because all I had to do was learn the fingering; I'd learned how to read music from the piano." One of Kelly's earliest models on sax was a player who lived across the street: "Sherard Smith, I think his name was. He had a nice tone, I liked the sound he had. Well, everybody had a nice tone in those days . . . but I liked the way he played; he had a nice, soft tone." He came to enjoy the playing, also, of Otis Finch, a tenor saxist in a local band, Hartley Toots' Honey Boys. He was not initially influenced by the great jazz tenor players of the 1930s for the simple reason that most of them weren't renowned when he was starting out, or at least, whatever renown they may have had in Harlem or Kansas City or wherever had not yet made its way to Miami. Hearing some of them for the first time was a revelation for him.

He recalls: "I listened to the radio broadcasts from the Savoy Ballroom in New York. I remember hearing Chu Berry with one of the bands. And I called my grandmother; she had a laundry, her own business, and I went running back there and said, 'Grandma, come with me, come with me!' She said, 'What is it?' I said, 'I want you to hear something, I want you to hear something!' So I called her to hear Chu Berry. 'Hear that? That man's playing the tenor saxophone. That's what I want to sound like!' But I wasn't really emulating him. Because this man across the street, I'd hear him more often. I'd only probably hear Chu Berry like once a month or so.

"Then I heard Coleman Hawkins and I got to like him. Then Dick Wilson came to Florida. The big bands started coming down to Miami. Now they'd only come down there like probably once a month or something. They couldn't come too often because the town couldn't stand it. They couldn't play in the white neighborhood, they could only play for blacks. And blacks couldn't stand but so many dances out of a month, you know. But every time a band would be there, I'd be right there listening to the tenor player. So then you got a band, Teddy Hill—they came down there and they stayed down there a month. And they were trying to build Miami up for that type of music, you know."

Kelly got hooked on big band swing several years before Benny Goodman broke through in 1935, launching the Swing Era. He was inspired by the black swing band leaders who were then on the cutting edge of American popular music. Within a couple of years after he had started on tenor sax, Kelly recalls, he was proficient enough to get together with others, mostly around his age, in a 14-piece big band. Kelly emerged as the leader of the band, known as the Cavaliers, when he was about 17 years old, in 1933. He led the band, to the best of his recollection, for about five years. The Cavaliers played locally in the winter. In the summer they traveled to one-nighters throughout Florida and neighboring states. The band included two other Miami teens who were to go on to make names for themselves in jazz: bassist Grachan Moncur, who was the same age as Kelly, and drummer David Francis (later to become better known as Panama Francis), who was three and a half years younger. Francis, Kelly recalls, was the youngest member of the band; he sat on a box to play the drums.

Kelly was still listening, still absorbing influences from tenor saxists he heard. In 1937, Count Basie's Band began recording and broadcasting frequently, and that brought to Kelly's attention saxist Lester ("Prez") Young. He notes: "When I listened to

Prez play, that did it! I said, 'Well, I got to learn to play like *somebody*,' you know. But I never did believe in copying people's style of playing. I played it probably a little different. I won't copy just note-for-note what they're playing. I liked Coleman Hawkins' tone; I liked his big tone. And I liked Lester Young's ideas. So I got a cross way of playing. I got a little bit of Prez, a little bit of Coleman Hawkins, a little bit of Dick Wilson, you know." To this day, Kelly notes, he listens to Lester Young's recordings often. He gets a great kick out of Young's playing, he says. Kelly names one other important musical influence: "A lot of my ideas come from Louis Armstrong. I liked a lot of things he played on trumpet. People wouldn't know that a lot of things I'm playing is more leaning towards Louis Armstrong than a saxophone player."

Around 1937 or '38, Kelly's band broke up. Some of the sidemen, including Francis, went north. Kelly didn't yet feel ready to make the move. He recalls: "A lot of people from up north asked me, 'Why don't you come to New York, man? You play too good to be down here.' I'd say, 'No way, man. There's too many good tenor players.'" Kelly went to Tampa, Florida, to join an octet led by Andy Martin (billed as "Andy Gump and the Jamsters" because of Martin's resemblance to the comic strip character Andy Gump). Kelly, who was always interested in arranging, not just in playing, was particularly impressed by Martin's ability to write arrangements while standing and chatting with his friends.

For several months, Kelly played in Zach Whyte's Band (which also included tenor saxist Dick Wilson) in Richmond, Kentucky, quitting when he received word that his grandmother had fallen ill. "That was in 1938, because I remember that very well, when she took sick. I went back home and my grandmother died in 1939.

"Then I worked with Hartley Toots' band, traveling the road with him. Miami was his home base," he recalls. And at some point, Kelly got to appear in two low-budget motion pictures made for black audiences, both of which were directed by Arthur Dreifuss and featured singer Mamie Smith. "The people Mamie Smith was doing business with had brought her down to Florida to make a movie. They got me to be in it, playing piano. But I actually wasn't playing. I was just mimicking, like I was playing. I made two movies: *Sunday Sinners* and *Murder on Lenox Avenue* [both released in 1941]," he notes. "I saw one of the movies when I came to New York. I saw it again on TV about a year ago—Channel 13 had brought back some of those old things—but I couldn't tell who I was."

Kelly formed a small band, which was fronted by Ivan "Loco" Rolle, who later became Jonah Jones' longtime bass player. But it was hard to hold on to the good players. He felt frustrated, and finally, in 1941, he made the move to the New York.

"I came to New York to join Al Cooper's Savoy Sultans," he recalls. "Cooper wanted a tenor player and I stayed with him until I went into the service (1941–44)." Kelly had known Cooper from years ago, in Miami, before Cooper had even taken up music. Cooper and bassist Grachan Moncur, who had been in Kelly's band, the Cavaliers, were half-brothers. And Moncur had been a member of the Savoy Sultans since its creation—in fact, he had been a co-founder—in 1937.

"When I joined," Kelly recalls, "it was a nine-piece band: two cornets, three saxophones (two altos, a tenor) and a complete rhythm section: piano, bass, drums and guitar. The members when I was there were: first trumpet, Pat Jenkins; second trumpet—well, cornet actually—Sam Massenberg; first alto, Rudy Williams; third alto and clarinet, Al Cooper. I replaced Skinny Brown on tenor. In the rhythm section was Cyril Haynes on piano, Jack Chapman on guitar, Razz Mitchell on the drums, and Grachan Moncur on bass."

For nine years, the Sultans were the house band at the Savoy Ballroom, that famed dancehall stretching from 140th Street to 141st Street on Lenox Avenue in Harlem. "The Savoy drew a mixed crowd. It was half and half, during those days. A big place, hold like around 2500 people, something like that. A hell of a place—with two bands every night," recalls Kelly. The Savoy had a reputation for having the best dancers to be found anywhere—not just the regular paying customers, but also a troupe of young professionals, Whitey's Lindy Hoppers, who kept coming up with exciting new moves (the men lifting their partners onto their backs, or pulling them over their shoulders, the partners moving together and apart in choreographed group routines). The high-flying dancers at the Savoy—the amateurs and pros alike—inspired the jazz musicians that played there, and the musicians in turn inspired the dancers. The music and the movement fed off of one another.

A jump band *par excellence*, the Sultans placed an emphasis on rhythm. If you wanted musical subtleties and nuances, carefully shaded instrumental colorations, you looked elsewhere. But if you wanted a band that would inspire you to Lindy Hop till you dropped, there was no beating the Sultans. One of their numbers was titled "Getting in the Groove" and they were masters of doing just that, as they stretched out with repeated call-and-response sax and brass riffs. Their records, it's often been said by those who heard them live, barely hint at what they sounded like when they built up to full steam at the Savoy.

"This was different from the bands I'd been in before, because they had their own unique style; they had their own way of playing," Kelly recalls. Their jump music initially threw him; he was nervous, at times, trying to fit in. "When I first joined them, for the first month or two I couldn't get accustomed to the way they would phrase the notes and how they anticipated things. I couldn't feel it. But after that, I got to kick right along with them.

"That was about the best band, I mean all-around band—I mean as far as deportmanship and getting along with people—that was the best band I've ever been in. Because I've been in some bands, man, I was glad to get out of! I mean, guys were so narrow-minded, some bands. Here, everybody was like brothers," Kelly notes. "They would come to work with the idea of playing. Not just shucking, you know.

"I wrote a couple arrangements for the band. But the main arrangers were Jack Chapman, the guitarist—he was the number one arranger—and Cyril Haynes, the pianist." Kelly remembers some of the Sultans' popular numbers as being "Jump, Jump, Jump," "Jumpin' at the Savoy," "When I Grow Too Old to Dream," "Boats," and "Frenzy." Kelly played on such records by the Sultans as "Norfolk Ferry" and "Second Balcony Jump" (both February 28, 1941), and "Let Your Conscience be Your Guide" (with a vocal by Kelly) and "Fish for Supper" (both December 29, 1941).

The Sultans have been overlooked in some books on the era. But musicians appreciated their cohesiveness and gusto. Dizzy Gillespie, who sometimes sat in with the Savoy Sultans, remembered them as "the swingingest band that ever was." And trombonist Dicky Wells, who played opposite the Savoy Sultans at different times as a member of Count Basie's Band, remembered them as "a living headache to everyone. They could swing and make most bands happy to play 'Home Sweet Home.' When a band like that was on your tail, the night never seemed to end. They didn't know the meaning of letting up."

Kelly notes: "The Sultans didn't care what other band came in to play at the Savoy—they'd shower down on them! One time, Gene Krupa came and the manager, Mr. Buchanan, gave Gene Krupa a choice: 'We could either have the Savoy Sultans playing opposite you the weeks that you work, or we could have Lucky Millinder.' Gene Krupa said, 'I'd rather have the Sultans.' Buchanan says, 'I think you'd feel better with Lucky Millinder because the Sultans don't let up.' So he says, 'No, that's what we want. We want someone to make us play!' Man, we had a week of fun—the two bands battling each other.

"Now, here comes Count Basie. He asked Buchanan, 'Who are we playing against?' So Mr. Buchanan smiled and said, 'Well, you'll be playing against the Savoy Sultans.' Count Basie said: 'Them pesky Sultans again!' We used to give him a fit. I had a lot of fun in that band."

In his autobiography, *Good Morning Blues*, Basie cheerfully recalled "those bad Savoy Sultans" who "ran the hell out of us. I don't ever want to see them cats no more. Every time we came down off the bandstand, they were right back up there swinging. . . . Every time we'd turn that mike loose they'd grab it. And oh, man!" Basie added that he'd turned down an invitation from Norman Granz to do a tour with the modern-day Savoy Sultans led by Panama Francis because—based on his memories of the

George Kelly. (Photo by Bill Walters.)

The Savoy Sultans, circa 1941. From left to right: Pat Jenkins (trumpet), Jack Chapman (guitar), Rudy Williams (alto sax), Sam Massenberg (trumpet), Alex "Razz" Mitchell (drums), Grachan Moncur (bass), George Kelly (tenor sax), Cyril Haynes (piano), Al Cooper (alto sax/leader). (Courtesy of the Institute of Jazz Studies.)

drive of the original Sultans—he was sure they'd "outswing anybody right now."

Kelly notes: "A lot of those big bands playing opposite us were booked by the same agents that owned the Savoy: Moe Gale's agency. I don't say Count Basie, but Cootie Williams, Lucky Millinder, Tiny Bradshaw—all of those bands were booked and controlled by Moe Gale's. Gale kept them on the road a lot, but would bring them in like a couple of weeks, then send them out again and bring in another band for a couple of weeks. But the Savoy Sultans stayed there; we were the house band. We used to ask to get out. We wanted to get out on the road too, you know. So Al Cooper would take the band out to Chicago and stay like a month. We went out to Los Angeles and stayed a month. And then we did some one-nighters around upstate New York."

The Sultans never developed the great fame of many of the bands they played opposite. They didn't travel very much, nor did they get the national exposure that came from radio remote broadcasts. "The bigger bands broadcast from the Savoy Ballroom. When I was with the Sultans, the Sultans didn't broadcast," Kelly recalls. Their function was to keep dancers happy at the Savoy, and they did that remarkably well.

In fact, Kelly believes that one reason the management kept the Sultans at the Savoy so much, rather than send them out on the road, was because the Sultans were such favorites of the Lindy Hoppers at the Savoy. "They'd lose all their enthusiasm with those other bands; it seemed they couldn't get the feeling from the other bands like they did from the Savoy Sultans—the dancers, you know," Kelly says. "A lot of the movie actors used to come up to watch those Lindy Hoppers dance, you know. Bing Crosby. And what's her name, she's a movie star, she had her legs insured? I forget. A lot of them came in." The Savoy kept him pretty busy, but there were times—such as when the Sultans were booked for an engagement at the Palace Theater—when he'd have some free time to play at jam sessions around town.

One of the jam sessions Kelly remembers best occurred just after he first got to New York. "A guy says to me, 'If you're new in town, you're supposed to go up to Minton's Playhouse and jam with the fellows.' I said 'OK.' I was game. So there were four saxophone players on the stand: one guy, then another guy, then me, then another saxophone player. So, they set this thing up. I didn't know who the last saxophone player was. I had known him, but I hadn't seen him in a long time and I'd forgotten what he looked like. But I noticed this first guy was playing subdued like, so I won't let loose. I felt, 'They're trying to trick me into something.' Then he got a little stronger and this other guy got stronger, so I stayed where I was; I didn't get no stronger because I didn't know what this other fellow next to me would do. Then those first two guys got off and just left me and this other guy on. I got a little bit stronger and then this guy got stronger. And I got a little bit stronger and he got stronger. And I started saying, 'Who in the hell is this cat?' Then he got real strong.

"I stayed up there playing until he got off, and everybody gave me a nice hand, said, 'Give George Kelly a nice hand.' And while we're getting our hand, he says, 'And let's give Don Byas a nice hand.' Seemed like every strand of hair on my hand went up—I said, 'Ow! What am I doing up here with him?' But he was nice." Byas was, in 1941, one of the most respected tenors on the scene, having recently taken Lester Young's former chair in the Basie Band. Kelly adds that Byas became supportive of him, telling some fans who questioned what Al Cooper saw in Kelly that he knew Kelly could play; he'd *heard* Kelly play. "So that gave me some confidence. I'd dug Don before, because he had come down to Florida with Andy Kirk's band."

Kelly was glad he'd made the move to New York—the greatest musicians in the world were here—and glad to be based in the very ballroom that had seemed the center of the action to him since he'd first begun listening to remote radio broadcasts from it as a boy in Miami. New York was also free of the segregation he had known all of his life, in Florida and in the other southern states in which he'd played. Kelly still found himself periodically running up against some racial prejudice—not as much or as blatant, certainly, as he had known in the south, but rankling nevertheless. And even minor incidents could feel jarring, perhaps because he hadn't expected to be encountering them up north.

Kelly still remembers, for example, stopping in a 10th Avenue bar in midtown, and asking for change of a quarter so he could make a phone call. "I told the bartender, 'Will you give me change for a quarter?' And he just stood there with his arms folded, looked at me. I thought, maybe he didn't hear me. So I said, 'May I get change for a quarter?' Then one of the customers said: 'Oh he's not going to change it. Give it to me, I'll get it changed for you.' So I gave it to him and he called him by name and said: 'Give me change for this quarter.' The bartender gave it to him. I said, 'Well I'll be damned.' "

Or, another time, in the late 1940s, Kelly remembers chatting with the black attendant in the men's room at a club where he was working when a fellow walked in and asked if there wasn't another men's room for white customers. "He says, 'Well, where I'm from, they've got one for white and one for colored.' So I say, 'Well, I know where you're from, but you're in New York now.' So one word led to another. And he hit me in the stomach." The club's management, Kelly recalls, took care of such troublemakers; they wanted musicians to be able to work without being hassled.

Jazz musicians, of course, operated in a subculture generally less prejudiced than the society at large. Jazzmen tended to treat each other with mutual respect, regardless of color. But there were still some insidious forms of prejudice in the music business, such as contractors for Broadway pit orchestras, radio orchestras, recording sessions, and other well-paying jobs, for example, who hired mostly white players. The fact that some jobs were hard to get for black musicians didn't matter much to Kelly's career in the early 1940s. He had steady work at a top place—*the Savoy*. Who could have asked for more? And who could have ever imagined that coming to an end?

After two years in the service, however, Kelly found quite a bit had changed in the music business. He reclaimed his old chair in the Savoy Sultans, but the band broke up almost immediately afterwards. (He only recalls two gigs with the band after the war.) Cooper felt the band had lost its identity, due to changes in personnel caused by the draft. And tastes in music were shifting.

Rhythm-and-blues was gaining adherents in some quarters, be-bop in others. The ever-swinging Sultans had had their time.

With G. I. Bill of Rights financial assistance, Kelly studied arranging, composition, and theory, skills he was called upon to use shortly after joining his next group, Rex Stewart's septet. Stewart's entire book of arrangements was stolen from his car. Stewart noted not long afterwards that Kelly "sat down and wrote a whole new book for us non-stop within two nights and one day. . . . He's bound to make it BIG! I can recognize an outstanding musician when I hear him play half of a chorus or have a look at his charts. Kelly is something else, yes sir!" Most of the recordings Stewart's group made for the Blue Star label were arranged by Kelly.

In subsequent years, Kelly used his talents in composing and arranging numbers for small groups he occasionally led, and in writing such originals as "House Rent Party" for Louis Jordan, "Don't Be On the Outside Looking On the Inside" for Sarah Vaughan, "Silver Lie" for the Ames Brothers, and various arrangements for Gene Krupa, Buddy Tate, and others.

From about 1947 to 1950, Kelly played sax in bassist Lucille Dixon's Quintet, mostly at the Savannah Club in Greenwich Village. He recalls: "You know who was in that band? I got him in the band. Fats Navarro! Then after Fats left, I got Taft Jordan in the band. We had Tyree Glenn, too, and Sonny Payne. A nice little band. Swing. I was on TV once—a Frank Sinatra special—with this same Lucille Dixon," Kelly recalls.

"And one time when I was working with Lucille Dixon somewhere out there in Queens, Tony Bennett came in—this was before he was known. And we had a girl singer with us then, Phyllis Branch. So Tony would—like he'd be imitating, he'd take his handkerchief, and he'd put it in his mouth and have it down like a saxophone, you know. So he says, 'Can I sing a song?' I say, 'Ask the girl. It's her band.' So she says, 'Yeah all right.' So he calls some songs that we knew, and he sang with us—before he got to be known. Later, one day I was walking down Broadway and I looked up in the sky, and I see this plane flying with an advertisement trailing behind it: '. . . and Tony Bennett.' I said, 'Damn! I know him.' And I thought, by him getting popular like that, he would have forgotten me. But one day I had to deliver some music to somebody at the Zanzibar, at Broadway and 49th Street, and Tony Bennett was there. And he said, 'Hi, George!' I said, 'Damn! He didn't forget.' I saw him again when I was working with Cozy Cole at the Metropole [in the 1960s]. He had a ringside seat. He spoke to me again. My wife said, 'He spoke to you!' I explained to her how we happened to have met, way back before he got known."

After leaving Dixon's group, Kelly went on the road with singer Babs Gonzalez for a couple months, then worked with guitarist Tiny Grimes for a couple more months and then "just jobbed around—no special gig. . . . I've been on recording dates with Sarah Vaughan, Nellie Lutcher, Rose Murphy, the chi-chi girl, she plays piano and sings in a high-pitched voice. I was on dates with Tiny Grimes, Jay McShann, Cozy Cole—a lot of different dates where I wasn't the leader." He made some hard-to-find sides under his own name for the Apollo and Winley record labels. But work for Kelly was far from steady. Like most players whose styles were well set before the advent of bebop, Kelly never really got into bebop; his preference was for older-style jazz, music with melody and a beat that the layman could easily follow.

Things got slow enough in the late '60s for him to take a day job for the first time in his career. "That was around 1967. I took a temporary job. I didn't want no steady job because if anything would break for me in music, I was going to quit. So I took a temporary job and something broke for me to go to Europe with Jay McShann. So I went with Jay McShann; we were over there two months—a quintet with McShann and Tiny Grimes." And Kelly sometimes subbed for Buddy Tate, with Tate's rhythm section, at the Celebrity Club in Harlem, when Tate got a gig of his own elsewhere.

For some years (Kelly believes it was from about 1970 to 1976), Kelly accompanied—on piano not sax—one of the groups billing themselves as the Inkspots and singing songs popularized by the original Inkspots of the 1940s. It was hardly the best use of his talents—and there were sax players no more talented than Kelly getting a good bit of work as saxists—but at least it paid the bills. Even though he did not get to play sax on the job, he notes, "I'd take my horn with me, because any time we'd find a jam session, I'd go and jam." Did he like touring with the Inkspots? His voice trails off after: "Well, the money was all right, but I didn't . . ."

The traveling, he recalls, grew wearying. "I'd been away— all over, out of the country, up in Canada, like six years. When I came in on a break—we were off for like two weeks—I asked Phil Schaap [the disc jockey, jazz historian, and recording engineer], 'Do you know anyone who wants to record me? I'd like to make a recording before it's all over.' Phil said, 'I'll record you.' Which he did. But it never came out." However, Schaap helped Kelly get booked into New York's West End Cafe as a leader, and he became a recurring booking there, starting about 1977, which brought some renewal of interest in him. "I gave up with the Inkspots then. I just went full-time with my own group, you know. I said, 'Well, I'll just stick with this. If I make it, I make it.' "

Kelly became a key element in the new Savoy Sultans, which Panama Francis organized on an ongoing basis in 1979, staying with the band for five years. He played tenor sax, transcribed original Savoy Sultans arrangements off the old records so that the new band could play them, adapted arrangements played by Chick Webb's 1930s big band to the nine-man instrumentation of the new band, and also provided catchy new arrangements of old favorites such as "Panama," "Ja-Da," and "Mack the Knife" for the band.

Finally Kelly left Francis, understandably preferring to lead his own group rather than remain a sideman. He uses the billing of "George Kelly and his Jazz Sultans" today. Kelly notes: "The main people in my group now are Candy Ross on trombone, Ronnie Cole on drums, Richard Wyands on piano, Peck Morrison on bass, and myself. Then sometimes we augment the group into a septet, and we add Irvin Stokes on trumpet and flugelhorn and Norris Turney on alto saxophone. So that means I have a four-part horn section and a three-part rhythm section."

Since the late 1970s, Kelly has been heard on a number of recordings. He's featured with Panama Francis' Savoy Sultans, for example, on such albums as *Gettin' in the Groove* (Black and Blue 33.320), *George Kelly and Panama Francis' Savoy Sultans in Cimiez* (Black and Blue 33.161), *Grooving* (Stash ST–218), and *Everything Swings* (Stash ST–233). He's also starred on such albums as *Fine and Dandy: George Kelly with the Paul Sealey Trio and the Harlem Blues and Jazz Band* (Barron VLP 405) and *Stealin' Apples: George Kelly, Artie Miller, and the No-Gap Generation Jazz Band* (Dharma GFL 1123) (both labels are rather obscure). In addition, he's been heard as a sideman on albums with Carrie Smith, Roy Milton, Humphrey Lyttleton, and others.

Perhaps the most readily available album of Kelly's is a 1984 studio recording, *George Kelly Plays the Music of Don Redman* (Stash ST–40). It's also the only one that shows real planning in terms of repertoire. Producer Bernie Brightman came up with the idea of Kelly doing an all-Redman program, and Dick Ables served as A&R man. Kelly says, "They were noticing that everybody was bringing out other people's music, so being they were friends of Don, they wanted to keep his music going, too. Then they figured I had a kind of sound that some of Don's tenor saxophone players had. And Don was a friend of mine anyway. I used to call him the Little Giant. In music he was a giant. I never worked with him. I met him when he came to Florida with his band. Any band came to Miami, I was always up under the reed section. So then I found out that he played saxophone and arranged; I was up under him—listening, talking. I always talked, you know, with musicians." Redman got to record such instrumentals as "Chant of the Weed" and "Cherry," and sing on "Gee Baby, Ain't I Good to You," supported by sidemen Glenn Zottola, trumpet and alto sax; Richard Wyands, piano; Bucky Pizzarelli, guitar; George Duvivier, bass; and Butch Miles, drums. The album helped draw further attention to Kelly. Kelly may also be heard on such albums as *Echoes of Harlem* (Stash ST–265), a live recording of a 1985 "Highlights in Jazz" concert at N.Y.U. that co-starred Doc Cheatham (Kelly's features are "Sweet Georgia Brown" and "Body and Soul") and *I'm Shooting High,* a 1987 studio recording by the Red Richards-George Kelly Quintet (Sackville 2017) featuring mostly Louis Armstrong-associated numbers.

In recent years, Kelly has played often, as time has allowed, with the Harlem Blues and Jazz Band. In the company of contemporaries, he can kick out with one uninhibited chorus after another of "C Jam Blues" and other oldies.

In 1983, Kelly acted and played (backed by his rhythm section) in the Robin Williams film *Moscow on the Hudson*. The song they performed in the movie was one of Kelly's originals, "Did Try Blues." And Kelly has been making trips to Europe every year since 1977, sometimes on his own, sometimes with others, ranging from fellow reedman Kenny Davern to the late singer Helen Humes; he's developed a following in Europe (he notes he's made some recordings abroad not available in the U.S.).

What does Kelly like doing when he's not playing music?

"Writing music. I get a kick out of just sitting down and writing music. Arrangements. Sometimes a tune will strike me and I can't get it out of my mind. And ideas come to me on what to put into it. And I'll just go ahead and start writing on it. Sometimes I write and I stop writing because of loss of ideas. Then other times I write and it seems like the ideas just flow fluently; I've seen myself write the whole day up into the morning, like around five, six o'clock in the morning," he says.

"Other than that, I like to go to sports sometimes. I like baseball. I've gone to see the Mets play a couple times this year. I used to go to the ballgame when the Dodgers were here at Ebbets Field at least twice every week, when I was in town. And after they left, when the Mets came along, I used to go out there quite a bit, too. But when I started working for those Inkspots, it got away from me."

Kelly gets a kick out of playing, from time to time, at New York's Cat Club on 13th Street and Broadway, where hundreds—everyone from yuppies to old-timers—gather on Sunday nights to dance to Swing Era sounds. Two of the Cat Club's best-known regulars are Frankie Manning and Norma Miller, who a half century ago were key members of Whitey's Lindy Hoppers. When they begin Lindy Hopping as a couple, or Manning begins making moves by himself which are emulated by others following him on the dance floor, for Kelly it feels like old times indeed.

"Sometimes I think interest in this kind of music is coming back—and sometimes I don't know," he reflects. "I hope it is.

They're trying to get some jazz stations to play that kind of music. It may take time, but eventually it may come back, because I've played a lot of colleges where the kids are interested in it. And once you get the kids interested, well, they influence the parents to buy what albums they want." Kelly says he's very much enjoying what he's doing. "My grandson says, 'Grandpa, when you retire, will you give me the horn?' " He smiles at the remembrance before adding: "And I say to him, 'Who told you I'm planning on retiring?' "

1985

Hiding in Plain Sight

"Whatever happened to Mahlon Clark?"

That was the question posed to me one day by an older friend of mine, a jazz buff who's worked in newspapers and radio, and even a bit in TV (helping produce some Benny Goodman specials years ago).

I had to admit I'd never heard of Mahlon Clark.

"Oh, he was great. I really expected him to be the next Benny Goodman," my friend said casually. (*The next Benny Goodman?* That remark alone was enough to lodge the name "Mahlon Clark" in my mind.) Clark had been featured with Will Bradley and Ray McKinley, he told me. But he first took real notice of Clark, he said, one Sunday jam session (at Ryan's, if memory served him) in New York before the war. Some of the best reedmen anywhere were gathered—Buster Bailey, Edmond Hall, and Sidney Bechet. And Mahlon Clark, whom nobody had yet heard of, held his own with all of them. "I'll never forget it," he said. He was convinced Clark was among the very best of the upcoming players. But then after the war, Clark—as far as my friend was concerned—vanished completely. So much jazz talent. It was a mystery to him.

Not too long afterwards, I received an invitation to cover the 1985 Conneaut Lake Jazz Festival. I was interested in attending.

I had heard that in the past few years, producer Joe Boughton had built it up into one of the better traditional jazz festivals around. I scanned the list of talent Boughton had lined up this year. There were some well-known artists: Billy Butterfield, Eddie Miller, Joe Wilder, and so on. And then I spotted "Mahlon Clark."

If I had seen that name up until a few weeks before, it wouldn't have meant anything to me—but now my curiosity was piqued. I couldn't wait to tell my older jazz-buff friend that soon I would be seeing (and hearing) the elusive Mahlon Clark.

"Mahlon Clark. . . ," he said, as if he had quietly assumed that Clark must have passed on 40 years earlier. "Mahlon Clark. . . . " He asked me to find out where Clark had been hiding all those years.

At the Hotel Conneaut, on the afternoon before the festival is about to begin, Joe Boughton introduces me to Clark and we go out to the front porch of the hotel. We've scarcely sat down when a jazz devotee from California introduces himself and says he has one of Clark's 78s from 1945. Clark seems almost surprised that someone would still have the record. Then we start talking.

I ask him who his earliest inspirations on clarinet were.

"Benny Goodman," he says simply. "That's it. Period. And most of the clarinet players, if they're truthful, will tell you the same thing. I never will forget, back in the '40s in New York, Irving Fazola and I were sitting at a bar one night and we were talking about clarinetists. He said, 'You know we talk about this guy on clarinet and that guy, but there's one guy that plays better than any of us—always has, always will.' I said, 'I know who you mean.' He says, 'Benny. You know, guys can do other things, but he's the best. He always will be. He started the whole thing.'

"And it's true. I think, as far as I was concerned, certainly. I loved Johnny Mince. I used to listen to Johnny Mince, and Fazola. I'll even like, I like Pee Wee Russell; for what he did, I loved Pee Wee's playing. I used to copy everybody. Still do!" Clark laughs. I ask him if Artie Shaw had been an influence, too.

"Artie Shaw was an influence, yeah. Very melodic, beautiful

player. Yes he was. I had occasion to front his band one night . . . the 1944 band, after he got out of the navy. He had to go someplace one night and he called me. I was like 21 or 22 and I fronted the band; that was a big thrill."

Clark was born in Portsmouth, Virginia, in 1923. He was 15 when he first began playing with bands professionally, playing in little clubs around Portsmouth and Norfolk. He went on the road at age 17, as soon as he got out of high school. He spent a year touring the South with Dean Hudson's territory band.

He was but 18 in 1941 when he joined the Will Bradley Band, co-led by drummer Ray McKinley. The band had been formed just the year before. It was an impressive, clean-sounding outfit, boasting rich intonation and a precise attack. George Simon raved in *Metronome* (under the headline "Will Bradley's Band Best of 1940 Crop"): "It possesses a freshness and crispness found in practically no veteran groups, plus a sureness, based on musical accuracy, that's startling for an outfit as young as this."

Its key players included Bradley (who was considered by Glenn Miller to be the nation's number one all-around trombonist), McKinley, pianist Freddy Slack, and a young tenor saxist (who was also required to double on clarinet) by the name of Peanuts Hucko. George Simon noted in *Simon Says: The Sights and Sounds of the Swing Era* that Hucko, then at the very start of his career, "couldn't play clarinet well enough, so they finally fired him. Today he's one of the world's greatest jazz clarinetists." Lee Castle (then Castaldo) joined in '41, giving the band a strong hot trumpet soloist.

Clark was in the band, playing alto sax and clarinet, when it made such 1941–42 recordings as "In the Hall of the Mountain King," "Sleepy Time Gal," "From the Land of the Sky-Blue Water," "Booglie Wooglie Piggly" (with McKinley on vocal), "I'm Tired of Waiting for You," and "Request for a Rhumba." And he was getting noticed. George Simon observed in *Metronome*, in November of 1941: "That young Mahlon Clark is really turning into one helluva fine clarinet player!"

I ask Clark what Bradley and McKinley were like to work for.

"They were fine. They argued a lot," he remembers. "They

had differences of opinion as to how the band should be running. When you have two leaders, naturally you're going to run into conflicts. And they were co-leaders. Ray liked to play boogie. He was the king of the big band boogie in those days. ('Oh, Beat Me Daddy . . .' and all that stuff.) And Will loved to play ballads. It's true; he played a beautiful ballad. And Ray played great boogie drums. And you always had this kind of bickering as to which tunes to play. They finally had a blowup. But it was a real good band.

"Will was a beautiful trombone player. He never practiced. Never. I was with him a year. I don't recall him ever playing his horn except when he was on the job. We'd have a week off. He'd come in and play just beautifully."

With players of the caliber of Bradley, McKinley, Slack, Castle, and Clark, it was inevitable that a spirited small jazz combo (a band-within-the-band) would emerge. "We did a record called 'Basin Street Boogie' that was a big-seller," Clark recalls. "Lee Castaldo on trumpet and Will on trombone and me on clarinet and then McKinley on drums and Felix Giobbe on bass and Billy Maxted on piano. Freddy Slack was with us originally, but he'd already left by then." The musicians were billed on the record as "Will Bradley's Six Texas Hot Dogs."

"Freddy Slack was the pianist the first couple months I was on the band. But he was a bad boy and we finally had to let him go," Clark remembers with a laugh. "He'd be late for a show and, you know, things like that. So they had a parting of the ways. He went to the coast and he did beautifully. He started working at Capitol (he led his own band) and did the stuff with Ella Mae Morse. You know, I still work with Ella Mae once in a while out on the coast. She's still in there punching, and singing good. She's a great gal. I worked with Ray McKinley out there with her a couple of summers, a week at a time at Disneyland."

In his April 1940, *Metronome* review of the Will Bradley Band, George Simon offered a guess that it might prove to be "just about the finest outfit in all dancebandom." But the band never realized the potential that Simon (and others) saw in it. Its co-leaders were unable to agree on the direction it should take. Early in 1942, McKinley left to form his own band.

Bradley continued on his own for awhile, but with diminishing returns.

"I left the Will Bradley Band and I went with Ray McKinley. When Will and Ray separated, I went with Ray. He took me with him and a couple of other guys. We formed a new band and we recorded for Capitol—some of the first records they made for Capitol. And we did some other records for Eli Oberstein; he had a record company at the time, and he was a big record man. We did Hit Records or Elite records. We did a bunch of those. And then a bunch for Capitol. And then the strike came, the recording ban. McKinley's records—the ones he made on Capitol back then—didn't sell too well. But we did 'em. I remember 'Big Boy,' 'Hard Hearted Hannah'—he did those before anybody really had brought them back. He liked them and he recorded them. And we did some pop tunes as I remember, like 'Manhattan Serenade.' These were all with his big band.

"He went with the Glenn Miller army band, which I was supposed to go with. But I wound up on the coast—I don't think Ray ever forgave me for that. For he had me all set to go in the military and I decided to stay on the coast. And then when he got out, he formed a new band. And that was the Eddie Sauter era—Eddie Sauter the famous arranger. And he had him and he wanted me to come with him, and his new band." McKinley did well commercially with this band. But Clark declined to go with him. "I was starting to work radio and stuff in Los Angeles," Clark recalls. And he got an opportunity to record a few instrumental sides leading his own small group.

"That was in '45–'46. Ben Pollack formed a record company called Jewell Records. And it didn't last very long. (He also had Boyd Raeburn and he had Kay Starr. Kay Starr did her first solo records with him.) And our Mahlon Clark Sextette did two dates for Jewell records. We did eight tunes and he only released four of them. Because the company didn't have too much money behind them. One of them did fairly well, a tune called 'I'm a Dreamer (Aren't We All)'—or 'I'm a Dreamer, Montreal,' as we'd say," Clark adds with a laugh. "And that sold pretty well. But the company went under right after that." The Mahlon Clark Sextette consisted of Buddy Cole (piano), Phil Stephens (bass),

Nick Fatool (drums), Nappy Lamare and Dave Barbour (guitars), when, in September of 1945, it recorded "I'm a Dreamer (Aren't We All)," "Atomic Did It," "East Lynne Jump," and "Can't We Be Friends."

Clark also had a contract leading small-group sides for anonymous transcription work. "At the time I was doing a bunch of transcriptions for Capitol. Capitol Records had a transcription library. Where they'd send these transcriptions out to all the markets, have the piped-in music, and the radio stations played them. I used to do a lot of those. With Red Norvo on vibes. They would say just a sextette [on the transcriptions]. And Nick Fatool did them with me. And Red and Al Hendrickson, Buddy Cole. That was a lot of fun. We'd go in and rip off 10–15 tunes at a time. Don't rehearse them, just do them. Maybe get an ending and change keys at the last chorus or something like that." It was enjoyable work, but it brought Clark no public recognition. He never was aggressive about making a name for himself. Nor did he ever really aspire to be a leader, he says. "I was kind of a follower. I don't know, I just like other people to take the—I just kind of follow orders. I'm one of those people, as far as music goes."

He also felt that there wasn't much of a future for the type of jazz he liked to play. He had arrived on the scene a bit too late. There wasn't going to be a "next Benny Goodman" now. Bebop was the up-and-coming thing—and there didn't seem to be much room for a clarinet in bebop. Swing was losing ground. "Bebop came in, see," he recalls. "I had always been sort of a semi-Dixieland player. And bebop came in, about '46–'47. And there was really no place for clarinet that seemed to fit. And I couldn't play bebop anyway. I couldn't keep up with the chords. So I just said: To heck with this. I'm not going to do something halfway. So I decided I'd just forget the jazz. If somebody calls me for a date, I'll do it. But as far as pushing myself and staying in the jazz field, no. That's when I really decided just to cool it and stay in the more or less legit field. Which I did for many years."

Radio work was tempting, Clark recalls, because it meant "the chance to stay in one place. My wife and I wanted to buy a house, and settle down and have kids and stuff like that. I got into radio and then, very shortly after that, I wound up on a staff job at Paramount studios. I was there for many, many years. It was security. Nice music. Playing a lot of legit music and a little jazz—not much—background music for pictures. Worked with a lot of great composers. One of the first pictures I did over there, I remember, was with Aaron Copland. And I was just—couldn't believe—here I am, oh, nothing, working with Aaron Copland, the famous composer. I was just thrilled. Oh, there were a lot of good experiences over there." Clark got to act as well as play in one film, entitled *The Rat Race*.

He also did a good deal of record session work. As with the film and TV soundtrack work, his contributions earned him no public recognition, even though he was heard on many popular albums. He was working with a number of top musicians who were, like himself, big band veterans. "I worked with Billy May a lot out there. And Nelson Riddle. I've done a lot of stuff with him over the years. Specials, records, you know, Sinatra stuff, Nat Cole, all kind of different artists. I kind of made up my mind that I wasn't going to play any more jazz anyway, so I just—I melded right into the thing and just started doubling more, playing bass clarinet, trying to play flute a little bit. I just got out of the jazz and went into the studios and raised a family. I kind of regret it now a little bit," he says.

Clark did have one job for awhile, he notes, where he was certainly seen by plenty of people, although he didn't get a chance to really show what he was capable of. "I was on 'The Lawrence Welk Show' for six years," he recalls. "I was the lead alto with that band. I didn't play much clarinet on that band. I didn't get to solo very much. They had a good clarinet player there at the time named Don Bonnee and he was second alto and played second clarinet and he played the jazz. And there was no place for me there, for clarinet. And I didn't particularly want to, either, because Mr. Welk's very picky, picky about his jazz. And [Clark laughs] I mean, I played a little too modern for him. As a matter of fact, he told me that. But anyway, after Don left I inherited the clarinet chair. About a year and half there it was touch and go. Like I say, Mr. Welk is very particular about his jazz."

228

MAHLON CLARK

Mahlon Clark. (Photo by Chip Deffaa.)

Mahlon Clark (at right) with Artie Shaw. (Courtesy of Mahlon Clark.)

MAHLON CLARK

Mahlon Clark sitting in with the bands of Henry "Red" Allen (top photo) and Oran "Hot Lips" Page. (Courtesy of Mahlon Clark.)

Tenor saxist Eddie Miller, clarinetist Mahlon Clark, and trumpeter Billy Butterfield made up a memorable front line during the 1986 Conneaut Lake Jazz Festival. (Photo by Chip Deffaa.)

232

Actually, Lawrence Welk hired a surprising number of superior musicians over the years. But—at least from a jazz fan's point of view—the whole was usually less than the sum of the parts. Welk's band often sounded stiff, mechanical. Welk kept a tight hold on the reins. "It was a pretty good band. Man for man, it was good musicianship in the band. But there you're under such tension all the time that you never can relax," Clark notes. "But that was all right. It helped raise my kids."

So where had Mahlon Clark been hiding? For six years, anyway, he had been playing weekly for millions of viewers on a nationally broadcast television show. But jazz buffs who might have known of Clark's work in the '40s probably weren't tuning in. And if they had happened to tune in, chances are they wouldn't have realized that the trim, graying fellow with the glasses playing lead alto was Mahlon Clark.

In recent years, Clark has also served as lead alto for Tex Beneke, for Beneke's West Coast big band dates. "Tex has a set band in Los Angeles. And I play sax with him there. I used to play the clarinet chair, and then I got tired of it. I was the contractor at that time, so I decided to put myself on the lead alto, and get a clarinet player," Clark recalls. "I work whenever Tex works out there. We do a couple, three dates a month maybe. He moved out there about three or four years ago and settled down in the Newport Beach area. He works out of there. And then he flies around the country and he works out of Chicago and New Orleans and different places. He's very active for his age." (But when Beneke flies East for dates, Clark stays on the West Coast. Beneke uses different musicians for gigs in different parts of the country.)

There's a syndicated TV special around, featuring Tex Beneke and his Orchestra, plus singers Helen O'Connell and Bob Eberly. Taped at the Hollywood Palladium in 1980, it still gets periodic airplay. If you happen to catch it, you can spot Clark on lead alto, and also soloing a bit. He does a great job on Jimmy Dorsey's theme, "Contrasts." (The soundtrack of that show is also available as a double-album set from Silver Eagle Records, 777 North Palm Canyon Drive, Palm Springs, CA 92262.)

"Working with Tex Beneke is really the only steady big band

thing I do out on the coast. The rest of it's little small groups and clarinet. I didn't really keep up with jazz until I just started back the last four or five years, playing jazz again.

"Well, for the last four or five years, I still do some TV, film, and occasional movie work, and an occasional record date. But I've been doing more of what I really love the most—that's play jazz. I've just got through doing the Sacramento Jazz Festival, with the Dick Cathcart-Pete Kelly Big Seven. And I did the Los Angeles Jazz Festival last August. Oh, I did one in North Dakota, a few months ago. I'm enjoying doing things like the thing here—Conneaut Lake."

I ask Clark if he often gets to the New York area.

"No, never. It never happens," he says. "I've been back there once since in the early '40s. I stay strictly on the coast. I did go back to my home town of Portsmouth, Virginia, and did a jazz concert with a big band there a couple months ago, with Tommy Newsom, who's from the same hometown as me. Most of my work is around my home area. I do a lot of jazz work, nightclubs and different things. I live in Santa Monica, which is just outside of Los Angeles. I work a lot with Johnny Varro, the piano player. Whenever John has anything, he always calls me on clarinet.

"Now, here I get into my 60s, I'm finding a new life in jazz. I'm really enjoying it."[1]

Clark's relaxed, melodic playing was very easy to take throughout the three days of the festival. I don't think he produced an unpleasant sound on his clarinet the whole weekend. He blended well with Billy Butterfield and Eddie Miller. And I particularly enjoyed his gently swinging playing over brunch. It's nice to have Mahlon Clark come out of "hiding" after so many years (even if that "hiding" included a stint on Lawrence Welk's television show), and let the jazz community enjoy what he has to offer.

1985

---

[1] In October, 1987, Clark released an album—his first recording in years under his own name: *Mahlon Clark—Hiding in Plain Sight* (Gome Records).

Pop Music Was a Comedown

After sparking the big bands of Benny Goodman, Les Elgart, and Woody Herman, Sonny Igoe decided he had had enough of life on the road. He settled down in northern New Jersey to spend more time with his family, working the New York scene with small groups led by Charlie Ventura, Billy Maxted, Phil Napoleon, and Pee Wee Erwin. For a decade he was a staff musician, first at NBC and then at CBS. And he was a mainstay of New York recording dates. (He remembers once having to drive his car to four different Manhattan parking lots in one day, as he hustled from studio to studio to cut albums, record jingles, and meet his TV commitments.) And, since the mid '50s, Igoe has been among the most in-demand of drumming teachers. He pioneered the use of two-track audio recording and playback in drum instruction, and added video as soon as the technology became available. He is the author of a book, *Get Your Fills Together*. He has a waiting list of students eager for the lessons he gives at his Emerson, New Jersey, home.

After four decades in the business Sonny Igoe can pretty well do what he pleases. He no longer has to take the freelance dates for jingles or recording sessions playing music he does not believe in. Each Monday night, in the Emerson High School band room, Igoe gathers with a crew of 17 top musicians—many, like himself, survivors of the Swing Era—who make up "The Dick Meldonian-Sonny Igoe Big Swing Jazz Band." They run through charts played by Count Basie, Buddy Rich, Woody Herman and others, as well as charts crafted by leading contemporary arrangers specifically for this band. The Meldonian-Igoe Band has given benefit concerts, and has put out two albums on Progressive Records. Igoe notes there's no money in it for any of the musicians. But it's a chance to play the music he likes best. And he says he'd rather be co-leading a big band for free than getting paid to record music he can't stand.

In his basement studio—the wall adorned with photos of friends and professional acquaintances including Gene Krupa, Carol Burnett, Butch Miles, Charlie Callas, Benny Goodman, and the Muppets—Igoe reflects on his career.

He says he is one drumming teacher who firmly believes that "drummers aren't taught, they're born," and offers himself as an example. He is a natural drummer, he says, who got started at age five or six. "I was guilty of breaking into the house next door, where the son was a drummer in college and had a drumset at home. He used to let me play on it. One day I broke in there about six o'clock in the morning and started beating on the drum and waking everybody up," Igoe recalls. His folks promptly bought him his own drums.

Igoe remembers waiting as a teenager for the new records of Benny Goodman (with Gene Krupa on drums) to arrive at Agel's Record Shop, in his home town of Ridgewood, New Jersey. Igoe was 16 years old in 1939 when he won a Gene Krupa drum contest. "My father thought it would be great if I would go to school and be a lawyer. But Gene Krupa told my father it would be a waste of time for me to be a lawyer, that I should really pursue the drums. He sent me to a teacher in New York, a fellow by the name of Bill West," Igoe recalls. He's still grateful to Krupa.

From 1942 to 1946, Igoe played in bands in the Marine Corps. It was a wide-ranging musical education for him, since most of the best professional musicians were getting drafted. He had a chance to play along with, and learn from, top sidemen. After the war, in June of '46, he joined a big band led by Tommy Reynolds, today a booking agent.

At Christmas break, Igoe caught Les Elgart's Band at the Meadowbrook. "There was a saxophone player and a trumpet player in the band that I had worked around with before the war. And before the last set, one of them came running out and said, 'Hey Sonny, Les just had a big fight with the drummer and fired him, and we fixed it up for you to play the last set.' So I went up and played the last set. The upshot of that was, I went to work for Elgart the next night. And that's how I got started in the New York area," Igoe says.

After Les Elgart, Igoe played in Ina Ray Hutton's Band, before moving on to Benny Goodman in 1948 and '49. "I was thrilled to death. I had two of my life's ambitions there. One of them was to play with Benny Goodman. The other was to play the Paramount Theater *with* Benny Goodman. And I got a chance to do that. We did the Christmas show, going from '48 to '49. And it was great—people standing in the aisles and all that kind of stuff. Benny hadn't had a band in a couple of years, and this was like a homecoming for him, at the Paramount Theater. It was standing-room-only all the time," Igoe recalls.

Igoe was now playing all of the classic arrangements—"Sing Sing Sing," "King Porter Stomp," "Sugarfoot Stomp," etc.—that he had memorized when Goodman had first recorded them with Krupa on drums. (Igoe adds that when he first started playing, "if you closed your eyes, you'd swear it was Krupa." He changed his playing over the years, after being impressed by the approaches of Max Roach, Art Blakey, Buddy Rich and Don Lamond.)

Igoe recalls that one critic wrote that he was the best drummer Benny Goodman had had since Krupa. But not all agreed. He got some wildly varied write-ups when he first broke through big as a drummer. "You can't let critics bother you," he says. "I remember when I was first with Benny Goodman, I had a terrible write-up in *Down Beat*. The first time. The guy said Igoe was a nice-looking boy and plays with a lot of enthusiasm, but sometimes he got too carried away, or whatever the comment was. And I was really down in the dumps about it. We were in the Paramount Theater, and Benny said to me: 'Well, they spelled your name right. There's only one person you have to worry about. And that's me. And I like the way you play. And it's my band. *That guy will never have a band.*' "

By reputation, Goodman was far from the easiest of band-leaders to work for. But Igoe says he and Goodman really never had any problems. He notes: "There was always this big thing about Benny Goodman and what they called 'the ray.' That he would kind of stare at somebody. Well one night, we were playing up in Canada and I was right in front of the band, and Benny had his clarinet stand right next to me. And all of a sudden I look up and here he is, staring right at me. And I can hear the guys in the band saying, 'Uh oh—looks like it's Sonny's night in the barrel.' And he's just looking at me. And I'd look away, and he's just staring. He's not even saying anything or moving a muscle. He's just staring at me. And the people are waiting, waiting to dance. And I'm looking around. And I couldn't take it anymore—so I just reached over and I passed my palm in front of his eyes, up and down. And do you know that he never moved a muscle? He didn't *know* I did that. Well, I thought the band would come apart when I did that. That ended *'the ray.'* Right there. Because he didn't even know that I waved—and from then on, I never worried about him looking at me. Because he was just staring off in space. And he said one night, when we were at the Hollywood Palladium, 'You know, all this story about the ray—a lot of times I'm thinking about something else besides the music. And I just start to daydream a little bit.' I always had a good time working with Benny."

Then Igoe went with Woody Herman, with whom he stayed for nearly three years. Herman had cut back to a small group when Igoe joined, but he soon reorganized a big band, which became his famed "Third Herd." Members included such fine musicians as Conte Condoli (trumpet), Bill Harris (trombone), and Dave McKenna (piano). Herman had gone pretty heavily into bebop the previous couple of years. Now he was returning to playing more straightforward contemporary swing. Igoe was

Sonny Igoe. (Courtesy of Sonny Igoe.)

The Benny Goodman Sextet at the Hollywood Palladium, March or April 1949. From left to right: Buddy Greco (piano, vocals), Benny Goodman (clarinet), Wardell Gray (tenor sax), Sonny Igoe (drums), Clyde Lombardi (bass), and Doug Mettome (trumpet). (Courtesy of Frank Driggs.)

in the band when it recorded sides such as "Music to Dance To" (by Al Cohn), "Sonny Speaks" (by Sonny Berman), and "Starlight Souvenirs" (by Ted Shapiro, Reg Connelly, and Lewis Ilda), all of which were recorded for Capitol. For an excellent sample of Igoe's drumming with Herman, listen to "New Golden Wedding" (by Jiggs Noble), which was recorded in 1951 for MGM.

Igoe has only fond recollections of Herman. "He would always expect that the drummer would play the right tempo, no matter what he'd beat off. That was the first thing he told me; the first night I joined him, he said: 'I always beat off the wrong tempo. When you know the right tempos, you play the right tempo, no matter what I do.'"

Igoe came off the road, after touring with Herman, to see the birth of his first child. He hoped to be able to find steady work near his home in northern New Jersey. But the jobs did not materialize, and after a couple months of virtually no work— just before his funds ran out—he accepted an offer to rejoin the Herman Herd on a tour of one-nighters. "And when I left home, I left my wife with what I thought was $119 in our checking account. And I made a terrible mistake. Instead of $119, I had left her with $1.19. That was our entire estate in 1951. And she had to call her sister to borrow some money because the baby had a cold and she had to get medicine," Igoe remembers. Touring once again with Herman paid well, but it also meant that when Igoe saw his daughter for brief spells in the first year and a half of her life, she did not recognize him. And that did it, he says; that forced him to finally give up life on the road. He wanted his children to have a chance to know who their father was. And he also tried to instill in them his appreciation for music. "When my son Tom was born," Igoe recalls, "—the first day when he got home from the hospital, I put him in front of the hi-fi and put on a Buddy Rich record."

Igoe played with Les Elgart again briefly in the mid '50s, when Elgart was in New York. And he played a good bit of Dixieland drums in all-star groups at Nick's, the celebrated Greenwich Village traditional jazz club.

Igoe says he likes to tell his students that they cannot afford to fluff off on any job, because you never know who might be hearing you or how they might someday be able to help you. In 1958, he recalls, he got a call to play drums in the orchestra of "The Garry Moore Show," one of the big variety shows of its time. The call led to Igoe's being hired as a CBS staff musician, eventually doing everything from "Candid Camera" and "Play Your Hunch" to "The Jackie Gleason Show" and Carol Burnett specials, and working as a substitute drummer on the Ed Sullivan and Merv Griffin shows. Igoe said he got quite a surprise one day when he sat down with the orchestra leader on "The Garry Moore Show," the man who had gotten him started in playing for television.

"He said, 'Sonny, you don't really remember me, do you?' And I said, 'Well, I know I've seen you around . . .' And he says, 'Yes, but you don't really remember me, do you? Remember when you were with Benny Goodman at the Paramount in 1948 and '49? I was the *piano player for the comic on the show.* I loved the way you played then. And I told myself, whenever I got my own band or could use you, I was going to call you.' Now this is *ten* years later. And this fellow's name is Irwin Kostal. And he was the orchestrator and the conductor on 'The Garry Moore Show.' The most marvelous musician I think I've ever met. I keep telling my students: You never know who's hearing you. You can't afford to really go in and fluff off a job."

Igoe admits there were times when he has not always followed his own advice. He had no use for a lot of popular music, and made no attempts to hide his feelings. He recalls playing on record dates with Fabian, Frankie Avalon, and other teen idols of the '50s. He found the new trends in pop music a comedown after the polished professionalism of the swing he had played with Benny Goodman, Woody Herman and company. But the heyday of the big bands was by then clearly history; the money was in records with titles like "Splish Splash." "I was on one date and I was really sick of it. Playing twist music and all that stuff. There were a bunch of guitars on the date. (All *the* New York recording players of the day—Bucky Pizzarelli, I remember he was there.) And we got the word: 'Okay fellows, let's run this down.' And we played it down, and jeez, it went off pretty good.

And the guy in the booth says, 'Okay, let's try it again. Hey Sonny, you know, it really sounds like you don't mean it.' And I, being one of these persons who usually says what he thinks, I say: 'Well, to tell you the truth, I don't.' I never got called by those people again—even though on the next take I played the hell out of it. But I really didn't care. Because that's not what I really like to do. And I spent a lot of dates with Fabian, who was a very nice young man who couldn't sing. Somebody had to stand in front of him to mouth the words, because he had no sense of rhythm, you know, at all. It was just a waste of time. But you'd play this thing over and over, hoping that he'd get it the next time.

"People tend today, I think, to equate popularity with being good. If it's popular, it's good. But jeez, I can't believe some of the stuff I see on MTV. They call that music. It's unreal," Igoe says. His idea of music was the sort of stuff being played by Herman, Basie, Goodman, and Kenton. And there was less and less of a market for that kind of music.

"I was getting a little disillusioned with the way you had to play then, on the records. You know, rock 'n' roll was really here then. And you had to play so much straight eighths with heavy back beats, and all that crap. I just couldn't stomach it," Igoe says. "Rock is all built on straight eighths. Nobody played that, years ago. If you played that, you were considered corny. But now, it was like a whole different bag." He was bothered, too, by the way that even the old pros seemed to be trying to rough up their sound. "One time I was on a record date for Perry Como. And the orchestra got there at ten in the morning and we ran over two tunes. And they were simple, simple tunes, trite stuff. It took us about 15 or 20 minutes to run these things down. Then we waited around an hour and a half for him to come, and he listened to the tunes and he said, 'Jesus fellows, they sound too good.' You know, here you spend all your life trying to be good and trying to play clean and that sort of thing, and now somebody comes around and tells you that it's too good. Well, you know, he wanted a certain thing, I guess, and we weren't doing it. It was too polished. And that was the way things were going. And I didn't like it, and so I sort of phased myself out of recording."

Economics dictated his growing involvement in teaching. Without touring, it was simply not possible to make a living playing just the music he liked. Gigs that were the most satisfying musically often were not financially acceptable. He recalls playing in an all-star group in the early '50s at the old Downbeat Club on 54th Street. "And the lineup of the band that I was playing in was: Bill Harris and Kai Winding were the trombone players, Charlie Mingus was the bass player, I was the drummer and the piano player was a fellow named Harvey Leonard. Opposite us in the other band was Charlie Parker, Max Roach, Percy Heath was the bass player, I forget the piano player. The job was from nine to four—we played alternate sets. Those people were all well-known jazz players—and we all made $12 apiece," Igoe says. For his livelihood, Igoe increasingly came to rely on teaching, first in New York City, and then later at his home in New Jersey.

In Igoe's basement studio is the Slingerland standard four-piece drum set that he has used for years. Facing it is a video camera, a television monitor, and a couple of tape recording decks. He notes: "I was one of the, I guess *the* first teacher in New York using an audio playback system with students. I'd have them play with an arrangement. We'd record it, with the music on one track and the drums on the other track, and I would play it back and I'd be able to show where they're off. Now I can do the same thing with video. The video's a great teaching aid." He stresses: "I don't tell anybody what kind of style they can play. I've got to give them the tools so that they can do what they want to do, and do it better than they ever could have without having met me."

He comments that while the music he's most comfortable playing is big band jazz and Broadway show music (he'll occasionally sub in Broadway pit orchestras), he can appreciate good drummers playing in different genres. He has never cared for the drumming of some very popular rock figures, such as Ringo Starr. "But I hear a lot of things today that I like. From different groups like Spyro Gyra, and funk groups and things like that, that type of drumming. And what they loosely call 'contemporary.' Gadd. And Harvey Mason. Absolutely incredible," he says. "Some of those guys sound like they have 12 arms and 10 feet."

He advises aspiring musicians to listen to a wide variety of recordings and play along with them. "That's the greatest way to practice. When I was a kid I had every record that Benny Goodman, Tommy Dorsey, Count Basie, Glenn Miller, every band you ever heard of made." And he practiced until he could re-create the work of all the leading drummers. "A lot of young drummers don't listen to enough music. And they don't sit down and play with records. You have to have an inspiration. You have to look up to Steve Gadd, to Buddy Rich, to Elvin Jones, to whoever you want to look up to. You listen to those people and you try to play along with them, so you can get an idea of what they do, of how they anticipate, how they set up figures, how they play breaks. That's how a drummer gets an ear."

Igoe comments that there are limits to what any teacher—no matter how good—can do for an aspiring drummer. "You can't put ideas in a person's head. I've had guys say, 'You're going to teach me how to play a drum solo.' I can't teach you how to play a drum solo. To play a drum solo, you have to want to show off. I've had guys who've told me that they want to play a drum solo, yet they come in here and they're so inhibited they barely can say hello to you. You have to want to show off, number one, to be a successful soloist. Number two, you've got to have some ideas. And number three, you'd better be able to execute them. That's where a teacher comes in, and makes it easier for you to play. But the ideas? You have to have the ability to improvise. Most drumming is improvisation 99% of the time anyway."

There's no escaping it, Igoe stresses: there's just such a thing as being a natural drummer. "And if you're a natural drummer," he says, "—there's nothing you would rather do."

In the Emerson High School band room, the musicians are slowly assembling. It is Monday night—the traditional off-night for musicians. The 17 men gathering here—most of whom are gray or balding—usually play nowadays in clubs or in Broadway pit bands, do freelance studio work and/or teach. They all love the big band sounds. And if there are few places left where they can play in big bands for pay, they are happy to play in this band on Mondays for free.

"Bring back the big bands so I can work again!" exclaims lead trumpeter Paul Cohen, half in jest, as he takes his chair. He's a veteran of the bands of the Dorsey Brothers, Raymond Scott, Artie Shaw, and Count Basie. He recalls, too: "I played with Sonny, in Woody Herman's Band, in Bop City back in 1950."

Igoe says that his own days of touring with big bands are long behind him, but he's not about to give up the music he believes in most. For more than a decade, these weekly get-togethers have provided him with an important release.

Igoe comments that his son, Tom, recently passed along his greetings to his old boss, Woody Herman, who is still on the road at 70-plus. Herman's current Young Thundering Herd was playing in England, Igoe explains, and so was the Glenn Miller Orchestra—now with none other than Tom Igoe as its drummer. "My son," Igoe adds with pride, "is a natural drummer."

The musicians are about ready now to get into the night's work. Dick Meldonian, the co-leader of the Meldonian-Igoe Big Swing Jazz Band (who's played sax in many Broadway pit bands, as well as in bands led by Benny Goodman, Stan Kenton, Nat Pierce, Charlie Barnet, and Woody Herman), is busy altering a chart, assigning parts. "We'll have two tenor choruses on Cliff, two on Gary, then the rhythm section before we come back in," he directs. A handful of onlookers have gathered in front of the band to watch.

"This is not a nostalgia band," Igoe says. "We don't play 'In the Mood.' " He nods to Meldonian: *Let's begin.*

Down in front, Meldonian quickly counts off the beat—and suddenly a wall of sound hits the few spectators. The brass soars, filling the cramped rehearsal room—it's like having the Stan Kenton Orchestra in your living room. The number is an up-tempo swinger, one of many written especially for this band by Gene Roland, an arranger long associated with Kenton, who also arranged for Count Basie and Woody Herman.

Igoe's drumming gives the ensemble a crisp rhythmic lift. He's mostly on the hi-hats now, pushing the band along hard. A broad, boyish grin spreads across his face. The grin stays there throughout most of the night.

"Our kind of music is pretty much extinct," he tells you later, during a break. "But I've been in music all my life. I can't imagine not being in music. You never stop."

1984

Jazz and Legit

Nineteen-year-old Joe Wilder was playing trumpet in Les Hite's band in 1941. When the band played a dance in Topeka, Kansas, a woman came up and introduced herself to Wilder. She was the wife of saxophonist Frankie Trumbauer, Wilder recalls. "And she said to me: 'You know, you remind me of a trumpet player named Bix Beiderbecke.' And I mean, I had evidently heard Bix Beiderbecke, but I didn't know him as such. Then she said, 'He worked with my husband and he made a lot of records. Maybe after the dance, if you come by my house, you'll hear some of these records. I'd like you to hear this trumpet player, Bix Beiderbecke.'" Wilder didn't know the Beiderbecke records then; after all, Wilder had been born in 1922, which would have made him only five years old in 1927, when Beiderbecke and Trumbauer made their best recordings together, and just nine years old when Beiderbecke died in 1931. But Wilder and a couple other musicians from the band went over to the Trumbauer home and listened to the records. "That was my first introduction, really, to Bix Beiderbecke," Wilder notes.

Joe Wilder doesn't really play like Bix Beiderbecke. (For that matter, he doesn't play quite like any trumpeter other than Joe Wilder.) He doesn't have Beiderbecke's rare gift for lyricism.

And—having been born nearly 20 years after Beiderbecke—he naturally works in a more modern manner. And yet we can understand how his playing made Mrs. Trumbauer think of Bix.

For Wilder, like Bix, is a jazzman of notable restraint. His work is marked by subtlety, by self-control. He treats melodies with respect, flowing with them. He doesn't try to dazzle us with torrential outbursts. And he often conveys an air of detachment. "I learned to play very lightly and delicately," Wilder says, adding that his style—so different from that of most trumpeters—developed at least in part by chance.

We sense in Wilder's work (as in Beiderbecke's) a grounding in European musical values. As a young trumpeter in Philadelphia, Wilder says, he would really have liked to have taken lessons from players in the Philadelphia Orchestra. But that was financially beyond his reach. ("My Dad could barely feed us at the time; this was just after the Depression," he notes.) So—as the next best thing, to his way of thinking—Wilder availed himself of opportunities to sit in with small woodwind ensembles, playing classical music (which sets him apart from most jazz musicians). "There were small groups, there would be, like, a woodwind group and sometimes a clarinet player wouldn't show up, or the flautist wouldn't be there. And they'd need someone to play the part. So then I would take the trumpet and try to play those parts. And it also helped me with my transpositions. But playing the trumpet in a woodwind ensemble, you had to learn to play very softly; you couldn't go in with the full force of the trumpet. And so, in doing this, and trying to play and relate to what they were doing, I inadvertently developed the ability to play very quietly. It was of necessity. It wasn't that I set out to do it. But then it became a plus for me later on."

Wilder worked the big bands: first local bands in Philadelphia, then big name bands such as Les Hite's, Lionel Hampton's, Jimmie Lunceford's, and Count Basie's. He recalls: "Most of my buddies were saxophone players. And I kind of liked the way saxophone players play and I guess to this day, I try to play somewhat like reed players on the trumpet. You know, they have sort of a flowing style that they play in."

Wilder has never been exclusively committed to jazz. He is a musician who sometimes plays jazz but is as comfortable playing music for Broadway shows or TV soundtracks, or playing classical music, when the opportunity arises. When I spoke with him, he was working at the Conneaut Lake Jazz Festival. A few weeks before, I had heard him backing Maxine Sullivan at the 92nd Street "Y" in New York, as a member of Dick Hyman's Perfect Jazz Repertory Quintet. Not too long before that, I had caught him re-creating solos of Charlie Shavers and Frankie Newton for an evocation of the old 52nd Street scene at the New York's Vineyard Theater. But such jazz engagements are fairly infrequent for him. His bread-and-butter work these days is playing trumpet in the pit orchestra of the Broadway hit *Forty Second Street*. Wilder notes that his earliest training and interest was in legitimate-style trumpet playing. His interest in jazz developed later. The clear respect for melody that we find in his jazz work no doubt stems from his initial training in legitimate playing.

Wilder was born on February 22, 1922, in Colwyn, Pennsylvania. He was around eight when his family's home burned down. His family moved to Philadelphia (where he grew up), to live with his paternal grandparents. "My Dad was a musician already. He originally played cornet and then he played Sousaphone, and later on he became a bass violin player. And he decided that I should be a musician.

"I guess I was about ten and a half, eleven, when my father started me on cornet. And I studied with a teacher who taught my Dad. He was a black teacher and he was a musician. He had been concert cornet player in the Army band: Fred Griffin. And he was a superb player. He was like the equivalent of Del Staigers at that time. And he was very strict. And I guess from him I learned a lot at that time," Wilder recalls.

But not jazz?

"Oh, no, no, no, no. He was strictly legit. He used to play with the Masonic Band and the Elks Band. Because he was a first-rate cornet player. And you know, they had marches and things they used to play. And they'd have the trumpet playing, 'When the Saints Go Marching In.' And he'd be playing the high parts, and things like that. It wasn't really jazz. It was just sort of embellishment to some marches. That's basically where I started.

"I played in school, and I was on a children's radio program in Philadelphia, the Parisian Tailor's children's program. This program was begun by Sam Kessler and Eddie Lieberman. The two of them decided that Horn and Hardart's—you know, the restaurant chain—had a children's program, but there were only white children on that program. So Sam Kessler and Eddie Lieberman decided that maybe there should be a black children's program. And they started one called 'The Parisian Tailor's Kiddies' Hour.' And so my father took me down to audition for that, and I was accepted. Almost everybody other—they were all singers and dancers and telling stories and things like that. That program, on Sunday mornings at 10 or 11, got to be very popular.

"We used to play at the Lincoln Theater in Philadelphia. This was on radio, of course, but we had an audience in the theater. And the Lincoln Theater was also where all the name bands played in Philadelphia. And since they had the blue laws—you couldn't have a show on Sunday because we were so saintly at that time—it was in their contracts that since the bands didn't work on Sunday, they had to play for us on Sunday morning, on this children's program. So we were backed by every name band that came into Philadelphia and played the Lincoln Theater. They all played for us. And Louis [Armstrong] came. And Don Redman. Every name band. Jimmie Lunceford. You know. Cab Calloway. Even Duke's band. Duke didn't come himself to play for us, but the band did—some of the members of the band. They backed us on the radio show. The program was an hour. I'd say they allotted each kid maybe five or six minutes. And a lot of us were regulars, every Sunday. I was about 12."

So circa 1934, young Joe Wilder was playing trumpet on the air with some of the very best bands in the country backing him. He's no doubt the only professional working today who can claim to have played with such top bands as a mere boy. He adds, though, that at the time he took it for granted. "I mean, as far as I was concerned, it was just a band playing behind whatever it was we were doing. But it really enhanced it. That's what made the program so popular. [He laughs.] People were hearing these bands behind us!

"And of course they called me 'Louis' [as in Armstrong] then, because I was playing trumpet. And when Louis came, I remember the first time he came to play. He saw me and of course he gave me a pass to come to the theater and hear him. He said [and now Wilder imitates the famous Armstrong gravel-voice]: 'Here kid, you come and listen to Pops.' And he gave me a pass and told me I could come every day.

"But I was interested in playing like Del Staigers. Del Staigers was a cornet soloist. And I thought that was great, because my teacher played that way, see. And that's all I was interested in." To Wilder, the cornet work of a concert soloist like Staigers was more "proper" than the sort of jazz Armstrong was playing.

"So I only went once or maybe twice and heard Louis, that week that he was in the theater. And I never went any more. He had a big band. I think it was Luis Russell's band; he was playing, fronting that band."

Wilder didn't want to play jazz. "Oh no, I wasn't even thinking in terms of jazz. All I knew was that when you played cornet, you know, you played these solos: 'Carnival in Venice' and 'Bride of the Waves' and all those things." Wilder's musical heroes were not from jazz or popular music. "Del Staigers was the one I admired.[1] And then of course my teacher, Fred Griffin, he was superb.

"I played in high school bands and things. I went to the Jules E. Mastbaum School in Philadelphia—it's like the Music and Arts in New York. I was up there with Red Rodney, Buddy DeFranco, and guys like that. They were my guys at school. Buddy De Franco was great. We were all proud of him. I think it was Tommy Dorsey who had an amateur musicians' contest all over the country. And they picked the guys who could play jazz the

---

[1]Staigers' fine tone and all-around technical proficiency earned him such jobs as membership in the Victor house orchestra (under the direction of Nat Shilkret) of the 1920s and '30s, recording everything from the music of operettas and Broadway shows to dance music, as well as backing vocalists. He displayed exactly the kind of versatility that Wilder would later become known for.

best, and they got a chance to tour with the band for a week or
whatever, and Buddy won it in the Philadelphia area, when we
were in Mastbaum. And like he was our idol, because Buddy
really made it, you know. And he was a fine, legitimate clarinet
player. Exceptionally good."

How did Wilder start getting interested in playing jazz or
swing music?

"Well, my father had some friends with whom he had played.
Who had like little small bands and used to do club dates. My
Dad would go on jobs where they had two trumpets. He was
playing with a lot of bands around Philly. And then my father
decided, well maybe I should learn to read some of the jazz music
that guys were playing. And in almost all the bands, the stock
arrangements had three trumpet parts. So my father started
dragging me along. He would say, 'I just want you to sit there
next to the trumpet players. You listen to the way they play, and
look at the music. And see if you can understand the way they're
playing these things.'

"So I would do that. Then after a while, he'd say: 'Is it OK
if the kid brings his horn?' And they didn't want to offend my
father, I guess; they'd say it's OK. And I would go and I'd sit
there and play a couple notes or whatever I thought I could play.
I'm sure I didn't do it well. At one time, I remember, the first
trumpet player—he saw me coming, he didn't know I heard
him—he said to one of the guys, 'Oh my God, here comes Wilder
and that blamed kid again.' [He laughs.]

"And you could hear bands all day and all night long on
radio. My father, being a musician, he listened to all these bands.
We heard Gus Arnheim's Band, which was an *excellent* band. And
we used to hear programs from Mexico. The Baja bands. That
you could hear playing every day. My father would say: '*Listen* to
these trumpet players.' These guys would be double-tonguing
and triple-tonguing like it was going out of style. And I'd be
trying, you know, to imitate them. Through listening. And I
guess that's what got me interested in *all kinds* of music. Because
I was exposed to it all. As a kid, I was exposed to it. Not realizing
that later on it would be an advantage to me.

"And my father would say, 'You listen to Adolphus Cheatham'—they were so formal in those days—'first trumpet with the Cab Calloway Band, if you want to know what a first-trumpet should sound like.' " (Adolphus was the actual first name of the man known to jazz fans as "Doc" Cheatham.) Wilder adds: "I've told this to Doc, but I don't know if he believes me."

After working with local bands, and going on the road with Les Hite, Wilder joined Lionel Hampton's Band (1942–43). He has mixed feelings about his association with Hampton.

"Well, it was a great band. They added me to the band. They had three trumpets and they wanted to add a fourth to the section. When I went in, it was Ernie Royal, Karl George, Joe Newman, and I. So it was nice. And Illinois Jacquet. Dexter Gordon. Ray Perry was playing third alto and violin. Jack McVey was the baritone player. And Marshall Royal was playing lead. It was a tremendous band, an exciting band. That was the probably the youngest black band around, and certainly the swingingest band at that time. So I was kind of lucky to be in there. I played some lead and I played some solos.

"But as far as Lionel, I was never very fond of him. I was disappointed when I found out the kind of a person he was, you know, towards the fellows in the band. He sort of had an attitude towards the fellows in the band that you can't work any place, because there are so few places for black musicians to work, and if you don't like the way I treat you, you're out of a job. It was sort of a reverse slavery in a way. I mean, he was paying the guys very little money, considering what they were earning. Because at that time, we could go 50 miles from one town to the next and the hall would be jammed. People would be fighting to get in. We played in West Virginia, I think a place called Bluefield, West Virginia, or Beckley, and the people were trying so hard to get into the ballroom that they had literally a riot outside. And I think two guys got killed. Just fighting, to try to get in to hear the Lionel Hampton Band. And at that time I was getting $11 a night. And being threatened, if I asked for more, with being fired, you know. So he has never, unfortunately, been one of my favorites. I was with him before I went into the service in '43, and then I went back with him when I came out in '46. I was in the Marine Corps. I became an assistant bandmaster of the

Montford Point Marine Band. Montford Point, in North Carolina, was where they first started with black marines."

Who were the trumpeters Wilder might have liked around that time?

"Oh, Dizzy Gillespie and Charlie Shavers. Louis, of course. Harry James. Billy was up—well, I didn't know Billy Butterfield personally at that time, but Billy was around then. There were a lot of really first-rate players. I liked Dizzy, because I knew Dizzy and I admired him. But I couldn't play like Dizzy. So I was never interested in trying to play like him. But Charlie Shavers was somebody I—and Benny Carter, who at that time was playing trumpet; he was a good trumpet player. But Charlie was the guy—I was fascinated by him. Because he did so many things. Well, first of all, Charlie was with John Kirby. And I grew up with Billy Kyle [Kirby's pianist]. I grew up with Billy's brothers and his sister; they lived around the corner from us. So we always regarded Billy as one of our big celebrities in our neighborhood. And when Billy would come home, sometimes Charlie Shavers would come out to his house. Billy would call up and say, 'Tell Joe to come around; Charlie is here.' And Charlie always encouraged me; he was awfully nice to me. So I was kind of thrilled with him. I was only a teenager at that time, and Charlie was in his 20s. I guess if I had wanted to play like anybody, I would have hoped to have been able to play like him. Which is not possible, either. But it gave us something to shoot for, you know. He was so versatile.

"I came out of the service in '46. I went back with Lionel Hampton, played with him for a short time. I left and I worked with Dizzy Gillespie, in Dizzy's big band. Oh, Dizzy's one of my good buddies—I mean, somebody I really like. I knew Dizzy in Philadelphia. I knew him before most of the guys knew him. I knew him, I guess, before he and Charlie Parker got to know each other. And I knew Charlie in Annapolis, Maryland, in 1942."

Wilder moved on to Jimmie Lunceford. "Oh, that was a great band. Reunald Jones, who played lead with Basie later on, was in the band, and Al Grey. Joe Thomas and Earl Carruthers, of course, were still on reeds. Jimmie was rebuilding the band. I liked Jimmie. Awfully nice. Very intelligent man. I was with

Jimmie in '47, at the time he died. I stayed with the band a while after he died, because Joe Thomas and Eddie Wilcox, they were co-leaders of the band, trying to keep the band together. Then I went with Lucky Millinder." In 1947–48, he worked with Herbie Fields, and then Sam Donahue. "Sam Donahue—it was funny because that band was styled after the Lunceford Band. It was like joining Lunceford's Band again, because they played a lot of Lunceford arrangements, and the style of the band was similar."

By now, though, the big band business was clearly drying up. Wilder was working in Noble Sissle's large house band at the Diamond Horseshoe nightclub in 1949, when he got a call to play trumpet in the pit band of a forthcoming Broadway musical, *Alive and Kicking*. Sissle let Wilder go, since there were almost no black musicians playing in the theaters and it was an important break for him, and took him back when the show closed just seven weeks after it opened. Wilder got hired next to play in the theater orchestra for *Guys and Dolls*, which ran for three years. And that established him in the Broadway orchestra scene.

Why did Wilder want to work in pit orchestras? "Well, because it was just work! And it was steady work. And it was fortunate for me that I decided that I wanted steady work, rather than fame and fortune—or fame without the fortune, because you weren't going to make much of a fortune traveling all over the place, you know. I became, I guess, the first black musician to go out and play lead with a Broadway show. I did *Silk Stockings*, the Cole Porter show, I did *Most Happy Fella*. Both of which I played first trumpet on."

In the meantime, around 1951, Wilder had begun studies at the Manhattan School of Music. He also played principal trumpet with the school's symphony orchestra. He got further practice reading symphonic music with rehearsal orchestras around town.

"I did some concerts with the Municipal Concerts Orchestra with Julius Grossman. And I did Haydn, a couple movements of the Haydn trumpet concerto with the ABC Symphony on TV. And things like that." Wilder states he enjoys playing symphonic music no less than jazz. "If you're playing with a nice group or a nice ensemble, you can enjoy either one of them. Of course, it's kind of exacting if you're doing concert playing."

Joe Wilder. (Photo by Chip Deffaa.)

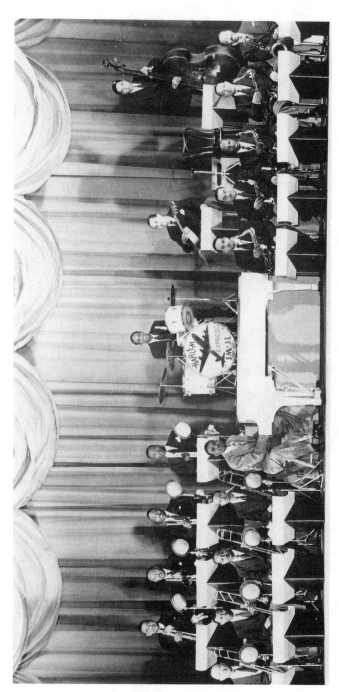

Joe Wilder (top row, third from left), playing trumpet in the Jimmie Lunceford Band. When this photo was taken at the Apollo Theater, not long after Lunceford's death on July 12, 1947, tenor saxist Joe Thomas (front row, second from right) and pianist Eddie Wilcox were serving as co-leaders of the band. (Courtesy of Frank Driggs.)

But Wilder had not given up on jazz. In 1954, he joined Count Basie. "Joe Newman was basically doing all the jazz solos. They needed somebody to help relieve him of the work, you know, so many solos. And that's when they hired me to come in. I wasn't in Basie's Band that long, either—about six months. I get a lot of credit for being there, because I was in that particular band of that era. That was a swinging band. And I liked Count. He was really a nice guy—cheerful."

Did Wilder feel Basie's piano playing contributed a lot to the band?

"Oh sure. The whole thing, you know, was built on the simplicity of his style. And the band, for the most part—it had a certain simplicity. It had a lot of force and all that. But there was a certain simplicity in the Basie Band that differed from any other band, you know, and a certain relaxation about the way they played. And they did swing."

But Wilder realized that at this stage in his life, constant traveling had little appeal for him. He quit the Basie Band to stay in New York, doing Broadway shows, record dates, commercials, and radio and TV work. He may be heard on albums with Sarah Vaughan, Lena Horne, Harry Belafonte, etc. "I like playing behind singers," he says. "Just playing enough to enhance what they're doing and not take advantage of it, you know."

Billy Butterfield, Wilder recalls, helped get him into network radio and TV work. He subbed for major variety and talk shows, and for soap operas, on a non-staff basis, beginning in 1953. In 1956, he became the first and only black musician on staff at ABC. He worked a wide variety of radio and TV shows—everything from soap opera to "Voice of Firestone." Nowadays, Wilder is a regular in orchestras for major specials produced in the East, such as the Tony Awards show and the Miss America Pageant. He has earned a reputation as a dependable, technically proficient, and versatile player.

But his versatility has come at a price. He is not committed to jazz the way a pure jazzman is. And that lack of commitment is often perceived by the listeners. If called upon to solo in a jazz setting, Wilder will play in a wholly professional and appropriate—but often rather impersonal—manner. He does *not* sound like a man burning to tell you his story.

Through the years, he has alternated between legitimate work and jazz, and has played on more than his share of radio and TV commercials, as well. He could play at more jazz festivals, if he wanted to. "But I really don't like to travel," he says. "If my wife were here with me, then it wouldn't bother me. It bothers me when I'm traveling by myself, because then I just get tired of being away from my family."

He has no preference, he makes clear, between playing "serious" music and jazz, so long as he's in good company. And so long as he feels interested. "But it's a psychological thing: If I'm not in the mood, then I would just as soon not touch the horn at all—as far as improvising or going out and doing anything, solo-wise. Playing in a section, it wouldn't make any difference, you know."

1985

Maintaining the Touch

There are some fellows who always sound like they're competing for the title of "world's noisiest drummer." Not Oliver Jackson. He's more apt to draw you in to listen to him, with inventive, subtle playing, than to force you back with bombast. Give Jackson a break where you'd expect most drummers to cut loose and he's likely to surprise you—maybe patting the drumheads low and musically with his hands rather than his drumsticks, or doing a whimsical tap dance on the rims and cymbals with his sticks. He understands dynamics, the use of drama, and he understands *effects.* He can get more different sounds out of a standard Slingerland drumset than most young drummers would probably think possible. But he's always got power in reserve. And when he's got you lulled—pow, he'll break through with the energy he's been keeping under careful control all along.

Jackson's worked with many of the greats: Earl Hines, Charlie Shavers, Erroll Garner, Roy Eldridge, Oscar Peterson, Benny Goodman, Sy Oliver, Lionel Hampton—the list goes on. He's currently a member of George Wein's Newport Jazz Festival All-Stars. He's drummed on more than 300 albums, he says, according to a discography prepared by European admirers. And he's equally comfortable in the drummer's chair of a big band or a small group.

If you ask most drummers to talk about their work, chances are they'll start with terms referring to rhythm and power. They'll talk about the beat they try to lay down, how the drummer is the timekeeper for the band, and how he's got to take charge of the band, drive it along. But if you ask Jackson to talk about his work, he'll tell you first off that he's striving for "a *melodious* sound, a sound that's compatible with whatever I'm playing with."

"My approach to playing the drums," Jackson explains, "is to play them like you're playing an instrument. Like you're playing piano or something. To try and get harmonics with them, with your sound. You know, because you've got four things you're working with: your left hand, your right hand, your left foot, your right foot. So really, you could play four-part harmony there. To approach the drums like a musical instrument. Sonny Greer, playing with the Duke Ellington Orchestra—and I had a chance to play with them myself on occasion—Sonny Greer set the pace. Like the drums are for effects. Not to keep time. It's like in a symphony orchestra. You have a conductor; he keeps the time. And the percussion section is just for effects. It's another voice. It's like another section. Like a reed section or a woodwind section or a brass section. You play and you play for effects, to get certain sounds. In jazz, they always say the drummer keeps time—but everybody is supposed to keep their own time. Sonny Greer's thing was to play drums as effects." And if from time to time you can catch the audience by surprise with the effects that you produce, Jackson adds—so much the better. Otherwise, he states, "drums can become *ponderous*." "Ponderous" is the last word anyone would use to describe Jackson's deft work.

"A lot of drummers," Jackson adds (making it clear from his tone of voice that he is not "a lot of drummers"), "—*beat* their drums. They *beat* 'em!" (He sounds quite put off by the idea.) "That's like beating your old lady. The drums start screaming on you: 'Oh, you're beating me!' You have to always maintain a *touch*."

Jackson's been maintaining the touch, as a professional, for most of his life. Born April 28, 1933, in Detroit, Michigan, Jackson started taking drum lessons when he was 11, decided within a year he'd make drumming his life's work, and began gigging professionally by about age 14.

Why drums, as opposed to any other instrument? "The school system provided music classes. I didn't have any money to buy an instrument, so I started taking drum lessons because you only needed a pad (not drums) to take the lessons," Jackson explains. "I used to go to the Paradise Theater all the time, from when I was nine years old on up. I saw all the big bands there. And all the drummers that were playing. I saw Big Sid [Catlett] with Louis Armstrong, and I saw Gene Krupa (he used to come downtown), and I saw Lionel Hampton many times, and Cozy Cole, and Jo Jones came through with the Basie Band, what have you. I saw Andy Kirk's Band. I saw all the greats.

"I knew right away, after about a year of studying, that I wanted to become a professional musician. Because at that time, Detroit, where I grew up, was like a southern town up north. There was a lot of discrimination going on. And by the time I was 12 years old, I realized then that I could never be a fireman, or I could never be a policeman, or that I could never be a lot of things, even a garbage man, because at that time, black people weren't allowed, didn't have these kind of jobs. Every kid wants to be a fireman or a policeman or something like that, but I realized then—when I was around 12 years old—that these things were not available for me. Because this was even before Jackie Robinson even got into the baseball scene. So I said, my best thing for me to do is just to stick with music, because I saw a way out of the situation that I was in, through music. By seeing all the guys at the Paradise, I said, well at least there is a future in entertainment with me." And there was music in the family, Jackson adds. His father was a chef who also was a part-time musician. His brother, Ali Jackson, was a bass player. (The two brothers periodically worked together until Ali's death in 1987.)

"I started working around Detroit, and playing for the singers and dancers on Hastings Street, which was a big entertainment street—every bar had a band in it—so at 14, I was working at night and going to school during the day," Jackson recalls. "Then I got a gig with Wardell Gray, the tenor saxophone player, at the Bluebird Inn. See, with so many musicians and so many jobs around, all the older cats had to take younger cats. I met Billy Mitchell and Elvin Jones. And Lucky Thompson was there in Detroit. And Doug Watkins, and Barry Harris, Donald Byrd, Kenny Burrell, Tommy Flanagan. We all grew up together around that time. (Thad Jones was already out with bands; he's a little older than we are. But he would come back into town once in a while, and we'd meet him. Hank Jones and Milt Jackson had left Detroit, too. But the melody lingered on, as they say.) I started working around that time with all these type of guys, all over," Jackson says.

"By the time I was in high school, I was working at the Juana Club on Woodward Avenue—they had a lot of dancing girls there—playing shows. Everything was a show, then. Very seldom did you just get a gig, playing in a jazz club. You had to be a well-rounded musician, in order to make a living. Not only play jazz, which was my preference, but also to be able to play for singers and dancers, and to know show business. Nowadays you can't see these things. There's no more cabarets, tap dancers, shake dancers, jugglers, comedians. You had to play for everything. So I got a well-rounded basic playing experience there in Detroit at that time. I was very fortunate.

"One thing about playing shows, you learn how to give of yourself. You're always putting your individual thing in it, but it takes a lot of cooperation and a lot of sacrifice to play for singers and dancers, because usually they're not expert musicians. So you have to bend and learn all the different tricks. Like when you're playing with a tap dancer, you can't keep a strict tempo, because the tap dancer's tempo changes according to what steps that they're doing. Now they'll slow down when they're doing like a buck and wing, and when they're free-styling they'll speed up, back to the regular tempo. So you have to watch, because you have to hit these things, you know, make accents. Then you take some singers, they sing way behind, but you have to still go straight-ahead. Because they'll make up the time, like the way a Billy Eckstine sings. Or a Sarah Vaughan sings. You think that they're out of meter, but it's just—well, little tricks like this mean a lot."

Jackson says he was very fortunate, too, in the formal music education he received growing up. He notes: "We had a symphony orchestra in Detroit, but they performed only 13 weeks out of the year. So all of the members of the symphony had to teach school in order to subsidize themselves. But by them being low on the totem pole and not having tenure, they had to teach in the ghetto schools and in the worst schools. They didn't get the lucrative jobs or the most prominent jobs in Detroit. So consequently, we had very, very good teachers. My percussion teacher in high school was the principal percussionist with the Detroit Symphony. And my theory teacher was the principal bassist with the Detroit Symphony. The head of our music department at Miller High School was a guy named Mr. Goldberg, and he was also like affiliated with the symphony as a librarian and a musician. And Mr. Alvey, my percussion teacher, would take me with him to symphonies. So those of us that really wanted to learn had a great opportunity because we had actual professional musicians who were teaching in school. Nowadays that doesn't happen. Most of the people that are teaching haven't been performers."

Jackson graduated from high school in 1950. But beginning as early as 1948, he spent his summers on the road with bands. "The first year I went on the road, I was about 15, with Candy Johnson and his Peppermint Sticks. We went all over Ohio. And then in the summer of 1950, I went out with Gay Crosse and his Good Humor Six. And we did a tour, Ida Mae Cox was singing. That's the first time I went to the deep South. Gay Crosse had a band that was covering like the Louis Jordan Tympani Five style. John Coltrane and Tommy Turrentine were in the band, too."

One of Jackson's close friends ("we practically grew up together") is drummer Eddie Locke. They both attended Miller High School and they both went on to Wayne State College (today Wayne State University). Around 1952–53, they worked up a two-drummer vaudeville act. They decided to present themselves as all-around entertainers, not just drummers. Drummer Cozy Cole, then touring with Louis Armstrong's All-Stars, gave them pointers as they rehearsed their act. Billed as "Bop and Locke—Versatile Percussionists" (Jackson became "Bop" for the time being), they entertained in clubs, resort hotels, and theaters, off-

and-on for several years. "It was what the agents called then an auditorium act. We sang and we danced and we had platforms built for the drums. We went on a circuit, up in Canada; we even came to the Apollo, later on," Jackson recalls. In between those bookings, the two accepted whatever gigs they could find individually, as jazz drummers. Jackson became a member of Yusef Lateef's group for a couple of years, recording a number of albums with him.

Jackson and Locke moved to New York permanently in 1956. "And at that time," Jackson says, "that was the end of vaudeville and the auditorium acts, like all the live stage shows. And the calypso craze came in, and so there was no work for the type of act that we had." They decided to try and make it just as drummers, rather than as entertainers. (They also took day jobs for the time being, to try and cover expenses in New York. For a year or a year and a half, Jackson worked in a stationary store, his first and only job outside of music.) Legendary drummer (and former Count Basie star) Papa Jo Jones was one who recognized their abilities as drummers right away. Jackson recalls: "Eddie and I were staying in the Alvin Hotel and we ran out of money; we couldn't pay the rent. This was about '56. So Jo Jones let us come and stay with him. We lived with Jo Jones for about three years. And during those three years, Jo turned me on to a lot of gigs," Jackson notes. Jackson was soon thoroughly immersed in New York's midtown jazz scene.

"First I got a job in the Metropole and started subbing for Zutty Singleton," Jackson recalls. "I met Zutty Singleton, George Wettling, Tony Parenti, Charlie Shavers, Coleman Hawkins, Roy Eldridge, Conrad Janis, Joe Muranyi, Cliff Jackson, Claude Hopkins, J. C. Higginbotham, Henry 'Red' Allen, Sol Yaged. . .all these guys I met then. That was like about '57. Ray Bryant was working there. There were a lot of people who worked in the Metropole, everybody came. I met Gene Krupa there. (And Gene was instrumental with me getting with the Slingerland drum company in 1958. He recommended me to the company and I've been with them ever since—I gave an endorsement; they gave me some drums and what-have-you. Gene was one of my favorite people, a great personal friend of mine, and such a nice man.) I

OLIVER JACKSON

worked at the Metropole a couple of years. I got a chance to meet
all those guys and play with all these different type of people,
there and at other places in New York. And Gene Sedric, I met
him, and Buster Bailey (baddest cat on the clarinet that ever
picked it up), Pee Wee Russell, Bobby Hackett, Pee Wee Erwin,
Earl Hines, Erroll Garner, Oscar Peterson, Dorothy Donegan,
Marty Napoleon. I'd be around these kind of people who were
the originators of this kind of music. Jimmy McPartland and Bud
Freeman. And Red Nichols and his Five Pennies—they were on
the same bill with us; I think I did sub with him one night at the
Metropole. I met Buddy Rich there. Everybody was there. And
I started working over at the Embers with Teddy Wilson. Here
in New York, I played all over. I got involved in a lot of studio
work, too, because I could read. I worked at the Roundtable with
Tyree Glenn, and I've worked all over. Even some rock 'n' roll
things up at the Apollo for Earle Warren." (Eddie Locke's career,
it might be noted, similarly blossomed. He too worked the Metropole and other midtown jazz clubs, often with Roy Eldridge
and Coleman Hawkins; he has found steady demand for his
services since the late '50s.)

Jackson notes he learned a great deal in the three years he
lived with Jo Jones. "He's a fabulous percussionist. He knew all
the tricks," Jackson says. "That's all we did was play drums. He's
another kind of teacher. You learn from him by talking. He'd
show you something one time, and it might take you a year to
learn how to do it."

Jackson comments that one thing Jo Jones taught him right
off was that you shouldn't try to use the same drumset for both
small and big bands. And that leads into a discussion of Jackson's
equipment. "I have three sets of drums. When I'm playing with
a large orchestra (like a big band), I'll use—I learned this from
Jo Jones—I'll use like a 22"–24" bass drum, a 16" tom-tom and a
9"x12" tom-tom. That gives you a bigger sound. When I'm playing with different groups, I change the size of the drums. You
know, I have a 22" bass drum, a 20" bass drum, and an 18" bass
drum. According to what I'm doing. (The smaller the group, the
smaller the bass drum.) The bass drum is the heart of everything.
Because there's no way you can sit up in a band or a large

orchestra—I don't care how much electricity they put on it—there's no way you can sit up there with an 18″ bass drum or a 20″ bass drum, and play with a big band. Because they won't be able to *feel* you—not hear you, but they have to be able to *feel* you. Sometimes what I'll do is I'll put a tympani head on the batter side of my bass drum, and that fellow—you could hear that for 30 miles. But what that does is, that makes you get a round sound. And I use no mufflers. Because when you start muffling something—it's like if someone is speaking, and you put cotton in their mouth, then you're going to hear another kind of speech. So I never use mufflers in my drums. I play 'em wide open. But then, you have to always maintain a touch. Because this way, you can play from pianissimo up to triple forte, almost, and still *play* the drums and don't *beat* them. If you play them wide open, then that takes a lot of technique and a lot of control. To control that sound. Because either you can sound too loud or too soft," he notes.

Jackson learned much about maintaining the proper touch as a drummer, he says, during his association with the brilliant trumpeter Charlie Shavers. He was a member of Shavers' quartet (which also included Ray Bryant and Tommy Bryant) from 1959 to 1961. Shavers had originally made his mark in the late '30s and early '40s with his subtle, intriguing work in John Kirby's sextet ("the biggest little band in the land"). The powerhouse side of Shavers' playing came to the fore in his years as star soloist with the Tommy Dorsey Band, in the mid '40s and again in the mid '50s. Shavers' quicksilver changes from the gentlest to the most forceful, impassioned of sounds made a lasting impression on Jackson. "I learned so much from Charlie Shavers," Jackson acknowledges. "What a great musician he was! I learned different dimensions for the drums. You could use more power drumming with a trumpet player than, for example, with a saxophone player. Charlie was very famous for his playing with the John Kirby Orchestra, you know, and he still had that same thing; he was playing in mutes and things. And he knew how to take the trumpet, piano and the bass, and make it sound like about 15 pieces at times, and then make it sound very soft at times. He taught me a lot about dynamics. And clarity with the drums.

Drummer Oliver Jackson solos while alto saxist Norris Turney looks on. (Photo by Chip Deffaa.)

Oliver Jackson drums with George Wein (piano) and Slam Stewart (bass). (Courtesy of Festival Productions.)

Making the drums become like a musical instrument, which they are. Instead of, most people think it's like a disco beat. Drums were for, like, effects. And you don't have to play that loud. (One drum, you know, is enough for 110 musicians.)"

In 1962, Jackson went to Europe and Africa with Buck Clayton. "I did a lot of work with Buck, off-and-on, a lot of recordings for him. He's a great arranger, too. From 1962 to 1964, I was with Lionel Hampton's big band. I went to Africa with him, and then we went out to Las Vegas for about nine weeks, and we went all through the South and Texas, and all over," Jackson recalls. He has frequently returned to work with Hampton for gigs since then. "I always work with Hamp. I go in for a moment or two or something. Last year, I made another tour with Hamp. We did a tour with a quintet (Hamp and four rhythm) and we played with about fourteen of the major symphony orchestras in the United States. And then with the big band again. I did about two months with him—one-nighters—in '84. And I've been to Nice with him a couple of times, and to Europe with him a couple of times. And I played with Benny Goodman's big band, that was in the '60s also, at the time of Freedomland amusement park. And I've been out with Benny and his quartet, too.

"I worked with Earl Hines from about '65 to '70, about five years. Mostly a quartet (with Bill Pemberton, Budd Johnson and myself)—but we also did some things with larger groups, too. Every once in a while we played a festival, and organized a big band. We worked down at the Riverboat a couple of times with a big band, too. In 1967, we went to the Soviet Union. We had, I think, a seven-piece band, with Bobby Donovan on saxophone, Budd Johnson, Bill Pemberton and myself, Michael Zwerin. It was a tremendous success; we were over there for nine weeks, a long time. The people like jazz; they like anything that's western. We played all the big halls. And we also went to a lot of places that no Americans had ever been." Hines' band hit some pretty remote regions of the U.S.S.R., Jackson remembers: ". . . like 150 miles from the Mongolian border, where the Russians look like me. And we went to Mahatchkala—I don't know how you'd spell it; it's not even on the map, unless you get a very detailed map of the Soviet Union. And the people there had never seen black people before. They had to put up the barricades outside the hotel we were staying in, because everybody wanted to come and see us and try and talk to us, and touch you. The kids wanted to touch you to see if the color was going to come off."

Jackson says that Earl Hines and Erroll Garner (whose approach to playing piano, he says, came from Hines') were two musicians he found exceptionally difficult to accompany. Why? "They could play in like two or three different tempos at one time. According to the passages they were playing. The left hand would be in one meter and the right hand would be in another meter, and then you have to watch their pedal technique, because they would hit the sustaining pedal, and notes are ringing here, and that's one tempo going on when he puts that sustaining pedal on, and then this hand is moving, his left hand is moving, maybe playing tenths, and this hand is playing like quarter-note triplets, or sixteenth notes. So you got this whole conglomeration of all these different tempos going on. . . . I used to work with Erroll Garner maybe three, four times a year," Jackson says.

"I worked with Cab Calloway over in Nice one year (in the '70s). We had a big band; I went out with him, all down in Spain and what-have-you." In the early '70s, Jackson periodically subbed in Duke Ellington's Band. "Any time Sam Woodyard would get sick, I'd go in and play a couple days or something. Duke always wanted me in the band, but I was always too busy doing other things.

"Then I worked with Sy Oliver for six years up at the Rainbow Room, in the middle '70s. It was a great, great experience, to work with this gentleman because I learned so much from him about orchestration," Jackson says. (He adds that he occasionally arranges things for groups he takes out under his own leadership, but says he still has much to learn about arranging.)

Jackson notes: "You know, a lot of horn players, if they can't hear one-two-three-four, then they can't play, because that's what they're used to hearing. They're dependent upon the drummer. My professor in school used to make all the horn players—when we rehearsed the orchestra, he rehearsed them without drums, so they would learn how to play without them. The same way when I was with Sy Oliver's band. He used to tell me: 'Oliver,

you don't need to kill yourself, let these cats play by themselves.'
Then once I'd stop playing, the whole thing'd fall apart. Because
everybody's so used to hearing the drums keeping time for them.
He'd make the horns play by themselves, so they'd get used to
keeping their own time.

"I'm fortunate, a lot of people ask for me. People know that
I can do a variety of things," Jackson says. "I got some things to
do with Teddy Wilson later on this year, and with Jay McShann,
and with Dorothy Donegan—I often work with her. I'm going
to England with Ed Polcer's Condon Band and to Senegal with
Aaron Bell. Then I've been working with the Newport Festival
All-Stars, doing a tour in the spring and the fall with them. This'll
be the third year coming up. I've been working with Joe Bushkin
here in New York, maybe six or eight weeks this year. I guess I
work in New York, I would say, no more than about 18–20 weeks
out of the year. The rest of the time I'm traveling. Since 1978,
I've been taking a group over to Europe every year, like in the
spring, under my name. (This past year I took Norris Turney,
and my brother, Ali Jackson, on bass, and Claude Black on piano.
We did a tour with Arnett Cobb and Irvin Stokes. We worked a
couple of clubs over there and did some TV shows and things.
Went all down in Italy.) Then I usually go back over for the Nice
Festival. I've been to every Nice Festival with the exception
of the first one. And then I usually go back and work in Switzerland over the holidays. One year I was in Europe about
four times."

Jackson also has performed in public schools. "I got the
Johns Manville Corporation to sponsor us: Budd Johnson, Bill
Pemberton, Dill Jones, and myself. We were 'the JPJ Quartet'
(Jackson, Pemberton, Johnson and Jones). We made some albums, too. For about four years, we went to schools and gave
performances (not *clinics*), playing all of the places where they
had Johns Manville plants. The educational system is deplorable
in this country when it comes to music. (Well, in general, education.) How can you give a 'clinic' when nobody knows anything
about music, when they don't have a music teacher in the school?
When they don't have a piano in the school? So we were doing
mostly performances in most of the schools. We made a movie

out of it, too. We had our own jet aircraft. We'd go out twice a year with it. We'd go out and play a month or six weeks of schools, and then come back in the spring and do another month and a half. So we were working about three months a year doing that. I would always go into the school library, when we'd get to the school early enough—if they had a library—and there would be nothing under 'jazz.' So the kids, nobody knew who Louis Armstrong was. They knew nothing about jazz, because they're not teaching that."

On records, Jackson has done everything from rock to Latin drumming. He's played New York society weddings. He's even subbed, on occasion, in the Ringling Brothers Circus Orchestra. He enjoys doing a variety of things as a freelancer, and maintains he really has no one favorite kind of music. Jackson says: "When it comes to music, I like anything that's done well. I like Miles Davis. I like avant garde music. I like the fusion music. I like good rock 'n' roll. I like symphonic music. I like pop music. I like all music. If it's done well, it's good. Some people say they only like jazz. That's like saying, 'The only thing I like to eat is chicken.' You have a variety of foods that you like to eat, to drink. So I don't think you have to be monogamous when it comes to music."

Before the interview concludes, Jackson notes with pride: "I have three daughters. One is a lawyer. She lives in International Falls, Minnesota. And I have another daughter who is a psychologist. She teaches at Berkeley. And my youngest daughter is in Syracuse University, getting ready to graduate next May." None had an interest in going into music, he says, nor did he try to encourage them that way.

As for himself, he says, he has no regrets that he chose music—and jazz in particular—for his life's work. He reflects: "Jazz is one of the few professions . . . that the older you get, the more validity you attain. Now most people that are working in the corporate structure, when they get to be my age, they get worried about losing their jobs and everything. . . . I'm 52, and now people are just beginning to recognize who I am, you know!" He laughs. "My career is just beginning."

1985

Like Father, Like Son

These days it's getting hard to avoid Bucky and John Pizzarelli. They've become regulars at the annual Kool Jazz Festival picnic at Waterloo, New Jersey. You'll find them at Dick Gibson's Colorado jazz parties. And in recent years they've been the customary opening act when Benny Goodman's chosen to make concert appearances. They work both separately and together. They keep busy.

But Bucky Pizzarelli likes to tell the story of how he was appearing for the summer with his trio at New York's posh Hotel Pierre several years ago. He had been unable to make the date the night before. And a patron, perhaps a bit inebriated, approached the stand. "You know," the patron informed him, "there was some kid here last night trying to play like you."

The "kid" was John Pizzarelli Jr., now 23, making his New York debut. They no longer ask who "the kid" is. In the last few years, the Pizzarellis have emerged as a formidable and unique combination, appearing in concerts, at festivals, and on television, offering music that is fresh, but clearly rooted in the Swing Era tradition. They are also the only jazz duo using seven-string guitars. Music critic John S. Wilson of *The New York Times* noted as early as 1980, when John was just 20: "Father and son are a close, appreciative team. John Pizzarelli, not surprisingly, has many of the same qualities in his playing as his father and he has developed a technique to such an extent that it is possible, listening but not looking, to confuse the playing of one with the other." Usually, but not always, it is the senior Pizzarelli who plays the lead when they perform, with the younger Pizzarelli backing him up. And so it seemed appropriate that when I visited at their home in Saddle River, New Jersey, Bucky Pizzarelli did most of the talking, while John sometimes plucked notes softly on his guitar, providing a kind of dramatic underscoring to his father's words. They had recently returned from a week's engagement at Charlie's Place, Charlie Byrd's club in Washington, D. C., and had spent the day before in New York taping numbers for their next Stash album.

If the Pizzarellis share a common approach to music, suggests Bucky Pizzarelli (born in Paterson, New Jersey, January 9, 1926), it might be because they shared the same teachers. "I was taught by my uncles, Peter and Bobby Domenick, in Paterson, back in the '30s. And they taught my son in the '70s as well." The Domenicks inculcated Bucky Pizzarelli into the world of professional musicians at an early age. Bobby Domenick played with various name bands. When he played in a group led by Joe Mooney, a blind pianist/singer/composer remembered as a "musician's musician," young Bucky was allowed to sit in with the group. In 1943, Bucky Pizzarelli joined Vaughn Monroe's big band. Except for two years in the service, he stayed with the band for the next decade. He toured with the Three Suns trio in 1956–57.

From the late 1950s into the '60s and '70s, Bucky Pizzarelli found himself in great demand on record dates. As one of the leading session players, he recorded with *everybody*, from Frank Sinatra, Ray Charles, and Andre Kostalanetz, to Dion and the Belmonts and Neil Sedaka, to Carly Simon and Janis Ian. There was also steady work as a staff musician at NBC and ABC, working under such leaders as Skitch Henderson, Doc Severinsen, and Bobby Rosengarden.

But his first love was jazz. He played concerts at Carnegie Hall with George Barnes and Les Paul. He appeared by himself at New York's Town Hall. He recorded albums with some of the greatest names in jazz: duets with stars from the generation before his, such as Stephane Grappelli, Bud Freeman, and Joe Venuti; contemporaries such as Zoot Sims and Buddy Rich; and rising jazzmen of the younger generation such as Butch Miles and Warren Vaché Jr., proving himself a thoughtful, lyrical, articulate player in almost any context. He also gave seminars in jazz guitar at William Paterson College in New Jersey and authored a couple of books on technique.

John Pizzarelli Jr. (born in Paterson, New Jersey, April 6, 1960) got used to his father touring for gigs at an early age. In 1970, '72, '73, and '74, for example, the father made European tours with Benny Goodman. (The father has also played with Goodman at the White House.) In 1977, he played Japan with Zoot Sims. "And of course my father's played on TV a number of times," John notes. "I remember being in Florida and turning on the TV and seeing him on Merv Griffin, a couple thousand miles away."

John played in rock bands in his teen years. But he found himself sometimes sharing with his fellow teen musicians music he liked from an earlier era. For jazzmen had always been frequent houseguests at the Pizzarellis' home. From Slam Stewart, the humming bass player, John had picked up the old number, "Straighten Up and Fly Right." From his father and uncles, he had come to appreciate a slew of mostly forgotten songs composed by the late Joe Mooney.

He enjoyed the music of such contemporary artists as Billy Joel, Kenny Rankin, and Pat Metheny, but his father made sure he also had a thorough grounding in jazz. "He said: 'You have to know what's come before you,' " John explains. And the son soaked up the sounds from old recordings of George Van Eps, of Eddie Lang and Joe Venuti, of Dick McDonough and Carl Kress. And gradually, jazz won out over rock.

"Around 15 or 16, I began to get interested in jazz. Then in college, I had a chance to figure everything out," John notes. By the start of 1980, the father felt his son was good enough to debut with him professionally. They appeared jointly on NBC's "Today Show," have opened for Pearl Bailey, Benny Goodman and others, and have proven a solid club and concert attraction on their own. They work together when they can—at least once a week—while maintaining their own individual careers. Their act offers a diverse assortment of tunes. They'll play "Sutton Mutton," which the father used to play with the late Carl Kress, then perhaps follow it with Chick Corea's challenging "Spain," which the son "discovered" and started playing with a teen jazz group while in high school. John sings songs from the repertoires of Joe Mooney, Michael Franks, and Dave Frishberg. The Pizzarellis' material spans the decades nicely.

I ask them to tell a bit about their instruments and their technique.

Bucky says, "We play on a Benedetto guitar, which is made in Clearwater, Florida, by Bob Benedetto."

"And we use a Duo/Vox Amplifier and LaBella tape-wound strings," John interjects.

"I've been playing a seven-string guitar—the extra string is a low A below E—all along, for the last 13 years, and then John switched over on the spur of the moment; he just picked one up and started playing it," notes Bucky.

"Well in the duo, it gives you a walking bass line, and you don't need any accompaniment of any other sort," says John.

"And you're also able to play in difficult keys," adds Bucky. "You know, D flat, A flat. On the six-string, you run out of good bass notes in those keys. In fact, you can play in any key with a seven string—"

"—comfortably," John finishes the sentence for him.

Bucky continues: "And then, with the seven-string guitar—well, just yesterday, for the album we recorded, we did two Bix Beiderbecke pieces ('In the Dark' and 'In a Mist') that you can't do with two six-string guitars. I always liked George Van Eps, who played a seven-string guitar. And then we finally got to meet him—I guess it was '68. He was showing off the Gretsch guitar, and I went out and bought one. I was doing 'The Tonight Show' and I used it the whole time. And it came in very handy because sometimes you had to back up a singer and the keys don't mean a thing on that guitar. You see, when you're playing a solo on a

six-string guitar, you have to play it around open keys, like D, E
. . . in order to utilize the open string. If you ever want a good
deep bass note once in a while, you play in those keys. But with
a seven-string, you can play in all the keys comfortably. Oh, I'd
recommend it to everybody."

"The hardest part of it is just getting the guitar, really—
trying to get somebody to find one somewhere," John adds.

Bucky explains a bit of their technique. "With two guitars,
the way we play, there's no strumming involved. It's all picking.
And the chords are sustained. The part that John plays, mostly,
is a bass and a chord. But the chord is not strummed."

"It's plucked. I don't use a pick," John says.

"So maybe it sounds like an organ," Bucky suggests.

"When he hits one note, yeah, we got only about five notes
at a time coming out, because it's all individually, you know, the
way we play—it's the notes we pick, though—" John laughs.
"Those great notes. . . . He'll play the melody and we'll work out
a set of changes that works interesting around it. Try to do
something different, with the harmonies.

"Well, the tunes that we do are good, because there's so
many things that you can do with them. We're always thinking
of different ways to play all the arrangements. Instead of just
playing them straight out, we can switch around the harmonies
or the meters, or how I play the chords and he might play
harmonics, if he plays the chords, or if we play chords together.
And that's why it's fun to work together, too, because we're always
changing things."

The Pizzarellis don't rehearse much together, they say. "No.
The form of the song itself is more important than a rehearsal,"
Bucky believes.

"Just so that we know the tune," adds John.

"So once we know the tune," Bucky says, "he knows what he
should do, and then we go into the different colors. We go into
our bag of—let's try this on this, or let's try this sound, or let's
play it slower, and make it a ballad."

"We'll sit down and he'll show me the chords or something,
or what we'll do. We don't rehearse it too much," John says.

"Once we know the form of the song," Bucky reflects, "we can modulate, we can play in almost any key, whatever we want to do with it."

"There's always going to be the night when we finally get it, the way it's going to be," adds John.

Bucky is a great believer in spontaneity. "You see, if you make arrangements, they become slick, and you end up doing it the same way all the time. That's no good. You leave that form. If you get the form down, then you can play with it. Sometimes better things will happen, and sometimes they won't happen. But I'd rather take a chance that way."

Does Bucky have any advice he'd want to offer to young guitar players?

"I think what they overlook sometimes is that it's important more to try to understand the guitar than try to play like a virtuoso guitarist. Because a lot of them get to that level and they don't know what they're doing. They start with the technique and they end up playing too much. They really don't understand what the function of the guitar is, by itself. It can be used with a vocalist, it can be used as a solo instrument, as an accompaniment instrument—but they don't look into those areas. They say, 'Let's just do this with a guitar.' The young players have a lot of technique—" Bucky says.

"All the technique—" affirms John.

"—And no emotion," declares Bucky. "Because they learn these things in school. They learn this mode and that mode. And all of a sudden, one's playing faster than the other. And that's true with all the guitar schools—Berklee—I've never heard so many fast guitar players in my life. Well, I don't consider myself a fast guitar player. But there are so many of them around. . . . It's about learning how to play the guitar in an un-technical manner, you know what I mean?"

"I like the premise here—" John comments.

"A good piano player doesn't show off his technique, but it still comes off," Bucky says. "It's like a writer doesn't have to write a lot of words to tell a story. If you can tell it in one word or two words, it's better than using a paragraph."

John notes: "It's like the first time I heard Tal Farlow play.

BUCKY AND JOHN PIZZARELLI

He played phenomenally. He's all over the place. It wasn't on the par of some of the kids, maybe. He didn't hit every note, and he didn't complete every run but there was such emotion."

"His understanding came across," says Bucky. "For him, it's not technical, the way he plays. That's easy for him. You see, the kids learn this in school, and they become masters of that technique and try to apply that to everything they do."

"You want to put down any more music schools while you're at it?" John asks his dad lightly, adding to me: "He'll get it that way—all that controversial stuff."

Bucky says: "I think all the young guitar players have the same values. They go down the narrow street, and I think what they should do is just broaden their scope, try to listen to somebody that just might be able to show them these un-technical things, and might open some doors in their thinking of what a guitar can do."

What does Bucky credit with having helped make him such a good player?

"When I came back to New York, after I left the road—around 1958, I did a lot of recording sessions. Now I was meeting all the guitar players on these sessions—we were like three and four guitars every session, which was a new thing. Nobody ever used more than one in the old days. But now with the rock 'n' roll scene, one guitar was playing high, another one was playing low, another guy was making a funny sound. And I was sitting next to Tony Mottola, Barry Galbraith, George Barnes. So you got to know what makes them tick, and each guy had his own little thing. Like George Barnes would play one or two notes—if you heard him on the radio, you knew it was George Barnes. I can pick him out today, yet—any record that he's on, I can pick him out. The same with Tony Mottola, Al Caiola. . . . Barry Galbraith's rhythm guitar playing was impeccable—and his jazz interpretations couldn't be any better. You know, there's a way of interpreting a part. And that's what the young guitar players have to look into. Of how these players became so good. And they were all different kinds of players. When you sit next to these people, and you hear the sound that you never heard before, you can absorb those kind of things.

"And it's the same with Freddie Green—there's another great example of the rhythm guitar, who plays with Basie yet. And he's probably the only guitar player—you could take all the guitar schools in America, and I doubt if there are two guys that could ever come out and take Freddie's place in Count Basie's Band. Because they don't train them to do that, number one. There may be a few energetic ones that studied him on the side— what makes Freddie play so great. But that's another way of playing that's completely foreign to the new players—they try to do it with an amplifier. He's the best in his field, doing the best thing he knows how—and he's the only one that can be doing it. And he's still making a living at it. There were great rhythm guitar players, like Allan Reuss, Barry Galbraith, Tony Rizzi, Al Viola.

"When I first started out in Vaughn Monroe's Band, my role was just rhythm guitar. And occasionally a single-note line with the clarinets, or with the piano. A good guitarist would have to carve out his own situation with a band, you know, make himself more useful by doing extra things. Barry Galbraith did that. Barry was with Claude Thornhill, and whenever Claude didn't play, Barry played a lot of chordal things on his guitar, that nobody ever—you know, nobody played that way. George Van Eps did it with Ray Noble's band. If you ever heard some of those old records, you'd be amazed at the stuff that they—at the music that they played, little interludes and endings, and modulations.

"I *did* get a chance to play in Vaughn Monroe's Band. Mostly all the records we made were vocal records for Vaughn, but when we played on a one-nighter, we always played—we used to fake 'Stompin' at the Savoy' and a couple tunes like that, 'Lady Be Good.' And then when we got into a hotel, I would try to do some things for the dinner hour, real soft. That was a good outlet for a guitarist, to improve. That's the whole idea when you're with a band, not to be able just to play the book and get the money and run, but to see what you have to work with, and just make the guitar more useful."

Some of Bucky's best work over the years has been in guitar duo settings. I wondered how, for example, his partnership with George Barnes came about.

Bucky and John Pizzarelli. (Courtesy of the Pizzarellis.)

Bucky and John Pizzarelli, relaxing at home (top photo), and sitting in with Les Paul. (Photos by Chip Deffaa.)

"Well, as we played together in New York, we got to know each other, and we used to play little jobs here and there, weekends. We did a few things with a trio, four and five people. And when I bought the seven-string, George happened to be living here in New Jersey, right up the road. And one night we got together and we got a stack of songs, and we turned the tape machine on. He played the melody and I played the chords. That's exactly how it came about. We played one tune after another. And then the next day or so we listened to the whole reel. And we heard some great sounds in there. It was very exciting, because now we had a nice new rich sound and we decided to form this duet. Aside from the studio jobs we were doing, we would work in a place in New York called The Guitar on 51st Street and 10th Avenue which is no longer. So then we got a good review from the *Times*, and we went to an East Side club. We played the St. Regis for a year. And while we were there, we did a few concerts. That's the best way to do it. If you're going to do concerts, you've got to be playing every night somewhere. One concert we were on with George Benson, Tiny Grimes, Charlie Byrd, Joe Beck and Chuck Wayne, and John McLaughlin. They had a rhythm section for each guitar player, and then when they got to us, they said, 'Who do you want to play?' And we said, 'We don't need anybody, we got our own thing going.' We played so long. A double-jacket album came out and we're on one side of it. We were playing every night, so to go in and do a half hour was nothing. The hard part was picking out about 10 tunes from a repertoire of about 80.

"Then after George and I split—he went with Ruby Braff— Les Paul and I did some things: Carnegie Hall, Town Hall, the Metropolitan Museum, some clubs. Well, Les and I were neighbors. When George left, Les played with me for a week at the St. Regis. (He won't take a job that lasts a week any more— one night and that's it. But it's memorable, I'll tell you, when you do see him.) Playing with him was different from playing with George. Each guitar player puts you into a different bag. I don't care, there's always something different. George had a lot of space in his playing. But Les, once Les got rolling. . ."

Paul is another player that can be recognized from hearing

just a couple of notes. "Yeah, that's what makes them good," Bucky muses.

I wondered if, when Bucky and John became partners, they used material that Bucky had used in his previous duos with Barnes and Paul?

"Not so much the material, but the format is the same. It seems to work," Bucky says.

"We do a little bit of what he did with George Barnes, and we do some Carl Kress and Dick McDonough—the old guitar duets. We do Stephane Grappelli and Django Reinhardt things," adds John.

Bucky likes being able to offer a diverse program. "You have to think of the listener. Material's important. And I think humor, too," he says.

"We've got a lot of humor," notes John, who is responsible for most of it with his bantering between numbers and occasional singing of songs in a wry, self-kidding vein.

Who picks out the tunes they perform?

"He's basically the musical director. If I have any suggestions, he usually has the best way," John says of his father. One thing he likes, he adds, is the flexibility of their act: "There are some of the things that we do the same from night to night, but it never really comes off that way. We'll always throw in a new tune somewhere, or something that's different. And that's why it's fun to work together, too, because we're always changing things, screwing everybody up, somehow. Heh-heh."

What's it like for John, working with his father so often? Is that ever a problem?

"Yeah, actually it was a problem for a while, coming out of college. I'll be 24 in April. But at the beginning it was a little tough. I had trouble separating the person who everybody saw on the stage and who I was off the stage. Just because people always say—you know, when you open for Benny Goodman and stuff, you end up going to these places and you've got to talk to a lot of people. They're always going, 'And your father must be—' and you gotta stay in that persona, you know, and sometimes you don't want to be 'somebody.' Or you don't want to be like, 'Oh

yes, hello, hello, nice to meet you.' You just want to go in the
back room and say, 'I did my thing for you,' you know. It took
me a while to adjust to that. I'm just starting to. It was something
that I had to work out. And still do sometimes. Sometimes you're
not in a good mood, you don't want to have to do that kind of
stuff. But it's not tough in the sense of working with him; it's just
tough sometimes with what people expect from you. On a small
scale, you can sort of understand what the real big stars go
through. The guys who've got to be constantly talking to somebody, or they've got to be on all the time. But it's fun. We just
did two hour-long sets every night for a week at Charlie's Place.
By the end of the week, we were burning. We didn't even rehearse."

"It was a heavy place to play—" says Bucky.

"A top-notch club," affirms John.

"So you've got to be on the ball there," Bucky says.

1984

The team of Bucky and John Pizzarelli, which was quite
enjoyable in 1984, has improved as the rapport between father
and son has deepened, and as John has come into his own as
both a guitarist and entertainer. His playing has become more
muscular and his personal wit has become a real asset to the act.
What started out being largely the father's act (with the son in a
supporting role) has become a true partnership. John's light-
hearted, extroverted singing of such numbers as "I Like Jersey
Best" and "I'm Hip" provides a change of pace from some of his
father's meticulously played, almost crystalline-sounding, intro-
spective guitar features. They can go from an exquisite duo
rendering of Fats Waller's "Jitterbug Waltz"—the individually
plucked notes showering down like gentle rain—to a tongue-in-
cheek (and effective) audience sing-along led by John. They have
recorded albums both together and individually, for such labels
as Stash and Chesky. John may not be the guitarist his father is,
but his ability to communicate with an audience vocally makes

him an engaging performer, and no doubt contributed to his earning a regular spot on WNEW-AM radio in 1986 and winning a Manhattan Association of Cabarets Award in 1989.

Since the death of Benny Goodman on June 13, 1986, the Pizzarellis have regularly featured such Goodman instrumentals as "Goodbye" and "Sing, Sing, Sing" (managing to evoke the feel of the whole Goodman band with their two guitars) in tribute to him. At the 1987 "Jazz in July" festival at New York's 92nd Street "Y," the Pizzarellis were standouts, digging into "Sing, Sing, Sing" with a passion and ferocity that would have been inconceivable in the first few years of their partnership. In addition to their duo work, John has often worked at the New York club J's, leading his own trio. In 1991, he had his first engagement at New York's prestigious Algonquin Hotel and was signed to RCA Novus Records. The latest development in the Pizzarellis' act is its conversion, from time to time, into a trio, with the addition of John's younger brother, Martin, on bass.

Keep It Fresh

"The music that I play, I guess you'd call it an older style, but that's all I know. I'm playing what I like to play and trying to do it my own way. That's all I can do. I wouldn't do something that I didn't feel natural about," says Ken Peplowski.

The music that the 31-year-old Peplowski plays—and plays well—actually encompasses a rather broad range. He can play clarinet comfortably in a fairly traditional style—for he appreciates Jazz Age clarinetists such as Jimmie Noone, Johnny Dodds, and Don Murray—if playing in a small group led by a Jimmy McPartland or an Ed Polcer. He can take the role of Benny Goodman—his first idol on the clarinet—in a big band swing concert. He can pick up his tenor sax to duet with Scott Hamilton on an Irving Berlin ballad, and then switch to alto sax for a more modern number that reminds you he's also greatly appreciated the late bebop saxist Sonny Stitt. He's never tried to copy any musicians he's admired—he's never transcribed solos and memorized them, the way some players do—but he's valued the contributions of, and no doubt absorbed from, a wide range of jazz artists from traditionalists to modernists. At J's, the Manhattan jazz club where he frequently performs (and draws packed houses), he can move from the music of Duke Ellington to that of Cole Porter to that of John Coltrane, and back, and somehow

289

it'll all feel connected and it'll all feel current. Whether he's playing the newer or the older music, he still seeks to tell a story in his own manner, as best he can.

Since signing with Concord Records in 1987, Peplowski has been recording with growing frequency, both as a leader and accompanying musicians and vocalists. He is also becoming an increasingly familiar participant on the jazz festival and party circuit, turning up every place from Odessa, Texas, to Nassau, in the Bahamas, to Nice, France. In 1990, he won the first *JazzTimes* critics' poll as best "emerging talent" on clarinet. His blossoming career had its start, he suggests one afternoon as we chat at his Greenwich Village apartment, in a chance occurrence.

"It was just pure luck that I played the clarinet. It wasn't my choice. I just was given the instrument," notes Peplowski, who was born May 23, 1959, in a suburb of Cleveland, Ohio, called Garfield Heights. "My father, Norbert Peplowski, was an amateur musician who played accordion. One day he brought home a trumpet that was given to him; he tried it out, he didn't like it, and he gave it to my brother, who's two years older than me. My brother started playing the trumpet. The next thing I know, my father gets a clarinet from some relative. He tries to play that, he doesn't like it. I wind up with a clarinet. And I liked it right away. I think I was seven or eight and my brother would be nine or ten. I really took an interest in the instrument. Within about six months, we were studying at this local music store, and we put a band together with some other kids that were at the music store—a polka band, naturally, being the name of Peplowski and living in Cleveland—and we rehearsed and we started working.

"I think my first job was when I was eight or nine and we played at the local library—I still have a picture of this—and it was the first of many misspellings of my name. It said: 'local musicians Ted and Ken Replowski.' I've been playing professionally since then.

"Our band was called the Harmony Kings. Of course, we had matching tasteless shirts and, you know, the whole uniform. We were very popular around the Cleveland area, because we

were a novelty, being this kids' band. We were singing and playing, and we played weddings and dances, things like that, and
even some concerts. We used to go on a local TV show and some
of the radio shows. It was great training, because I was actually
writing arrangements and learning how to improvise. Actually
Polish polka music is very similar to Dixieland jazz in that you
have two trumpets playing in tandem and then you have a clarinet
improvising around it. So it was really great training. It kind of
like forced me—it's like learning how to swim by being thrown
in the water.

"I sat down at the piano at school and taught myself, you
know, where middle C was and I figured out chords, and I used
to write them out by writing out each individual note. I didn't
know that it was a C chord or a C–7, I just knew it by the sound.
Later, I figured out what everything technically was. But it was
really the best training I could think of. And it also taught us to
learn how to play for people, to entertain and to try to get people
to listen. We originally had two trumpets, a clarinet, an accordion,
a bass, and drum. Later that changed into a few different kinds
of bands, you know, and then like more of a wedding-type band,
and then we played rock music and stuff like that.

"But at the same time, I was listening to jazz music. Because
playing an instrument like the clarinet, you tend to listen to other
clarinet players. I remember probably one of my first jazz records
was a Benny Goodman record, which led me into listening to the
big bands. I just started listening to a lot of the big bands. And
they used to come into town—Woody's band, and Stan Kenton,
and even Maynard Ferguson. Benny came into town a lot, with
small groups.

"The next thing that happened, a few years later, after
playing the clarinet, I got a saxophone. And started messing
around with that. And all my life, pretty much most of my training and practicing has been on the clarinet and I find that most
of it transfers over to the saxophone. The first sax I got was a
tenor.

"For some reason, I could always sight-read things pretty
rapidly. So I'd always cheat and not practice my lessons. I would

be learning songs and practicing improvising and messing around at the piano, and then I'd go in and look at my lesson the night before and just come in and tell the guy I'd been practicing diligently when really I'd been working on everything else. Because I loved to just play through songbooks. I'd go through different tunes and learn how to transpose, just because we had to, you know, because we were playing off of C parts. This was when I was around 11, 12. And I worked a lot when I was in elementary school up through high school. We were pretty successful.

"My Dad used to drive us to gigs and set up the equipment, and make sure nobody would beat us up if we didn't play the right requests. It was fun. He didn't play with us—I think by his choice, because he knew he really wasn't good enough. I really look back fondly on those days because it was good music—you know, it really was—like the real, authentic Polish polka bands, there's some great musicians in those bands and it's very intense music. You could play dances that would last for six or seven hours and these people just do not want to go home. They're into the music, they love to dance, and they love to have a good time.

"I learned the tunes from reading them and from records; I'd take them off of records. And then we learned a lot of old standards, too. And we did like mini big band versions of some of the great old standards. And I learned a lot of tunes, because we played for older people and we needed to know those songs. And I've always loved—even now, I love to play for good dancers. I think that's an important ingredient in jazz music—you don't have to specifically play for dancing, but you have to have that feeling, you know, that people can groove to it, can feel the music. That's what I like.

"Almost as soon as I started playing, I knew I wanted to be a professional musician. I just fell in love with music and playing for people and entertaining. Now, that's kind of a bad word, to 'entertain' people. But I enjoy it. I love playing for people and getting a reaction from them."

Benny Goodman was always Peplowski's favorite clarinetist. But the list of musicians Peplowski admired and took some inspiration from is a long one. Who was important to him, besides Goodman?

"I liked [longtime Ellington clarinetist] Jimmy Hamilton a lot. I was really enamored with Duke's Band, right off the bat. And Jimmy Hamilton had a little of a classical kind of a sound, which I always kind of went for. And Jimmie Noone—I really liked him a lot, Edmond Hall. Artie Shaw I really didn't appreciate until later. I listened to him and I liked his sound and everything, but his playing left me cold until much later, when I really started to listen to him again and I said, 'Jeez, this guy, he's really just a completely different kind of player from the Goodman school.' And I really appreciate his playing now. He was his own man completely. And he had phenomenal control of the instrument and he had beautiful sound. And some of his solos— like that 'Stardust' solo will stand out as one of the greatest solos in the history of jazz.

"As I got older—when I was 18 or 19, or into the 20s—I started digging back further, listening to a lot of the older clarinet players. Johnny Dodds. And Don Murray from Bix's band—I like him a lot. And Jimmy Dorsey was a good clarinet player. And Albert Nicholas. I've always been a collector; I guess it's in my system—videotapes, records and everything. So, if I get something that I like, it always gets the wheels turning and then I start saying, 'Well, where does this come from?' And I read liner notes and they bring up somebody else's name and then I have to get that record. So I listen to a lot of the old New Orleans clarinet players and the different schools, you know, and Pee Wee Russell. And Buddy DeFranco, too, I like him."

Peplowski includes among his influences pianists and saxists and singers of various styles. "I listen to a lot of piano players. Like Teddy Wilson, Tatum, Phineas Newborn Jr. I really like a lot. I like the whole range of jazz, really. I like Bud Powell—just incredible, as a composer and a piano player, both. The clarinet has such a wide range—when you hear guys like Teddy Wilson, I mean you can almost play that way on the clarinet, because it's got such an incredible octave range. And I listen to saxophone players like Coleman Hawkins and Lester Young, Stan Getz, Zoot Sims, Charlie Parker. Sonny Stitt was a big guy for me, and later on I got to study with him and hang out with him a lot, which was a real inspiration for me.

"Singers have been a big influence on me, too. I'm a big Frank Sinatra fan. I mean, a big Sinatra fan. I've got tons of rare unreleased tapes and session tapes and videos. I think he's probably one of the greatest artists, period. One way I learn a lot of songs is by hearing the singer do the song, and it gives me the feel for the music. Lester Young said you should learn the lyrics to the songs. I really believe in that. And if you don't know the lyrics, at least know what they're about and know an approximation of the feeling. I love Sinatra. And Rosemary I love. Obviously Billie Holiday. I'm a big fan of Dinah Washington. And Jimmy Rushing. Bing Crosby, you know."

His musical pleasures don't come only from jazz and jazz-influenced performers. "I even listen to some rock music. I'm a big Beatles fan. People like Elvis Presley and Chuck Berry. Again, it comes down to, what I perceive as honest music I like. And it doesn't matter what kind of music it is." He responds to the joy, the vitality, and the feeling in some of the early rock 'n' roll. "That music can swing just as hard as anything."

But by the time he was in his teens, Peplowski's orientation as a player was set firmly towards jazz. "I used to play jazz music in the stage bands in school. Then when my brother started going to college, he used to bring home some of the musicians from the college and we used to jam and then we started playing out in some of the bars around Cleveland with jazz bands, you know, quintets, quartets.[1] When I got into college—Cleveland State—I formed a quartet and we played a lot around Cleveland.

"But I really did not enjoy college," Peplowski notes. "I mainly went there to continue studying with this clarinet teacher that I had through high school who I really liked a lot, Albert Blaser, a great teacher. I was going to college to get a degree in teaching and performance, and I just thought it was a waste of time for me. If you're a performer, you go out there and play.

---

[1] His brother, who plays Top 40-type music in the Cleveland area today, gradually grew more interested in rock.

You don't need a degree. And the best way to learn how to perform is by doing it."

When the first opportunity to leave college and go on the road with a real band came, Peplowski took it. He recalls: "About a year and a half into college, I played a job opposite the Tommy Dorsey Band—a concert in Cleveland with Teddy Wilson, my quartet, and the Tommy Dorsey Band. The leader of the Dorsey Band, Buddy Morrow, heard me and asked me if I wanted to join the band on lead alto. I said yes immediately, because I thought this would be my out, you know. I stayed on that band for about two and a half years.

"Buddy Morrow was a great leader. He taught me a lot about playing lead alto, about playing the saxophone, playing in sections, about responsibility, and discipline. He gave me a big feature spot on clarinet where I could do anything I wanted to do, which he'd never done before in that band. He gave me a lot of feature spots. We also did a record for MCA and he insisted that I have the lion's share of solos—that was on alto.

"He was a great guy. He opened up a lot of doors for me. He always talked me up with people that he knew, put in a good word for me. He tried to get me to lead the Artie Shaw Band. When they were putting the band together, he set up an audition for me at the Willard Alexander agency, thinking that it'd be a good idea to have some unknown young guy lead the band, just like Artie did when he came along. That didn't work, but still, I couldn't believe that he would do that."

It was while Peplowski was touring with the Dorsey Band that he had an opportunity to meet reedman Sonny Stitt. "He was always a big idol of mine. I was just knocked out by both his tenor and alto—and even baritone on some early records. And the fact that he had a unique style on both instruments, which I tried to do on the tenor and clarinet. He sounded different on both instruments, like he approached them differently; he didn't sound like a doubler. I heard him many times in my life. And because of his personal misfortunes, he would have a different mouthpiece, a different horn every single time I saw him, because he would pawn one or something got stolen. But he always sounded the same. And that impressed me. He always had this standard. And he always used pick-up rhythm sections, but he always had this high level of playing.

"Anyway, the Dorsey Band was at a Chicago hotel that a lot of musicians stayed at and we found out Sonny Stitt was there. So I just went downstairs and I got his room number and knocked on his door, about noon. He opened the door and he was in his pajamas, and I'm stuttering out, 'Gee, Mr. Stitt, I play with the Tommy Dorsey Band, could I possibly get together with you for some lessons?' He says, 'Oh, bring your horn down.' So we ended up spending the whole day together, about eight, ten hours. Like he'd have me play a tune and then he'd get out his horn and play back at me, and just try to show me things—he really couldn't put things into words as much as he could just demonstrate. But he was so positive and reinforcing.

"I asked him a lot of questions about his life, like how could he play with different rhythm sections, didn't it bother him to play with a bad rhythm section? He was playing with a bad rhythm section there in Chicago. And he said, 'Well, if you can hook up with one person on the bandstand, hook up with that person and block everybody else out. If you can't hook up with anybody, you play for yourself, like we're playing in the room. This way, the bottom line is, if you're at 100% and you're playing for yourself and you're being completely honest with yourself and you're making the best music you can make, that's all that matters. If you make yourself happy, you know you've done the job. If you're playing with a good rhythm section, then you can make music with them. Otherwise you can still play good music, just by doing it like we're doing in the room.'

"He'd gotten a lot of knocks over the years for being a Bird imitator—which I never thought he was, I always could tell the difference—and I asked him about that. He said: 'How could this be possible? We both came up at the same time and when we heard each other, we were amazed that we sounded so much alike.' I mean, there's no question he was influenced by Bird. But he said, 'Look, it doesn't matter what all these other people say when they put you down, because they're not musicians, and if you know you're being completely honest with yourself and playing the way that you want to play and you're being yourself, then that's the important thing. Nothing else really matters. Then you'll be happy with your own life.' And that really made such a strong impression with me. And that's my bottom line for myself. Not to get corny or anything, but I think if there's one positive thing I can say about my playing, it's that I try to be honest. And I try to give something of myself.

"And then we were watching TV and he said, 'You know, you can get music everywhere, out of everything. It all goes into your horn.' And I remember that there were some Olympics or some kind of sporting event on, and there were some weightlifters. He says, 'You see those guys? That's music.' Later on we were walking around the street and there's like guys, a bum laying on the street, and he says, 'See that? That's music. See that guy over there? That's music. It all goes into your horn.' It was very inspirational.

"And then later on, once in a while in my travels we'd hook up again. And the last time I saw him was at a concert at Avery Fisher Hall, and he had a big patch on his throat and it turned out he had cancer. He died just a couple of months later, I think. But he was playing great, right up to the end."

After a couple of years in the Dorsey Band, Peplowski felt ready to take on new challenges. "When it came time for me to think about leaving—it was a very hard decision because Buddy and I had gotten very close—I came up to him and I said, 'Buddy, I really feel like there's no more I can do in this band.' He said, 'Well, basically think of your career as a series of plateaus and if you find yourself moving in the same direction and you're stagnant, then it's time to move on to the next plateau. So I would tell you to leave.' Which was a great thing. He said, 'You should go to New York.'

"We'd played in New York a lot and the first time I came to New York City, I loved the town. If you're a musician, I don't care where you live, you know that New York City is one of the music centers of the world. So I had this dream about coming here anyway. And when I left the band, I had this set as my goal, to move here. I took a job with a road company of *Annie* for eight months because it paid real good and I just wanted to make some money, save up some money and move here. So I did that for eight months. It drove me nuts, you know, playing whole notes, the same music over and over. I mean, we were sick of this show about three days into it. And it was a really wild touring company, too. All I can say is it's allegedly this wholesome family entertainment. But the excesses on this band and the touring company were like the worst rock 'n' roll stories you could possibly hear. Everything was going on in this company, because everybody was bored out of their gourds. So I did that for eight months and then I ended up subletting an apartment in New York from one of the actresses."

Peplowski drove to New York from Cleveland with a car full of furniture. "The apartment was on Ninth Avenue between 49th and 48th, and the day I moved to New York was the day of the Ninth Avenue Street Fair. Welcome to New York! I had to park blocks away. I paid a guy like $40 to watch everything. I moved it piece by piece to a fourth-floor walkup. And then, probably two weeks later, someone smashed in all the windows in my car.

"I moved around a few other times and I've been down here [in Greenwich Village] for about five years. And I love this neighborhood. This is really nice and quiet.

"When I first came to New York around 1981, I only knew a couple of people. There was a guy who played on the Dorsey Band with me, Mark Lopeman, a saxophone player. I called him up and said, 'Is there anything you can give me?' So he recommended me as a sub on a big band out in Long Island he was playing with. And from that, I just got some other jobs and more and more jobs, just by word of mouth.

"Because I played clarinet, I got a lot of Dixieland calls when I first came here and people thought of me as a traditional player, which is kind of a mistaken idea. Not that I mind it—because I love that kind of jazz, too—but I like to play the whole range. Max Kaminsky called me for a whole bunch of jobs. And Jimmy McPartland—I did a nice cruise with him, to Bermuda, with Bobby Pring and Carol Britto. And Ed Polcer, as soon as he heard about me, he was very nice to me. He called me for some subs at Condon's and then gave me a lot of work after that. He really recommended me to a lot of people—which he still does. He's really into helping out people. I was doing a lot of that kind of work, which I was glad to be able to do, but at the same time I wanted to move into some of the other things.

"I had a great time playing at this organ room in Freeport, a place called Mr. Hicks. It was tenor, organ and drums, and they had some great organ players that were coming there. Bobby Forrester played there a lot, a guy named Reuben Wilson who did some records for Blue Note, and some other people. Roy Haynes would drop in sometimes. That was a great place. It was an all-black club and sometimes I was the only white guy in there, but you never felt any racial—never any problems. It was a real good feeling there, and real hard-driving music. You played from ten until two or three.

"And I started subbing on some big bands and getting better quality jobs. I mean, some studio calls, you know, for movies and commercials and things like that. And I started playing with Leon Redbone. I was on the road with him, on and off, for about three years. We'd go out for two months and then I'd be back in New York for a couple months. He'd take unusual combinations of musicians on the road. Sometimes there'd be cornet, myself, Redbone playing acoustic guitar, and drums—no bass. Other times we'd have bass or bass saxophone, drums, piano. You know, he's used everything. Sometimes he's got a band with a steel guitar, cornet, and himself. But I enjoyed working with him, because he's a very interesting guy, musically and personally, and he gets into a lot of different styles and kinds of music. And he pretty much plays and sings by instinct. He doesn't really have much formal training. So it's like playing with some of the old blues guys where you could play an 11-bar blues or a 13-bar blues, instead of a 12-bar. So you're always keeping your ears open. Or we'd go in and do some movie work, we'd just make everything up from scratch. And I would end up making up horn parts and just overdubbing on different instruments, one after another, with no music. I like challenges like that. And I like to be thrust into a high-pressure situation sometimes. Redbone lives out in Pennsylvania. And he listens to a lot of different kinds of music, from like old opera singers to old vaudeville singers and minstrel shows, and a lot of different kinds of ethnic musics. And he really loves old jazz and he loves Jelly Roll Morton and all the old blues guys. Now I don't travel with him any more because I just got tired of being on the road. But I still work with him every now and then around New York.

"I got recommended to him maybe through Vince Giordano, because I played in Vince's band for about a year and a half, two years, and Vince was also doing work for Redbone. I'm not really sure. I was doing all this freelance work and playing with some big bands. Loren Schoenberg—I met a lot of people through his band, actually—and Dean Pratt, Bill Kinslow, Bill Conway's band, Swing Express—I still play in that band. There were a lot of rehearsal bands around New York.

"I was doing all these different kinds of jobs and everything, and Loren's whole band got auditioned by Benny Goodman. Benny loved the band and hired us; we were essentially his last big band. It was a working band and we rehearsed all the time and it became a really good band, a very tight band. Of course, he fired Loren pretty soon after, and some of the other people, but there was a core group of people that he kept on. I think just about everybody got fired once. Except somehow I was lucky, I squeaked by.

"The first rehearsal, Benny didn't show up and we thought he wasn't going to come. So I was playing his parts. Now I'm playing with my eyes closed, and all of a sudden I felt the entire band change. And I knew he was in the room. And I opened my eyes and I know he's right in back of me. So of course I couldn't play at all, you know, from that point. But he said, 'Oh, you play a good clarinet.'

"Benny and I hit it off very well. He called me up just about every day, asked me for advice, because he'd always be firing the drummer and he wanted to hire another guy. And I ended up just making a big list for him of about all the musicians left that I knew, so he could just consult that and call them. And we had lunch a few times. He sent me flowers when I got married. Christmas presents, things like that. We really liked each other.

"You know, people talk about his personality and everything. And now, it's in fashion to say what a terrible guy he was and everything. But with our band, I think most of the people that played for him have very good feelings about him.

"I wasn't intimidated by him because I respected him as a musician, but I wanted to play for him and I wanted to make music with him; and to make the best music you can, you have to be relaxed, and you have to consider yourself on the same level as the other person, whether you are or not. So I think he appreciated that. And he in turn respected us and he had big plans for the band. He wanted to do a record of all Fletcher Henderson charts that had never been recorded before. He was very excited about this band.

"When he died [on June 13, 1986], we had a year's worth of gigs lined up and they all wanted us to keep it going, to make some money. We just got together and we said, 'No, we're not going to do that.' We did one last job as a final tribute to him, like a month or two after he died, and we said that's going to be it. We didn't want to make a living off of his name. I feel so strongly about ghost bands and not making a living off of somebody else's name.

"I think if you want to do a tribute to somebody, the best thing to do is to just say, 'Listen, this person has been a big influence on my music and everything,' and just carry on in your own way. That's the best tribute you can do. Or do a concert where you play tunes associated with him but do them in your own fashion. Because otherwise it's like playing dress-up or something. It's treating the music as a dead music. It's putting it under glass. It's treating it like classical music," Peplowski says. "And the whole thing about jazz is that it keeps revitalizing itself. It keeps changing.

"I have the same problem with a lot of these repertory bands. I think in a lot of cases they put on boring concerts because everybody's trying to play the same solos as the record. And it's never going to be as good as that. And then where do you draw the line? Do you crack the same notes that Bix cracked or do you fix them or what do you do? I think it does a lot more service to the music to have a bunch of younger guys playing in that style and doing it their own way. And that's what's going to carry the music on. There are ways to continue it without having it note for note just like the record. I'd rather go listen to the record. At least that's fresh, you know. But to sit there and say, 'Well, Gene Krupa did this; I want you to do this, and play in this style.' It can't possibly be as good as the original. That's like remaking a classic Laurel and Hardy movie or something. Really. Can you imagine that? Or *Casablanca*—let's do it over again." Peplowski bristles at reviewers who write that he sounds just like Goodman. "If they hear a clarinet player with a good quote unquote classical sound, good technique and time, they automatically bring in the name Benny Goodman. But I don't think I sound like him and I've never tried to, because there's one Benny Goodman. There's one of everybody, and to me it does a disservice to somebody to cheapen their image by imitating them. I wouldn't want to be known as a Goodman imitator—and there are a lot of them out there. I even stay away from his repertoire, because you play 'Avalon' or 'Memories of You' and immediately people think of him. Unless somebody really wants to hear it or just on impulse I feel like playing the song."

When he practices clarinet, Peplowski mostly practices classical music, which allows him to cover the entire range of the instrument and gives him harmonic ideas he can use in his jazz improvising. He is not a great one for practicing, he admits; he feels he gets to play the clarinet plenty on the job. "And I think that it's important to have a life. If your music is supposed to be an extension of yourself, then it's good to have a life to put into the music."

Peplowski made records as a sideman with various leaders, from Redbone and Schoenberg on down. But finding a record company that would give him his first exposure as a leader—so essential to establishing one's reputation as a jazz musician—was not easy, he recalls. He was thinking of paying to put out an album himself, just to have something of his work on the market. One company to which he sent a demo tape gave him the run-around, which was frustrating. "The owner sent me back a letter saying he was interested—and then I couldn't get through to

Ken Peplowski. (Courtesy of Concord Records.)

Peplowski gained big band experience in the Benny Goodman Orchestra (top photo) and in the Tommy Dorsey Orchestra led by Buddy Morrow. The bottom photo, taken aboard the Dorsey Band bus, shows Peplowski, bassist Tom McLaren, and trombonist Phil Sims betting on a kiddie racing game Peplowski had bought to pass time on the road. (Courtesy of K. Peplowski.)

304

Peplowski plays with clarinetist Kenny Davern (top photo), and with cornetist Scott Black and singer/guitarist Leon Redbone (bottom). (Courtesy of K. Peplowski.)

Peplowski plays at the 1990 Bahamas Jazz Festival (top photo), and talks about jazz with Long Island school children in the bottom photo. (Courtesy of K. Peplowski.)

him! But then after I got signed by Concord Records and my first album was in the top 20 of the *JazzTimes* national jazz airplay charts, he saw that and said, 'Ah, geez, now I'm kicking myself.' And then I had some bites from his company and from other companies. You know, one company wanted to put out the demo tape I had sent them! And I just turned them all down because I'd rather be with a company where the people care about every single release. And Concord does. It's like a family there. [Concord president] Carl Jefferson has done a lot for me, and he really lets me do the records the way I want to do. He trusts me. And as far as I'm concerned, as long as he wants me on the label, I'll be there."

How did Peplowski wind up on Concord? "I was a sideman on Dan Barrett's first record for Concord, *Strictly Instrumental*. Carl was there producing and he had heard about me from Warren [Vaché] and Scott [Hamilton]. They had both recommended me to him. I gave him a demo tape that I'd made. He listened to it on the plane [flying back to California from New York]. He called me up the next day. He had me fly out there to talk to him. We had a real good meeting and we hit it off. And we just re-signed for another three years. I've done three records as a soloist so far: *Double Exposure, Sonny Side,* and *Mr. Gentle and Mr. Cool.* And then I did a lot of records as a sideman, with Hank Jones, George Shearing, Mel Tormé, and Susannah McCorkle. And I did a Peggy Lee record—all unpublished Harold Arlen tunes—that I understand is going to come out pretty soon."

On his newest release, *Mr. Gentle and Mr. Cool,* Peplowski is joined by Hank Jones, Bucky Pizzarelli, Frank Tate, Alan Dawson, and, on two tracks, Scott Hamilton. (He says he tries to follow advice given him by Buddy Morrow: "Always play with people better than yourself, so you can play up to their level instead of being complacent.") Peplowski notes: "We did the whole session in maybe five hours. Everything was one or two takes. I never overdub or do edits or any of that stuff. I think a problem with a lot of commercial records is they sound so sanitized and cleaned up and everything. Listen to any old record that you like—Louis Armstrong, Benny, Charlie Parker, anybody— there's mistakes all over the place. I like those rough edges. That's why people like jazz, because everybody's making things up on the spot; they don't know what's going to happen. And you're bound to make mistakes in that kind of music. But that's the fun of it, seeing how you can paint yourself out of these corners.

"Like we did a tune, 'You Do Something to Me.' I just said to Alan Dawson, 'You start it off. I'm going to come in, just improvise the first chorus, you and me; I don't know how it's going to turn out, and we're going to end it the same way, with just drums and clarinet.' It's a one-take tune and it's a very funny ending because we both didn't know how to get out of it. And he actually winds up playing with his hands because he dropped the sticks. And I played a funny thing at the end, and everybody laughed but I kept it in. If people think it's an arrangement, it's not. All my idea was, was that it'd be drums and clarinet at the beginning and at the end, and I didn't play the melody until somewhere around the last chorus. We had no idea how it was going to turn out. And there's no way you could do that again or fix things. You just leave all that stuff in. And I think people can hear that in a record. They still, hopefully, like that freshness.

"Even the sound sometimes on records is so clean it drives me nuts. Everybody's miked separately and in a booth. I asked the engineer to have us all in the same room on these records because that's the way the music is. When you go to a club, you don't hear five guys in separate booths; you don't listen through headphones. I want it to sound like there's a band playing in front of you, together, in a room with sound to it."

Peplowski is concerned about the future of jazz. Jazz would be a lot more popular, he believes, if younger people simply got more chances to hear it, but he feels they're being brainwashed into thinking Top 40 is all there is. "You turn on the radio and you've got one jazz station that's got bad reception, you know, and everything else is Top 40 or talk radio," he notes. "The whole concept of Top 40 and TV now is to appeal to the lowest common denominator of people. If you give somebody the same thing over and over, pretty soon they'll accept it, and after a while, they'll actually like it, like junk food, and then you don't have an appreciation for the other things. Jazz requires participation on

308

the audience's part. It requires them to think a little, and it requires them to kind of step into the artists' shoes. It's not music that hits you over the head, you know. But one thing I find is that if we get to the kids early, if we go into an elementary school or something, they love the music, because it's so much unlike anything they've heard. What other kind of music do people just make things up from beginning to end and it's never played the same way twice? There's nothing else like it."

While he appreciates some of the classic rock performers and groups (saying, for example, that the Beatles' creations showed "a very high level of creativity—everything they did was different"), he feels that too much of today's rock music "is calculated and thought out and commercialized; all the emotion has been drained from it. It's like people sitting around a board room deciding what factors to put into the song, to make it sound like the last one." He has the same complaint with a lot of jazz fusion music. While he's admired some fusion groups ("the Crusaders would get a funky sound and it'd be loose and creative"), all too often, he notes, "there's no looseness in that kind of music. If it's not a drum machine, it's the drummer trying to sound like a drum machine. And I don't care what anybody says, it's not natural—you don't walk that way, you don't breathe that way. And music is meant to shift a little, the time is meant to go back and forth a little. We're not precise people, so why should the music be that way? So that's why I don't listen to much current rock or jazz. There are still some people out there that are very creative. Sonny Rollins is just really creative. And Stan Getz, I heard his *Anniversary* album and I was just blown away by that. But a lot of this stuff, it just bores me to tears.

"Classical music, now, has also been drained of a lot of its emotion. The schools that they have now, they just teach you note by note and measure by measure, and they forget that you're still supposed to be playing the song. And it's supposed to have a lift to it. You're telling a story, you know. But that's my main beef about a lot of the more modern music.

"It's like the Emperor's clothes, that story all over again. These people go out to these clubs and listen to this music and they tell themselves, 'Oh we're listening to jazz and how great it is.' But let's face it, it's boring. It's not exciting music and that's why it's dying out."

He worries about the future audience for good mainstream jazz. "In this country, the ages of the audiences, they're getting older and older, the average age of the jazz audience for concerts and these jazz festivals and parties. In Europe, it's not really the case. You still see a lot of younger people over there. And I don't know why that is.

"A lot of the jazz parties have an elitist attitude where it's invitation-only and it costs a lot of money to get in, and that automatically excludes younger people. And I've been really trying to get some of these people to have like a special deal for students. Or if they've got a few empty tables, why not invite the local high school kids to come in for free? So I'm working on that, and there's a few other musicians that feel this way. Like we almost have to be activists now, in addition to musicians, for our own good. I've been doing some arts and education things. I did some things for the International Art of Jazz. And it's not just because I want to help the kids, although I enjoy that, it's for my own selfish reasons, too—that's the next audience.

"The only thing we can hope for in music is that people will just get tired of all this computerized stuff. That they'll get bored with it and, if anything, they'll turn back to jazz music just because it's a novelty to them; it's something different. We're starting to see a little bit of that. Like the younger people with money will go out to clubs or hire a jazz band for a private party. Right now a lot of them don't even bother to listen. There's some clubs in New York where the people just talk the whole time and then they tell each other, 'Gee, what a great club this is and what a great band.' But that's OK, as long as they keep coming and maybe a few of them will start to listen," Peplowski says. "Maybe things will turn around."

1990

"I Loved Doing So Many Different Things . . ."

It seemed extraordinarily apt to me that Dick Hyman was the musician chosen to score Woody Allen's motion picture *Zelig*. *Zelig,* you'll recall, told the story of a fellow whose features and personality kept changing to fit whatever context he was in. In a gathering of doctors, Leonard Zelig would become another doctor. In Chinatown, he would somehow become oriental. He kept turning up in expected places in unexpected guises. People would look at newsreel footage shot as far away as Germany, and lo and behold—there, once again, would be Zelig.

Hyman, who works regularly on Woody Allen's films, was hired, of course, because of his consummate professionalism. What made his participation in this film so apt, however, is that he's as close to a musical counterpart to Leonard Zelig as we're ever to find. He turns up seemingly everywhere, his musical style changing to fit the context.

I remember going to a Benny Goodman big band rehearsal a couple of days before the taping of Goodman's "Let's Dance" PBS-TV special. Goodman couldn't make that rehearsal. Who directed the band in Goodman's absence (sounding as if he had grown up playing those classic Fletcher Henderson swing arrangements)? Dick Hyman. Hyman has conscientiously re-created on record the music of James P. Johnson, Fats Waller, and

Jelly Roll Morton. Yet he also turns up on rock 'n' roll records. He has played on literally thousands of records of widely varied genres. In his frequent appearances as a solo pianist at the New York jazz club J's, he'll accommodate requests whether they're for numbers by Bix Beiderbecke or Thad Jones, two disparate composers whose music he handles quite sensitively. Although he may be best known for his work in traditional veins (he produces an annual jazz festival at New York's 92nd Street "Y" celebrating "hot jazz, ragtime, oldtime, and blues"), Hyman was also the first person to make a pop recording on Moog synthesizer ("The Minotaur" in 1969). He has publicly performed serious music by Copland, the Schumann piano quintet, and Gershwin's *Rhapsody in Blue*, not to mention his own piano concerto. Under the pseudonym of "Knuckles O'Toole," he's done honky-tonk piano albums. He'll sometimes pay tribute in concert to varied jazz piano greats such as Teddy Wilson, Earl Hines, Art Tatum, and Bill Evans by playing a single number in the readily recognizable styles of one master after another. In the film *Scott Joplin, King of Ragtime,* Hyman not only stood in for Joplin on the soundtrack, but also for every other pianist seen and heard in the picture! And if you check out the only known film footage of bebop giant Charlie Parker, there on piano—could Leonard Zelig have pulled it off any better?—is the ubiquitous Dick Hyman. He defies categorization. In his spacious midtown Manhattan apartment, Hyman reflected one afternoon on the development of his wide-ranging career.

"My big brother introduced me to what we now call classic jazz at a very tender age. I was about 11 or 12," says Hyman, who was born in New York City on March 8, 1927. He grew up in Mount Vernon, New York. "I remember the first records my brother brought home. They were 'Singin' the Blues'—and on the other side of that silver Brunswick by Frankie Trumbauer was 'I'm Comin' Virginia'—and a Bix and his Gang reissue of 'Somebody Stole My Gal' and 'Rhythm King.' " Those four reissued Beiderbecke and Trumbauer sides (recorded in 1927 and '28, truly peak moments in early jazz) fascinated young Hyman, who then played both clarinet and piano. He eventually came to focus exclusively on piano, but in his youth both instruments lured him.

"When I was a kid, I used to play clarinet along with records for hours on end. So I got to know all kinds of classic jazz very well—strangely enough, from the point of view of a clarinetist. I could mimic Johnny Dodds and Don Murray and Frank Tesche-macher and people like that very well at that time. I just loved to play clarinet along with those solos. But now that I look back on it, it was very educational. Because when you play over and over again with the concentration that only a very young person—or particularly a very young person—can give something, you really learn things. And I learned Louis Armstrong and I learned Bix Beiderbecke and I learned all the clarinetists. I learned the pianists, too. But you couldn't play piano along with my little phonograph too well. The piano was too loud. The phonographs weren't very loud in those days. So the piano developed some-what differently—not from playing along with the records, but from absorbing. This process of learning also included Fats Wal-ler records and Joe Sullivan piano solos. And particularly, I had the universal experience of being introduced to Art Tatum and his stunning records of 'Tiger Rag' and 'Sweet Lorraine' and all of those, at the same tender age. And also in my brother's collec-tion were old boogie woogie records: Pinetop Smith, Meade Lux Lewis, Montana Taylor, Albert Ammons; all the Solo Art records and the Hot Record Society reissues, and all of that stuff.

"All of this was happening to me in the late '30s and through the '40s." Hyman shows me a copy of the *Hot Jazz Discography* from 1938. "My brother was indoctrinating me. I knew every-thing. I still know an amazing amount of stuff from that book," he says, such as all of the personnel changes in the Fletcher Henderson Orchestra, to give one example. "I went to college in 1943 or '44, graduated in 1948. I was in the service for a year during that time."

Hyman was certain from the time he was a student at Colum-bia University that he would make music his career. "I could have gone on the road with bands at that time, but my parents very correctly insisted I stay in college and graduate. There was one point where I could have gone on the road with Buddy Morrow's

Band. All the bands were rehearsing at Nola's [Studio], which was on Broadway and 51st Street. It was very seductive but I didn't go with them. And the funny thing was that later on I got to know Buddy very well and worked with him in the studios. So it wasn't necessary for me to go on the road and not finish college in order to get to know him."

Hyman played in bands throughout college. "We were doing a lot of things on WKCR, which at that time was a campus radio station that—strange to understand—didn't broadcast through the airwaves; it was broadcast over the radiator pipes around the campus, through some system that I've never quite understood. I had a record show then, from time to time. Also we had jam sessions; we got people up to play with us. I remember Willie the Lion Smith came up one night. And Bob Wilber, who was a year or so younger than I was. We even have some acetate recordings of that stuff. We have a living room jam session with some of those people. I wasn't a member of the Scarsdale gang [that Wilber was a member of]—their pianist was Dick Wellstood— but I knew those guys; we were around the same age and I was friendly with Eddie Phyfe, who was their drummer. And there were a couple of memorable sessions at WKCR.

"My parents didn't object to my becoming a musician. My uncle, Anton Rovinsky, who was a concert pianist, became my teacher. I studied with him the most seriously that I studied with any piano teachers. After I got out of the service, I put in some valuable time with him. He was a recitalist of some reputation in the 1920s and '30s and mostly concentrated on teaching thereafter. I never saw myself as a classical pianist. I was always a jazz player, but I needed to study classical in order to improve my playing in general. So that was valuable time.

"And I won a contest on WOV, a jazz piano scholarship, and I studied with Teddy Wilson. That was when I was in college. He was and is one of my idols. And the other, of course, is Art Tatum. Other people I liked back then included Johnny Guarnieri, Art Hodes, James P. Johnson. Occasionally I went to a club downtown called the Pied Piper, to hear James P. Johnson and Willie the Lion Smith, who were both playing there—one of them with Max Kaminsky's Band, and the other at intermission, as they chose. And I got to know the Lion a little bit. He liked to acquire proteges. And I think I became almost a protege for a while. I remember going up to his apartment in Harlem. And then I remember he brought me down to, I guess it was to NBC, and had me play for somebody. I was probably in my first year in college, 17 or so. Well, it was all marvelous. But what was even more marvelous is that I was fortunate enough to get to know and work with all of these idols of mine later on, on a professionally equal basis. I mean, I now know Benny Goodman and Art Hodes; James P. of course passed on. I was very sorry when Johnny Guarnieri passed away. I got to know him early on in the '50s, and later toward the end of his life I got in touch with him again, when he had moved to California. And he even wrote and dedicated to me one of those pieces that I play now, 'The Virtuoso Rag.' So I guess that's the most satisfying thing. To be playing with the people who you grew up idolizing. That's the greatest privilege."

Hyman didn't put himself in any one musical camp. He found he could appreciate both older and newer forms of jazz. "Well, that was true then and it's true now." he notes. "Bebop came along pretty much when I was in the navy, which was in 1945. And I remember hearing those records, the first Dizzy and Bird records, in 1945. And we were beginning to play that way, too." Within a half-dozen years after his graduation from college, Hyman played at one point or another with such renowned swing musicians as Benny Goodman and Red Norvo, and such leading beboppers as Charlie Parker and Dizzy Gillespie.

"You know the film I made with Charlie Parker? I opened Birdland. And I was definitely a bebopper. I certainly was. But on the other hand, I had hung around with guys like Bob Wilber and Johnny Glasel, the Scarsdale pack. I was, I would say, on the edge of that gang. I was also a Westchesterite. So I was familiar with the Eddie Condon music. And I always had a big record collection, which I still have here, as you can see.

"When I went into Birdland, I actually went in with Max Kaminsky's [traditional jazz] band. They were putting on a broad spectrum of jazz presentation for the opening show at Birdland. There's a poster that I'll show you, advertising the opening show at Birdland with Charlie Parker. Bill Williams was the host. And Max Kaminsky's Dixieland was one band; Hot Lips Page, Stan Getz, Harry Belafonte were other people. That's how I got into Birdland. And I stayed on and worked with Lester Young for several engagements, and I worked with other people there, such as Flip Philips.

"I went to Europe with Benny Goodman in 1950. The band included Zoot Sims, Roy Eldridge, Toots Thielemans, Eddie Shaughnessy, Charlie Short, and singer Nancy Reed. It was very significant, the first really big-time thing that I had been asked to do. There's a tape of it I've gotten from a collector since, from an aircheck made, I believe, in Switzerland. It was pretty good, too," notes Hyman, adding he's returned to work with Goodman on various occasions in the years since.

Although there were periodic jazz club gigs to be had, Hyman made most of his living throughout the 1950s and '60s as a studio musician, playing for radio and television shows and on freelance record dates. Some musicians found studio work a grind but Hyman remembers it with great enthusiasm. It was all new to him, he was surrounded by pros, and he was learning. He insists: "Studio work in New York at that time was just about the most stimulating environment that a pianist or a musician could find. Well, it was very demanding—demanding that you know how to read music, that you could be able to play any style, that you play any kind of music—all kinds of things. And it was all live. Of course there was a lot of recording—much more than there is now—but there was live broadcasting; we were on the air live every morning.

"First I joined the staff of WMCA. And after that I moved over to NBC and stayed at NBC for five years [1952–57], as a staff pianist and organist. I conducted my first show during that time at NBC. It was very stimulating. The demands on you in those days were as varied as playing soap operas on an organ; playing some pretty hard light classical stuff on 'The Show of Shows'; rather complicated background music, here and there, for films; playing with Eddie Safranski's jazz group early in the morning—all kinds of stuff, on both radio and TV. We would do a live program from 7:05 to 8:00 a.m., if I remember right,

on radio with bassist Eddie Safranski's band, which had Don
Lamond on drums, Mundell Lowe on guitar, Artie Baker on
clarinet, Will Bradley on trombone—and Ray Conniff played
trombone for a while—and Mick McMickle on trumpet. We'd go
off the air on that, rush up to the studio on Amsterdam Avenue
and 64th Street, and then we'd do 'The Morey Amsterdam Show'
live from nine to ten o'clock. And that band was Milton DeLugg's
Orchestra. Phil Bodner was in it, Don Lamond again, Safranski,
Mickey Bloom was the trumpeter. After that we'd have breakfast
and then rehearse for the next day of 'The Morey Amsterdam
Show,' and then, depending on what NBC had in mind on their
schedule, I sometimes had game shows to play on organ, or a
soap opera, later in the afternoon. All live. Then there was 'The
Sid Caesar Show,' with Bernie Green's Orchestra. That was an
intense learning process, too. Because there was hard and interesting music. I learned a great deal about orchestration and
arranging, just by being on the spot. All of this was going on,
and there would be record dates, more than likely, in the evening.
We thought nothing of doing a record date at seven p.m. and
another one at midnight and starting all over again. So it was a
terrific time.

"I got to be an organist through Alvey West, who had a
group known as Alvey West's Little Band, and we did various
television shows and recordings with it. I first began, really, to
arrange professionally for Alvey on a show called 'Country Style,'
which was done on Dumont Television in Wanamakers. And also
on an NBC three-times-a-week show in which we accompanied
singers such as Eddie Fisher and a number of other people. And
also on that show the band had a number, and Alvey let me
arrange and feature myself in 'Carolina Shout' with the band. So
that was, I suppose, an example of merging of the fields, which
I've done ever since. That would have been around 1952 or '53.
I have the airchecks. I have all that stuff." He became Arthur
Godfrey's musical director from 1959 to 1962.

"The playing in jazz clubs had to stop for some time. You
couldn't do everything. And I concentrated on studio work for
many years, only occasionally playing jazz piano here and there,
or playing as part of a studio situation as it arose. Occasionally I

would play jazz gigs, more often than not with people I was working with in studio work—Mundell Lowe, for example, Safranski. I went into a place called The Composer for a couple of weeks at one point with my own group. I can't even remember who was in it," he says. Hyman paid a price for his seemingly endless studio work. He did not develop the immediately recognizable style of his own that fine, wholly committed jazz players do. And while he learned to execute competently any type of music requested of him, that is not the same thing as mastering a single idiom. He could earnestly give you anything you needed, but sometimes with the slightly studied, academic quality of one whose playing is not born from passion. But Hyman had no complaints at the time.

"I loved doing so many different things. I really did that for 25 years, just about. I really loved it all, the whole sensation of playing everything possible, everywhere in New York City," he says, with characteristic cheerfulness. "I rarely traveled in those days. I travel much more now. I didn't need to go out of town. It was just a wonderful, stimulating period. There was so much work. And all of us were just running around like crazy, from studio to studio. And furthermore, the work was of a sort which unfortunately musicians don't have now. It was live. That is to say, this was before the days of multi-tracking. You didn't have a situation where the rhythm section plays on one day on a recording, and then they think about it and they put in the violins the next day, and then they put in the horns, and then they take out the piano and they replace it with harpsichord. None of that was possible. Consequently the standards for playing were, I think, higher. And every recording session was a real performance, which is not at all the case now except for classical music or jazz. Pop recording was live. This is no longer the case; technology has altered that irrevocably. So the totality of the whole thing was great. And there was a marvelous camaraderie among us all. Some of the musicians I was close to were Al Caiola, Tony Mottola, Bob Rosengarden, Phil Bodner. Some of these people I'm still very close to, still play with. And there were all the guys on 'Sing Along with Mitch,' which went on for several years—Bob Haggart, who is now my neighbor in this building, Milt Hinton,

DICK HYMAN

Osie Johnson, Jerome Richardson, Al Klink, Bernie Glow, Mel Davis, Panama Francis.

"And with Panama in that period, I did a lot of early rock 'n' roll on Atlantic, for Jerry Wexler and Lieber and Stoller. I did things for groups like the Coasters. I can't remember the names of all those rock 'n' roll groups. But I went through the mill with all of that. I played triplets from here to the moon. Just endless, endless triplets. I got into the recording end of the studio business, having been more a radio and television guy, because I could play blues piano. Along with the triplets, you had to know something about playing the blues kind of fills. That came from having learned boogie woogie earlier on. Whatever it was that Atlantic was doing in those days, I was generally the piano player or the organ player. And that's how I first came to know Panama, who was the very hot rhythm-and-blues drummer at the time, the middle '50s. And we used to do the same kind of thing for the other companies. Columbia got into the act. And there were all the countless little companies trying to cash in. We did a lot of things for an outfit called Chancellor Records, with Frankie Avalon. It was called 'the Philadelphia sound.' And guys would come up from Philadelphia. Al Caiola was in charge of that operation. Frankie Avalon and Fabian were the people there. And it was funny music. I mean we all kind of laughed at it. It was paying the rent very nicely. But it was funny music. I've gotten fond of it in retrospect, because it's gotten very nostalgic now. But at the time it just seemed just funny. I still think it's funny music. We had a good time doing it, but nobody took it seriously. Maybe Frankie Avalon did, but we didn't take it seriously. We were seriously trying to get it to swing and the time was very good. Panama was certainly serious about playing the time; we all were. But it was just funny, crude music. It went with all the other stuff.

"And around that time, I got teamed up by MGM. I had begun to record under my own name for MGM, and they teamed me up at one point with Sam Taylor, who was the great rhythm-and-blues saxophonist. We made a bunch of albums together. By that time, I was into playing funky kind of Harlem blues organ. Which happened another way. See, the first job that I played when I got out of college was in a Harlem bar called Wells's, and I played piano there. It was a piano and organ place. The organist was a man named Charlie Stewart, but at one point Wild Bill Davis was the opposite organist. Various other people there saturated me with that blues-based playing of Hammond electric organ. So I began to be able to do that, too. And with Sam the Man, that's essentially the way I was playing: funky organ. There was double billing for Sam and myself. I also did a lot of that anonymously. But Sam and I made a number of records which were pretty fair turntable hits for a while."

Hyman recorded commercial music in seemingly every type of format, from cocktail lounge piano to jazz and pop trio dates. In 1955, following a successful recording of "Moritat: Theme from *The Threepenny Opera*" (the number better known today as "Mack the Knife"), on which Hyman played piano and harpsichord and whistled, *Cashbox Magazine* named the Dick Hyman Trio "the most promising up-and-coming small instrumental group."

"This was all pop business. But I was really into it then. You know, since then I've kind of abandoned the pop market. Or it's abandoned me," Hyman says. On Cozy Cole's hit recording of "Topsy," Hyman served as arranger and organist. "We recorded that one twice—the original mono single, then stereo arrived and we had to do it over again in stereo for the album issue. And if I'm not mistaken, we did it a third time, when Cozy changed contracts and we did it for Decca. The first was on an old label that went bankrupt, called Love Records." He found time to write arrangements, over the years, for artists as varied as Count Basie, Al Hirt, the Mills Brothers, J. J. Johnson, Doc Severinsen, and Bobby Cole. "And I was also playing on films. I don't remember the names of the sessions that I played on. And I got into writing music for commercials. Well I played them, hot and heavy, for anybody who called me. But also I began composing them, and conducting and arranging them." He recorded honky-tonk and novelty numbers under assorted pseudonyms, and notes that he was not the only pianist who recorded as "Knuckles O'Toole," the non-existent honky-tonk piano great whose records sold just fine. "And I recorded the first pop (maybe jazz) record on Moog synthesizer in 1969, called 'The Minotaur.' It was a real, very popular single. But the album was very popular, too. (The only thing that had come out on the synthesizer prior to this was 'Switched-On Bach.') Some of these things are not unlike avant-garde jazz. And I did one other album. For a while, I was playing synthesizer, and I played some of it live for Arnie Lawrence's group. And I did a bunch of it in the studios up to a certain point, when really my synthesizer went on the blink once too often, and I was more interested at that point in regressing to ragtime. And synthesizer specialists were appearing on the scene who knew much more about it than I did. So I have kind of gracefully retired from the synthesizer field."

In the early '70s, Hyman's career turned around. He became a familiar presence on the New York jazz scene, a musician the public came to expect to hear live—a one-man library of jazz past and present. His return to the field of live performing came about almost by chance, he suggests. He tells it this way: "A significant thing happened to me. My old teacher, Teddy Wilson, who was appearing at The Cookery [a jazz club in downtown Manhattan], was unable to make it one Sunday night, and [club owner] Barney Josephson called me up on a last-minute basis to sub for him. So I went in there and for the first time in years found myself playing solo piano in a joint. And I was really surprised to see how much I liked it! When Barney Josephson asked me if I wanted to go in there regularly as the Sunday night pianist, at first I hesitated. I really wasn't sure I wanted to go back to what I had left many years before. But I agreed to do it and I liked it so much that I kept doing it by myself for, more or less, a couple of years of Sundays. And I began to focus myself back onto solo piano playing.

"Around the same time, there happened the ragtime revival. With the movie *The Sting*, suddenly Scott Joplin music was in vogue. RCA got me to record the complete works of Scott Joplin. And my friend Sam Parkins, who was then associated with Columbia, called me to record what Columbia hoped would be a natural follow-up to the Joplin revival in the form of Jelly Roll Morton orchestral transcriptions. Jelly Roll's playing was tough—

tough playing with a lot of dissonance, a lot of harsh accents, and peculiar voicings. It took me a while to get with it. I did get with it. And I like it a lot now. (What I appreciated in it when I was a kid was less his own work than that of the whole band, the clarinet in particular.) So I found myself immersed in early piano music. The ragtime revival was in the air. I began to recover some of my James P. Johnson things which I had played when I was a kid, and I recorded an album for Columbia on James P. Johnson. And [starting in 1975] there was the New York Jazz Repertory Company stuff, including the Louis Armstrong concert that I arranged, which we took to Russia. Around that time also, I was doing some concerts, and I wrote my own piano concerto, which I still play in public occasionally with symphony orchestras. And I took the ragtime experience and put it into something I called 'Ragtime Fantasy.' And I play that with orchestras occasionally. I got focused on solo piano playing at The Cookery and recording, and early jazz, along with the interest in the New York Jazz Repertory Company. And I was also making records and performing occasionally with Soprano Summit, with Bob Wilber and Kenny Davern. And with this and a number of other ways, jazz became a lot more important to me. I sought it out, I focused more on it, rather than just doing the general freelance running around that I'd been doing. I sought it out. It felt good. And it's been focusing ever more finely since then.

"Now, I consider solo piano playing one of the very most important things that I think I can contribute. And I work on it very hard these days. And do a lot of it. The job I have now at Hanratty's every Monday night is comparable to what I had at The Cookery. I don't care to work every night at a club. If I do that, I can't do anything else, really. But one night a week suits me very well.

"And for quite a few years, we'd go into Michael's Pub once a year, with what I call the Perfect Jazz Repertory Quintet. (The Perfect Jazz Repertory Quintet was so-named by Whitney Balliett in a moment of compliment.) And in subsequent concerts, we'd do concerts of Gershwin, of Berlin, of '30s music, of Fats Waller, of Ellington, whatever. It's a repertory group. But not too strict. We just kind of function in a general area. The basic personnel

of the group is Joe Wilder (and sometimes Warren Vaché), Phil
Bodner, Milt Hinton, and Ron Traxler. In the first show at
Michael's, around 1978 or 1979, however, Bob Wilber and Bob
Rosengarden were involved."

Hyman has become known as an expert in the field of jazz
repertory. He approaches the task of dealing with the historic
jazz repertory as seriously as a classical pianist might the task of
dealing with the classical repertory. He notes, though, that there
are varied ways of re-creating jazz. "If I'm doing a history of jazz
piano, I do it as closely as I can to whoever it is I'm trying to
sound like. But I might loosen it up a bit if I'm in performance
on my own. I'm not going to play a Jelly Roll Morton like Oscar
Peterson, but I confess I might play 'Fingerbreaker' faster than
he did. I take care not to mix up styles, unless it's of my own
improvisation. If I'm playing Jelly Roll Morton, I'm doing my
best to play like Jelly Roll Morton—sometimes a little closer and
sometimes a little less close. I think it'd be disastrous to try to put
everything together. It would be disastrous to try to encompass
everything. Now, on the other hand, Jelly Roll Morton's tunes,
some of them, can be very well played in other styles. Mary Lou
Williams recorded 'The Pearls' once and everybody's recorded
'King Porter Stomp.' So you can take his compositions and you
can play them any way you want and they work very nicely, but
it all depends what game you're playing. If the point of the game
is to play like Jelly Roll Morton, you want to play like Jelly Roll
Morton," Hyman says.

"In doing re-creations, I think it's very important to know
what the game is. (A.) Are you re-creating something as close as
possible to what you hear on the record? (B.) Are you re-creating
it as close as possible to what you hear on the record but with
people improvising their own solos, presumably in the style? (C.)
Are you just vaguely playing it like the record? That is to say, are
you playing the song and maybe a few cues, a few little hints of
the record (which is pretty much what we do with the Perfect
Jazz Repertory Quintet, partially because of our instrumentation)? (D.) Or are you trying to be completely different from the
record, just using the same song? I used to do an impression of
Earl Hines doing 'Monday Date' and I didn't necessarily play

exactly what he played. I just played it in his style, using that song—which is another way you can go. If you know the style well enough, you can improvise in that style. And more often than not, that's what I would be wanting to do," Hyman says.

Although Hyman can offer good-faith simulations of just about any piano style, he seems clearly more at home working within some traditions than others. When he plays Bix Beiderbecke's music, for example, you sense he really understands it, relates to it—which, perhaps, is not surprising since some of the first classic jazz records he heard were Beiderbecke's. Hyman can play Beiderbecke's "In a Mist" note for note, following either Beiderbecke's original recording or the somewhat different published version that Beiderbecke and Bill Challis worked out after the recording was made. Hyman does not try to re-create the exact tempo and feeling of the original recording, saying he is dealing with Beiderbecke more as a composer than as a pianist. But he comes up with a quite fully realized performance of the music Beiderbecke composed.

He comments: "I think there are many instances where the composer doesn't really know how the thing should best go until it's been performed a while, maybe by other people. This is true, for example, with the *Rhapsody in Blue*; the original Gershwin recording is very indecisive in some areas and the tempos are peculiar. And I know myself that I have composed things and I don't really understand the optimum tempo or the interpretation for some time. In the case of the record of 'In a Mist,' I have had to play it note-for-note for [choreographer] Twyla Tharpe. She has a dance called 'The Bix Pieces,' and for one of the parts in that she had been using the actual recording. She decided to do it live. Obviously the point of that game is to play the number exactly as close to the record as you can. And I did that.

"However, when I'm playing 'In a Mist' other than in that situation, I have found other values in it. I would play it a little bit slower than Bix did, a little bit more lyrically. Not so slow that it turns into a Chopin nocturne, but a little bit less propulsively. Also, I think there's a good reason to believe that he was playing it maybe a little too fast in order to get it within the confines of a 78 record. That's possible. It's hard to say what 'moderato'

Dick Hyman. (Courtesy of Concord Records.)

Dick Hyman supervises a rehearsal of the Benny Goodman Band at New York's Marriott Marquis Hotel, 1985, in preparation for the WNET-TV special, "Benny Goodman—Let's Dance." (Goodman did not attend that rehearsal.) Band members visible in this shot include James Chirillo (guitar), Bob Haggart (bass), Ken Peplowski (tenor sax), Jack Stuckey (alto sax), and Chuck Wilson (alto sax). (Photo by Chip Deffaa.)

means on the tempo, especially since Bill Challis wrote it. But it's conceivable that it might have been a more meditative piece than he recorded. I take it from the text rather than from the record. I'm playing it in a gentler manner and in a more impressionistic manner. You know, sometimes players find interpretive values that are improvements on the original. Sometimes the original composers are not as good piano players as their interpreters, maybe. I'm not making a judgment in this case, but that's certainly the case. And composers can often be indebted to performers for bringing out things that they were incapable of playing but were talented enough to imply in their writing. But I don't do any inventing when I play those pieces."

Hyman has developed a following—fans who come to hear him play music of his choice without specifically trying to re-create past recordings, and who buy his new recordings of vintage tunes. "More and more, I do things in my own style," he says. "But my own style includes influences from a whole lot of other things. I like to do James P. Johnson or Morton or Joplin things pretty much the way they're written. I think that's as much value as playing Bach or Mozart or Chopin the way they're written. So I certainly enjoy doing that. But on the other hand, I think that what I can do uniquely is play my own elaborate improvisations in whatever combination Dick Hyman-style that I've evolved. And I have by this time put them together in a way which nobody else does, so it must be me." Sometimes Hyman will play a Scott Joplin composition exactly as written and then follow it with his re-interpretation of the piece. "But I make a point of announcing what I'm doing. First I play it straight and then I play, very often, a whole fantasy on it."

Hyman's reputation as a Joplin expert led in 1976 to a note-worthy film soundtrack job, which in turn led to an increasing involvement in films. "I did *all* the piano playing for the film soundtrack of *Scott Joplin, King of Ragtime* [1976], even the contest where there were four pianists. There was a long scene in which all the pianists had a cutting contest. We had two upright pianos brought into the studio, tuned slightly apart so that they'd sound different, so that they'd sound as though there were different players. And I did them in sequence, that whole thing. I also did the orchestration and the adaptation, and a fair number of original cues. However, when we made the soundtrack album, everything had to be redone because we hadn't done any one piece in full in the film. So we redid everything in fuller versions. And when it came time to do the piano cutting contest, although it worked out beautifully in the film I decided that for a record it would be better if Hank Jones and I played on two pianos. So we did what's called 'The Cutting Contest' as a two-piano thing with Hank and I, based loosely on the routine I had worked out before."

He has done the musical scores for such well-known films as *Moonstruck, Zelig,* and *The Purple Rose of Cairo.* He orchestrated the Broadway hit *Sugar Babies.* He's scored assorted TV dramas and documentaries, picking up two Emmy Awards along the way. He has also done characteristically conscientious work supervising the music in some films that never went anywhere. "I did an original jazz score for a minor film called *French Quarter,* which I once saw advertised as playing in a Florida drive-in. I think that's about the status of the film. Jelly Roll Morton was a character in the film, and they wanted Morton-esque kind of music, but they didn't want to pay for the real Morton music. . . . So I was asked to do pseudo-Morton music. And we did. We had a band with Bob Wilber and Pee Wee Erwin, George Masso, Panama Francis, I can't quite remember who the bass player was. The soundtrack was *very* good. But nothing ever happened with the film. I don't think the film deserved to have anything happen with it. And I did *Sunshine's on the Way,* another situation where it involved kind of a traditional jazz. George Masso, again, was on that, and we got Kenny Davern and Joe Wilder. Tommy Benford played drums. You know, he was the original Jelly Roll Morton drummer. I got him to play for the Twyla Tharpe 'Eight Jelly Rolls' dance, too, which we've done quite a few seasons."

Hyman has become, in recent years, the man who does the music for Woody Allen's motion pictures. How did that come about?

"I think that I was known around New York for having some expertise in old music. So that when *Zelig* came about, one of his producers called me. They didn't know quite how to proceed with some of their 1920s requirements, and I think they had heard me do something like that somewhere else. . . . I think they had heard me do it with Twyla Tharpe when we re-created the Paul Whiteman band for the Bix pieces. I think that was the beginning of it. But, however, I was known to Woody and to the producers, because I'd played piano in several films of theirs before. I've had something to do with his films as far back as *Everything You Wanted to Know About Sex But Were Afraid to Ask*. I played piano and organ on that, and piano on a number of others. But the first thing I really began to work with him on a full-score basis was *Zelig*. So I worked on *Zelig* and *Broadway Danny Rose* and *The Purple Rose of Cairo*, and very little on the last one, *Hannah and Her Sisters*; it did not have any score that I'm aware of (it probably had some phonograph records). It's about to come out now. I did play a little piano on that.

"We've begun the taping for the next Woody Allen film, which is nameless as always until the final days of production. But this film [since released under the title of *Radio Days*] is set in the milieu of the 1930s and many of the things that are involved in it at this point have to do with old radio programs. So we have recorded various songs of the period with different singers, and I've also done some fanfares for a mythical radio quiz program and a couple of soap opera backgrounds on organ for that sort of stuff. So far they're old songs, but the underscoring, of course, is mine. Whether there'll be new songs as there were in *Purple Rose of Cairo*, I'm not sure yet. We'll get into that more in the post-scoring. But this is just in advance, things that have to be done for the actors to hear as they either mime or react to pre-recorded music.

"And I've just finished 'Benny Goodman—Let's Dance.' It'll be on in March as a fund-raiser for Channel 13. I played piano and I also acted as musical supervisor for the television show itself," Hyman notes.

"These days I spend a lot of time playing concerts. That's the way things have gotten. And I enjoy it very much. I play much more publicly than I ever used to. I think what I like to do more than anything else is play solo piano. And I do it a lot, not only in Hanratty's, but I frequently make appearances as a solo pianist, or occasionally solo organist. Or frequently in duet with [cornetist] Ruby Braff on either piano or organ. Ruby and I are going to go to England to record a BBC television show in our cornet and organ duo format, as we did in the album *America the Beautiful*. And also, I'm going to do a couple other solo things for them. I'm going to do my history of jazz piano, which they have titled (with their British oblique humor) 'Honky Tonk Professor.' And a third program I'll do solo of just piano improvisations. And while we're there, Ruby and I will play a week together at the Pizza Express.

"Last weekend I played the *Rhapsody in Blue* with the Brown University wind ensemble. I play at a lot of jazz festivals and jazz parties with a whole gang of people. Many of us showed up on the S. S. Norway for a floating jazz party—two weeks of nice playing on the Carribbean. And I play the Kool Festival, the Dick Gibson party—I've often played at the one in Phoenix, I've played at Wilmington, North Carolina, Sacramento, Nice, the Conneaut Lake, Pennsylvania, Jazz Festival, the Midland, Texas, Jazz Party, the Northsea Festival in Holland, the Breda Traditional Jazz Festival in Holland. I have tried more and more to make it a single [rather than performing in a group]. In Breda, I did only single and it worked fine. In that place, of course, I concentrated on repertory (Zez Confrey, Jelly Roll, James P., and so forth), and rather less of the free improvisation that I would do on a Monday night at Hanratty's. And of course I would honor their gig by not trying to foist any bebop on them. I try to know what the game is that I'm supposed to be playing, and then follow the rules.

"I can play bebop if I'm playing at a festival with people like Clark Terry or Al Cohn, or Billy Watrous or Urbie Green or people like that. What happens at festivals like that generally is that the rhythm section has to be rather chameleonic. You have to go back and forth. Dave McKenna can shift, as I can. And other people who can do this are Roger Kellaway and Derek Smith and so forth. So depending on who the soloists are, you have to go somewhat in their direction, to make a happy party out of it. So I do play bebop, yeah. But I'm afraid I don't play much avant garde jazz. About the farthest I got in that was with

DICK HYMAN

[alto saxist] Arnie Lawrence and the Children of All Ages. We did a very free, no-form recording, and we did several concerts about 10 years ago. And it's quite nice, in its way. Just loose, anything-happens style—getting into a groove and working on it a while. Richard Davis was the bass player. I had my Moog synthesizer, too."

Hyman has become visible, too, as artistic director, host, and participant in the annual "Jazz in July" concert series. "I had an idea that New Yorkers hadn't been given enough of mainstream traditional jazz, even in such a broad presentation as George Wein is able to do. Somehow, that kind of music has been a bit slighted." He's presented artists such as the Classic Jazz Quartet, Panama Francis' Savoy Sultans, Bucky and John Pizzarelli, Carrie Smith, Buddy Tate, Al Cohn, Al Grey, Joe Wilder, Maxine Sullivan, Ed Polcer and the Condon Gang, and Vince Giordano's Nighthawks (playing late 1920s and early '30s arrangements by the likes of Bill Challis and Gene Gifford). In fact, all of the musicians profiled in this book could comfortably fit within Hyman's format. And he paces his programs remarkably well (and that's almost a lost art in concert production—his years of involvement with TV variety shows no doubt helped), moving briskly from solo or duo piano bits to full band jam-session-type things, to vocals, and occasionally to more ambitious undertakings, such as performances of rarely heard, longer, not-quite-jazz compositions ("Krazy Kat" by John Alden Carpenter or "Yamekraw" by James P. Johnson, for example). He makes a congenial and occasionally witty host.

Hyman has filled a need, bringing people concerts they weren't getting at any of the other jazz festivals in New York. He's drawn packed houses and raves from the critics. "We call it a festival of 'Hot Jazz, Ragtime, Oldtime and Blues.' And I worked out that title very carefully, so it would include some other elements, such as Maurice Peress' Paul Whiteman concert—not really jazz at all, but certainly what I call the edge of jazz, and marvelously oldtime, and marvelously well-done, too. It just seems to me that you lose something if you have an arbitrary cutoff point and say, 'You can't do this because it is on the other side of the line.' We're presenting joyful music with the

331

element of discovery. It's spontaneous; it happens as you hear it. It's the antithesis of popular music today, where people spend months in a studio putting down layers of sound," he says. Dick Hyman, onetime studio scene stalwart, seems quite content these days playing and sharing with audiences some of the music that first turned him on as a youth. "This is largely older jazz and ragtime," he notes. "This is a happy era of jazz. Everybody's supposed to have fun with it."

1985

Doing What His
Brother Taught Him

In a 1985 *Modern Drummer* interview, Mel Lewis commented that
the four major living big band drummers were Buddy Rich,
Louie Bellson, Jake Hanna, and himself. If Hanna's name is less
well known to the average individual than those of the other
three, that's no doubt because he, alone among them, never was
a bandleader; a sideman never receives as much publicity as a
leader. That he never established himself as a leader has more
to do with his temperament than with his abilities as a musician.
He simply didn't want the hassles of organizing and maintaining
a band. For that matter, he notes, he's never been one for aggres-
sively seeking out jobs, generally; he's simply taken offers as
they've come to him. That's the way he works—and he's
drummed for many of the greatest musicians in the business.
Although he reached maturity when bebop was at its zenith, his
own preferences have always been for swinging mainstream jazz
rooted in an earlier tradition.

Hanna was born April 4, 1931 in Dorchester, Massachusetts
(not in Roxbury, as has been printed in some standard sources,
he says). How did he originally become interested in being a
drummer?

"Well, I didn't really," he says. "Growing up, I liked playing
ball a lot. I was fair, that's all. But I loved it. I didn't care whether

In the Mainstream

I was playing field or hitting or running the bases, so long as I could play ball." What drumming he did in his youth, he suggests, was secondary to playing ball.

"I started hitting the drums at CYO, Catholic Youth Organization. I heard the church band, and I wanted to play in it. So I started playing when I was five or six—a little pee wee band, drum and bugle. The music was as simple as you can get: 'Our Director,' stuff like that. My brother—he was about five or six years older than me—played in the regular band, with trombones and clarinets, up in front of us. That was when we were little kids in the '30s. And I just kept playing a little. I didn't really follow music. I just played ball a lot. I never studied music.

"My brother showed me basically what to do as a drummer. I do basically the same thing today, without any variation. I was very lucky. When I was about 11 or 12, he showed me the right way to play the cymbal beat. Way back then, he showed that to me. And it was ingrained. I says, 'Oh, that's the way it goes.' I didn't know it could go stiff or loose or bad; he showed me the exact right way to do it, automatically.

"I still do the very basic thing my brother showed me, way back. And that's all I ever do. If Dixielanders want to play on top of that, that's fine; if boppers want to, it fits. No matter who I'm with, I just do the same thing. If they say, 'Give me this,' no, I go, shuhit-shuhit-shuhit-shuhit [he simulates keeping time on the cymbals]. That goes with whatever it is. I do the same thing, no matter who I'm with. I don't care if it's a combo or what."

Hanna says he wound up playing drums more when his family moved into a Jewish neighborhood in Dorchester, where he started meeting more youths who were into music. It was the same neighborhood, he says, that had produced such jazz musicians as Ruby Braff, seven years his senior, and Buzzy Drootin, 14 years his senior, both of whom had already begun making names for themselves. "A lot of Jewish kids loved good jazz music. I always loved a good band. And I started playing with those guys. There's an Irish section of Dorchester, there's an all-Jewish section. No Italian section. The Italians had to fight both of them! It was great. I really had a good time. All those guys, they loved to play ball too.

334

JAKE HANNA

"A guy who used to go out with my sister really got me going as a musician. He'd give me tickets to go see Benny Goodman and those guys during the war—there weren't many guys around in the bands (they were in service), but [drummer] Morey Feld and [tenor saxist] Vido Musso were there. And that's how I got to see them. My father was on the newspaper and he'd get me tickets to go backstage at the RKO. (He also got me press passes to the Red Sox. I saw my first pro game in '39. I remember everybody who was in the line-up, too.) I got my education at the RKO Theater in Boston. I'd hook school, sit there for the whole six or seven shows. [The theater presented movies, vaudeville acts, and featured spots by top big bands.] I'd watch that drummer play the acts. Buddy Schutz was with Jimmy Dorsey's band, Buddy Rich was with Tommy Dorsey—they were the two top drummers around. Jimmy Vincent was working with Louis Prima's big band then. Tony Pastor had a nice band. They all had good bands. I saw Woody Herman's band with Don Lamond the night that Neal Hefti got married to Frances [Wayne]—they were all leaping in cabs to go to the wedding, after the last show. I spent all my time there, watching Lionel Hampton, Count Basie—all good bands. That went up till about '47, then stopped. And I knew every act that came through," Hanna recalls.

By 1944, the year he turned 13, Hanna was drumming professionally. He explains: "Well, during the war, anybody could work. I worked when I was 13. They didn't care how old you were; they had to have somebody, man. People didn't want to dance to records. They wanted live bands: 13-, 14-piece bands. To play in a big band now is a luxury, a unique event. In those days, there were over a thousand bands working, especially after the war. Anybody could work then; I don't care how old you were. My brother was only about five feet tall and he worked all the time, underage, those real bad bars. And I was able to work all those joints, too, for $9 a night."

Who were the drummers Hanna emulated in his youth?

"Gene Krupa was my first big influence—very heavy. The next guy that influenced me was Kenny Clarke, and Denzil Best and Shelly Manne—the bebop era. Denzil Best for wire brushes. He was my first big influence—and Jo Jones, naturally. But I still try to get that sound that Denzil gets—a little different, so it'll be sort of like mine, you know. He was fantastic; great propelling style.

"Shelly [Manne] turned me around, in 1946 or '47. That was a new style of drumming I'd never heard before. I heard strong bass drumming, and the left hand was doing something totally different from the right; I said, 'Jeez, what the hell is that?' I met Shelly in 1947."

(Hanna adds that he wasn't influenced by Dave Tough back then—he never got to see Tough play—but that long after Tough had died, by listening to old recordings of Tough with Woody Herman, "Tough heavily influenced me. That was years later, when I was about 35 years old, he influenced me.")

Bebop was the new thing when Hanna reached maturity. His own preferences were for the music prior to bebop's ascendancy, however. He reflects: "The bop came in and when I finally started playing, I never got to play with the bands I like, you know. I had to play with Maynard Ferguson or somebody . . . it was all, for those days, quite modern, very beboppy."

What were the bands Hanna would have liked to have played with?

"The Woody Herman Band of back then [the mid '40s]. Eventually I got to play with that style of band, later on. I first played with Woody's band in '57, but that was a bop-oriented band and it never got swinging. But the band he had in '62, we played the stuff from '44—'The Good Earth,' 'Apple Honey,' 'Caldonia.' 'Four Brothers' from '48 or '49—we played all the stuff I liked. We just played that whole book. It was great. That's when I first got to play in a band I really liked to play in."

But that's getting a bit ahead of our story. Hanna put in a good bit of apprenticeship before getting to play with bands of the caliber of Woody Herman's.

"I played around Boston while I was in high school. When I got out, there was nothing. I wasn't good enough to play with anybody who was any good. I went in the service (the Marines) in March of 1950," he notes. Hanna drummed, both on the base (and having to beat a bass drum at maximum strength for an hour so troops could march to it was useful experience, he says) and also, as time permitted, off the base. Although he couldn't read music, he was able to play for the shows at a theater. "I knew every act. How? I had seen every act that came through the RKO Theater in Boston six years earlier. I knew the trampoline act. I knew the guy with the newspaper act (he sat there and read a newspaper—you know, some funny licks). I knew the two acts with the falling-away suit. I knew just what to do. Jeez. So I had that thing. It gave me a couple of dollars. I got out of the Marines in '53."

Hanna picked up experience wherever he could. "I joined Tommy Reed's territory band, and I sat down in Kansas City for a while with him, at the Muhlbach Hotel. I'll tell you how you got the gigs in those days. Either you hung out in musicians' bars or you played jam sessions. (They don't have many jam sessions any more.) Well, Ted Weems' band had a jam session out in some joint and one guy said, 'Jeez, the drummer's leaving soon. Will you be interested in going with the band?' I said, 'Yeah.' I was making $100 a week. I went with Ted for $20 or $30, something like that—very low. Of course, hotels weren't very much either: $25 a week, $3 a day. But Ted had a very good band. He had one of the better books I played."

Hanna went on to study at the Berklee School of Music on the G. I. Bill. He was a student at the same time as Toshiko Akiyoshi, Bill Chase, Charlie Mariano, Bill Berry, Gabor Szabo, and others who went on to make names in music.

He drummed for a stretch in Buddy Morrow's Band, which was then riding high with numbers like "Night Train." Hanna notes: "A guy named Walt Stewart was writing some real good arrangements for him. There were a lot of good guys in that band. Dick Johnson [the clarinetist/alto saxist who today leads the Artie Shaw Band] was a star, man. A real good player and a great guy. Jesus. You couldn't ask for a better human being than that guy."

Toshiko Akiyoshi hired Hanna to drum in her trio at the Hickory House in New York in the summer of 1956. He wound up working there every summer for about five years. Hanna joined Woody Herman for a brief stay in 1957. He joined Maynard Ferguson's big band in 1958, spent another summer with

Akiyoshi (he was always glad when he could get off the road for a bit), then took a job as the house drummer at the Boston jazz club Storyville. "I worked with Anita O'Day; her drummer, that maniac, got sick, so I worked with her. That was an experience. I'll never forget that, nor would I recommend it to anyone either. She's a *meshuganuh,* you know [he laughs]. She's a great gal, but she's real mad—whew! Was that off the wall. Anyway, that was nice. Then the Hi-Lo's come in. These are acts I didn't expect to be working with."

Playing with one band at Storyville convinced him of the direction he wanted to pursue in music. "The real good band came in—Buck Clayton, Vic Dickenson, Pee Wee Russell, Bud Freeman, Jimmy Rushing was the singer—and that band stayed there over a month. Wow! That's when I said, 'Fuck this bebop shit! What bullshit. It's all nervous, everybody showing off. Man, this is where it is!' I couldn't believe how good these guys played, and how easy it was to play with them. The people liked it better. I liked it better. They liked it better. The bartender liked it better. He was doing business. The waitresses liked it better. Everybody liked it better. I says, 'What's the use of trying to kid yourself, man? Hip is square. You wanna be hip, you're a square. Really.' That was 1959.

"And Marian McPartland came in. She sat in and she liked it, and she called me to go out on the road. I said, 'Yeah, time to get going again.' So I went out on the road with her a long time [about 1959–61]." A jam session in Columbus, Ohio, with Bobby Hackett and Dave McKenna led to Hackett inviting Hanna to drum with him at Condon's in New York.

"I said, 'You kidding? To get off the road again? Yeah!' In those days, you could get a place to stay in New York. I got a place for $80 a month, with cooking, on 48th Street. The Burnham. Barbra Streisand lived right above me. And from Bobby Hackett I went with Duke Ellington for 10 or 15 days, until they could find Sam Woodyard again.

"In 1961, I visited home in Boston and the Harry James Band was there," Hanna remembers. A musician from the band, who had been in Woody Herman's Band with Hanna a few years earlier, invited Hanna to go to a local record shop. When they got there, they found Harry James. Hanna's friend made the introductions. "And Harry says: 'The drummer with Maynard Ferguson.' I said, 'Gee, I haven't worked with him in a while.' Harry says: 'I'm listening to you now.' He was listening to a Maynard Ferguson album! Harry liked Maynard. He says: 'You want a job? Jackie Mills is going to leave. Join me in Vegas.' That's how I joined Harry James. Jesus Christ. Isn't that something?" Hanna comments, marveling at the one-in-a-million odds of meeting Harry James while James was listening to a record on which he was playing. "I was real lucky," Hanna says, "—or unlucky, depending on how you look at it. Because I didn't have any fun in that band. I loved the guys; they were great. But Harry was a pain in the ass. Just an egomaniac. It's never his fault. Everybody else makes mistakes. He doesn't make mistakes—and he made plenty of them! So what are you going to do?"

Hanna didn't consider James much of a jazz player. (A number of other musicians, of course, have rated James' abilities higher than Hanna does.) Hanna believed James "never swung. . . . His best years, I think, were with Benny Goodman, to tell you the truth. He had some very good commercial years with his own bands. I think he influenced more trumpet players than Louis—of that ilk, you know. Most of the lead guys play like Harry used to play, as far as I'm concerned. Now, Louis influenced a certain era, you know. But man, most of the guys you hear playing the lead stuff now in that style of jazz are like Harry James. It really was a big influence.

"But he was a disappointment. I liked the band. I loved the book. He used the Count Basie Book. And man, that's good for a drummer, you can either play or not play, you know. But you got to have the right guys playing. And Harry's band had nothing to do with Count Basie. The arrangements were the exact same, but it just came out real different. Real different. You know, the rhythm was not in Basie's class and Harry was not in Basie's class.

"I saw Count Basie after I left the band. He says, 'I thought you were in Vegas.' I says, 'I quit Harry; Buddy's with the band now.' 'Buddy Rich? Well, I don't mind Harry playing my arrangements, but I wish he'd let me play them first. [He laughs.] And I'll tell you another thing—that's a military band. They sound like a marching band. Even my boy Buddy ain't going to get that thing off the ground.' I says, 'Well, if anybody can, he will. But it ain't going to get off the ground.' Buddy did as good a job as anybody could do with that thing. And it still wasn't working."

What, in Hanna's opinion, was holding it back?

"Harry. Harry. Harry. Too much trumpet. Notes too frequent and too high. Too much trumpet. He had some good guys in the band. Ray Sims was good. Willie Smith, very good. My man Red Kelly was there. . . . I left James to go with Woody. For a lot less money, but a lot more music and a lot more fun. And it lasted a lot more years too," Hanna says.

In 1962, Woody Herman was about ready to throw in the towel as a big band leader. In recent years, it had grown increasingly hard for him to get the bookings he wanted. He had tried cutting back to a small group; demand was still somewhat slack, but his expenses were much less. Sticking to a small group appeared the only viable option left. Herman's big bands of recent years hadn't, generally speaking, been as strong musically nor drawn the attention that his big bands of the mid and late '40s and early '50s had.

Hanna was thus invited to become the drummer in the Woody Herman Sextet, not big band, taking the place of Gus Johnson Jr., who was about to leave. Hanna sat in, playing Johnson's drums. "I didn't sound too good," Hanna admits. "I was trying to play Gus Johnson's drums and I can't really reach his pedals; you know, he's so big. And I couldn't read. I sounded pretty bad. Woody said, 'Forget it.' And I say, 'Okay, I'll give you your money back.' "

But not long afterwards, Hanna remembers, "Nat Pierce [Herman's pianist/arranger, who was getting musicians for Herman] called me again, and says: 'Look, Woody's going to take a big band out instead of a sextet. Can you come out for a couple of weeks? I'm determined to have him use you.' Nat fought for me."

Herman figured he'd have a kind of last hurrah with a big band for a month—playing not the book he'd played in recent years, but the best material from all of his past bands—and then stick to a sextet as his standard unit.

"He didn't intend to have the band that long—only a month—and then he was going to go back to the combo permanently. But when the band hit New York City, after about two weeks on the road, it was in shape. Nat Pierce put it together like a watch and man, the band took off! And Woody's been working ever since with the big band. This thing just took off and there was nothing he could do about it. It was like getting on board a runaway train and you just have to hang on, man," Hanna says.

Hanna remembers vividly the night it became clear the band was something special. Herman was breaking it in on the road before coming to New York. After the third or fourth day, a tenor sax player quit. He was replaced by Sal Nistico. "And the first minute Sal hit—he joined the band in Dallas, Texas—boom! It took off. We had a hot player. And I took over. Charlie Andrus was there on bass. And [trumpeter] Bill Chase. Man. It took off. In just one night. It just exploded! People went crazy. Woody went nuts. He said, 'What the hell's happening? What have I got here?'

"He got the three of us in a hotel, in a bar in Chattanooga, Tennessee, on Lookout Mountain. He says to Sal, 'You are going to be my hot ride tenor player. You're not going to play any ballads, because you know I want to use you on the other thing, and you're going to blow till you get tired of playing, and you can play as long as you want.' He said he'd never before told a guy you can blow as long as you want. And he says, 'Bill and I are going to take care of this, and Nat's going to take care of that,' and he looks at me and says, 'You get carte blanche. You do anything you want to do on the drum. You can lay out, you can play, you can play on the tom-tom, you can play Dixieland, whatever you want to do. Carte blanche. The only other guy I said that to was Dave Tough. And you got it.' And that frees you, man. It's like taking a bridle off a race horse and letting him go. That's what he was doing. You can't tell a guy, 'Can you give me more of this or less of that.' The guy says, 'Well, what am I doing wrong?' A lot of leaders do that. No, Woody was just the greatest at that. And that's how that happened.

"He only put that band together so he could work the Metropole for three weeks. We were taking the band out for a week or two first, to blow it in shape. And within three days after we opened at the Metropole, we were booked for a solid year—all the way to the West Coast. Within three days. The word got around. Shelly Manne came in to hear us—and he called up everybody. Shelly was something else, man.

"This band was really the number one band in the country. Count Basie, Ellington, and this band were the three best bands. And I would feel sorry for those other two bands if they got up against this band. Mel Tormé said that: 'You better not put Basie and those guys up against this band. This band will blow anybody out of town.' At that time, Woody made a *strong* comeback.

"By the time we hit the West Coast, the band was booked forever, you know. We were working places Woody had never worked before. It was good. That band made a bunch of records for Phillips.

"Funny thing about the records, though. A guy named Jack Tracy was the producer on all of them. And he first got Woody to do a quintet album. Woody said, 'Well, I'll try.' Five stars. Won an award, you know. Great. And Woody says, 'I want to do another one like that—follow it up.' Jack says, 'Nope. We're going to record that big band of yours at the Metropole.'

" 'Naw, man, that band over there is not in shape; it's just a blowing band. We're ragged.' Jack records it in a studio. *Great.* Still, it's against Woody's wishes, you know. So he says, 'Let's follow up with another one in the studio.' Jack says, 'Nope. We'll do this one *live*.' Woody says, 'Oh man, you know we stretch out, we do tunes for 20 minutes, we can't.' 'I want to do one live.' Woody says, 'I won't allow it. Let's do the quintet record again.' Nope. We recorded live. A Grammy. Jack had more faith in the band than Woody did, you know. And then we came to a parting of the ways that shouldn't have happened, but that's another story."

The band was working constantly during the period Hanna was with it (1962–64)—mostly on the road, but with perhaps 12 weeks a year in New York. The New York bookings were necessary to generate publicity and other bookings, but were financially less rewarding—not that Herman cared much about money, so long as enough was coming in to keep the band going.

Pay adjustments were made during New York bookings,

Hanna recalls. He was one of the higher-paid members of the band, but he took a $50-a-week pay cut during New York bookings. There was less money to divvy up, and the lower-paid members had to be paid more in New York than on the road since the cost of living was higher in New York, Hanna says. "The Metropole only paid $4000 a week for the whole band and Woody. So we had to come down. Actually, the guys that made $125 a week, they would come up to $150. See, and the guys that made $200 or $180 a week would come down to $150. It's like a communist operation. So, the fourth trumpet player and the third trombone player made as much as the lead trumpet player, the drummer, and Sal Nistico—pretty weird but we didn't squawk.

"But I always lost about $75 on an engagement here. I always came out owing $75 because of the cost of living. You had to pay a hotel out of that. And eat. You always ate out. And booze bills, they could run up pretty good, you know. Especially if you started early in the day. So I'd come out having to borrow $75 to get out of town, after all the money. But it was still worth it. I was wringing wet every night—Jesus Christ. Four one-hour sets that we did there, one tune after another.

"We were all up behind the bar at the Metropole, single-file. Sanchez over there, me here. Bass, piano, trumpets—trombones way down there. There was a mirror. I could almost see them. But they were sort of in the dark down there. And only one mike. Single file. Lined up like this, sideways. We thought it was going to be a disaster. We said, 'It'll never work; we can't go in there with new arrangements, we have to rehearse everything on the road.' Woody says, 'The sound will bounce right off the mirror instantly. I know it'll work.' He was 100% right. I said, 'No, it's going to go blip-blip-blip-blip-blip'—but it didn't. It played like that.

"There might have been a delay for the sound down the other end from the drums, but Bill Chase always looked in the mirror and he watched the hi-hats going up and down like that, and that's how he got his time. He'd have to wait one beat to get the start. . . . Tempos here [he beats off a fast clip]. We always played that fast. One tune a set we played that fast. He'd just watch in the mirror like that. I was way down here and he was down, down there. I'd look at him and he'd look—pow!—and we'd hit. Benny Goodman came in and he says, 'How the hell do you do this, Woody?' And Woody says, 'It's all done with mirrors.'

"It was really something. We had a real good time there. All good guys in that band. As good a time as I've ever had in a band. And we played the whole history of the band. We played some new things, like 'Wine and Roses.' Some songs that Nat wrote very nice arrangements on: a few originals, some things Oscar Peterson did, a few things that Horace Silver did—Nat arranged these songs for these guys. And then we went back to one or two from the '50s. A couple of things from the Third Herd from the early '50s—you know, with Dave McKenna and Sonny Igoe and those guys. And then some from the Zoot and Stan band. And some from the original band. One or two from the very first band of the '30s. 'Woodchopper's Ball'—the exact same arrangement. He's had three or four different arrangements of this over the years. This was the original. . . . We didn't know how to play it. We had to go out and buy a stock chart for a buck. A whole dollar! And we played what was right on the paper, too. The original voicings. Jesus. For high school bands. That's what we played.

"Reading music was almost nothing with that particular band. Now it is important, because Woody has Eastman-style, very difficult arrangements. But in those days we used to get 'em as simple as we could get 'em. This was not a reading band. Everything was done—'Try this. Okay, we'll play this, you do that.' One time we went over to do a clinic at a school, and man, we couldn't get any of their music. We sounded so rotten. These kids are looking at us like: 'This is a professional band?' The guy that brought us over, he was sort of getting mad at us. He thought we were drunk. We were trying, man." But only a couple of players in that band were real readers, Hanna says. "I told them, 'I haven't looked at a piece of music in six years.'

"Arrangers get overrated anyway, a lot of arrangers. I think most of them ruin jazz today—along with the electric bass, you know. Everything's overwritten. Not enough room for the jazz guy. Most arrangers can figure ways to stop it from swinging.

You don't have any Ernie Wilkinses or Neal Heftis or Al Cohns around anymore. Very rare. Nat Pierce writes very good. Real good swinging stuff. Brookmeyer used to—he's writing so deep now that I think most of his stuff is unplayable. Or if you do get it right, then it really sounds bad. I don't know what got into him—or what didn't get into him.

"I stayed in Woody's Band two and a half years. Made my getaway in '64. I stayed in 'The Merv Griffin Show' for 10 years, man. Whew. Now there's the stupidest thing I ever heard of!"

Money was being spent freely in an attempt to establish Merv Griffin as a late-night TV rival to Johnny Carson. The show began its run with a truly star-studded big band (later in the run, the size of the band would be scaled back) conducted by Mort Lindsay. Hanna was delighted, not just with the financial security playing on the show promised him, but with the idea of working among such musical heavyweights as trombonist/arranger Bob Brookmeyer, trumpeter Bill Berry, and guitarist Jim Hall, all of whom were in the orchestra when the show first went on the air. "It was one of the best bands I've ever played with in my life," he says. The thing none of the jazz musicians could have anticipated was what little use would be made of their talents.

Hanna wasn't impressed with Lindsay's abilities as a leader, saying he tried to ignore Lindsay's directing—or misdirecting, as he viewed it—of the orchestra. He explains lightly the way some musicians—himself among them—coped with the situation: "You come in as loaded as you dare get, you know, in a way that you can still do the job; that way he doesn't bother you." And Hanna was much less impressed with the quality of the performers the band had to back.

He notes: "I thought the acts on the show were bad when we started, but a year later they were so awful, and 10 years later they were unbearable. We had a guy named Danny Meehan on the show and he used to whistle standing on his head. Then we had Donna McKechnie come on and we thought this was awful. I said, 'Jesus Christ, I played with Jimmy Rushing, man, Jack Teagarden. They're singers. Louis Armstrong. Those guys can sing. Jeez, these people sound like a bunch of idiots.' Nanny-goat vibratos, you know. The music was all like this . . . Charo, Sonny and Cher [he pronounces the names with utter distaste]. I mean, we're *playing*, this fucking band is a *live* band. We got good players. And now it's: 'Can you give me more of this?' As if you've just learned how to play. They want an ugly sound, a stupid sound. *Duhn-duhn*—we're clunking away and they're saying: 'That's it, that's the feeling I want.' And I'm thinking: 'You don't want *any* feeling is what you want, kid.' Jim Hall's going *sheesh*— he just had to put down the guitar and leave, one day, with Leslie Gore. He had to accompany her and he couldn't stand the music. He said, 'Pardon me,' went outside, just sat down on the curb and said, 'Jesus, what am I doing here?' I think Brookmeyer was the first guy to leave. Then Jim Hall. . . .

"And this guy, Danny Meehan, comes back on the show again after about a year—the same music, standing on his head, whistling, the same act—and he sounded like a million dollars compared to the acts that had been on in the meantime! We said, 'Jesus, it's a pleasure playing for this idiot. Man, that shows how bad off we're getting.' Enough was enough. We finally came down to the end in California—the show moved out there." Hanna was getting to do a good bit of freelance recording in California and he was receiving offers to play gigs that were musically far more intriguing than "The Merv Griffin Show."

"In '74, Oscar Peterson asked me if I wanted to go to Russia with him. I met him at a jam session on a boat, the Norway. I told him I didn't know and he says, 'I'll give you $1500 a week.' I says, 'Let's go!' I didn't get that kind of money before. So I went over to Russia. I just took a leave of absence from 'The Merv Griffin Show'—and I never came back.

"After that, I just started working with whoever—freelancing, and that's all I've been doing. I worked with Supersax; Joe Venuti, which was great; Bob Wilber and Kenny Davern ('Soprano Summit'), which was very good—I did two albums with them; Marty Grosz, he's exceptional; I worked with him and Dick Sudhalter recently, out on the Island. Now I'm supposed to do a trip to England with Kenny Davern and Dick Wellstood. . . . Guys call, ask me to work with them. I've never made a phone call in my life. I've never asked anybody for a job."

Hanna has played with artists of varied ages and idioms, everything from the Dixieland of Max Kaminsky to the straight-ahead sounds of Freddie Hubbard. "The ability to really play with anybody is to play with the bass player's feel," Hanna says. "That's all that is, it has nothing to do with whether you're playing Dixieland or bebop or whatever. Oh, the bop guys, they didn't swing worth a shit—so many goddam notes—Charlie Parker excepted, naturally; that guy could *swing*."

Who are some of the musicians Hanna particularly likes playing with?

"Scotty Hamilton's my very favorite guy to play with. Zoot Sims. Al Cohn. And [guitarist] Ed Bickert in Canada—a very, very good player. I like the bass player Steve Wallace. Carl Fontana. Anybody would like to play with these guys; it's so damn easy. Dave McKenna, naturally; he's going to sound good no matter what happens. Herbie Ellis. Ross Tompkins. Jack Sheldon. Fantastic. There's a great singer, too, by the way. I think he's the best singer there is. He's dynamite. But there's a lot of other people. Count Basie's very, very easy to play with. I worked with his big band, with Tony Bennett. I worked with Tony for a while. We won't talk much about that. At least the first two weeks when I joined, it was Count Basie's Band. Man, what a pleasure. They make it real easy. Especially Count Basie at the piano."

Has Hanna ever wanted to lead his own band?

"Big band? Oh, no! Jesus. How those guys do it! Too much headaches. I always wanted to have a nice little combo—and then let somebody else take it over, so I can play the drums. I don't want to get in the arguments for the money, and get the transportation. That's too much trouble," he insists. On the rare occasions when he has led groups of his own in New York or California, he says he was more concerned with getting the best guys to work with him than in making money. One time he and trombonist Carl Fontana were set to co-lead a quartet date at a restaurant, using Dave McKenna on piano and Herb Mickman on bass. Hanna recalls: "Dave McKenna's crazy about Herbie Ellis, so I said, 'I'll get Herbie, too.' Then [tenor saxist] Plas Johnson came and sat in. I asked him, 'What are you doing on the weekends? I'll put you on the payroll. The guy's giving me so much money;

I'll just take less for myself.' I paid the guys $450 for the night. It usually pays $250. Herbie says, 'You don't have to pay the guys that much.' I says, 'Are you or are you not the very best there is?' 'We're the best.' I says, 'Then you got to get the best money. I can't pay you like I pay a regular cat. You're the best, you're going to get the most.' Then Bill Berry came and sat in, so I threw him on the payroll, too. Carl Fontana says, 'Man, you better not have anyone else sit in. You keep hiring them if they sit in.' So I wound up with about a seven-piece quartet. And we broke it up! I didn't know it was going to sound that good. The ideal jam session. I can't do much from the drums back there but Carl Fontana put it together, and Herb Ellis. Between Carl and Herbie—they gave all the signals and the cutoffs, the ins and outs. They were perfect."

Hanna helped Woody Herman put together a small band for an engagement at New York's Rainbow Room, making sure Herman used Scott Hamilton and Warren Vaché. "Scott and Warren have a lot of stuff worked out. When you hire them, you've got an automatic book. You say, 'We'll do this tune.' Well, they've got three different alternate riffs on the same song. And they must have 40 songs in their heads. When you hire them, you don't ever look at the music. Scott doesn't know what a whole note looks like (Warren's a fantastic reader)—but Scott's got everything in his head. And they have these thousands of arrangements there," he says. At the time of our interview, Hanna had recently done some big band work with Herman; he was currently doing some small group dates in New York with Herman; then they were heading off to Europe and Japan.

Does Hanna, who's had considerable experience in both areas, prefer drumming with big bands or small groups?

"With a good big band, there's nothing like it. With a bad big band—there's nothing like that either! Whew! Boy! You got to have a waiter handy at all times: 'Bring me another! Make that two!' " (And as for Mel Lewis' assertion that Hanna is one of only four master big band drummers, Hanna says with a smile: "Mel doesn't get out of town too much! Jeff Hamilton is real good. Terry Clarke is great. Don Lamond, one of the greatest of all time, is still playing. Gus Johnson's great with a big band. So

Jake Hanna. (Photo by Bill Walters.)

Jake Hanna drums for tenor saxist Scott Hamilton (whom he calls "my very favorite guy to play with") and trumpeter Joe Wilder. (Photo by Chip Deffaa.)

there are a few guys.") Hanna says he likes working with a good combo—so long as it's a *good* combo. "If it's bad music, a combo's hell. You've got to be very choosy who you're working with. I am, anyway. Guys say, 'Can you work this job?' I ask, 'Who's on it?' 'Hey man, it pays $200 a night! What are you asking, who's on it?' 'Who's on it? I'll do it for $100, if you got the right guys. But I won't do it for any amount of money if you don't have the right guys. Not for $1000.' And I've turned down jobs that paid better money, just because they had the wrong guys on them. Singers are the worst of all. Singers! Christ!

"I worked with Bing Crosby—now that's a different story. He's great. That's like not playing at all, when he's singing. He plays the drums for you with his singing, you know. Perfect time. Best time of any cat I've ever worked with, including Sal or Zoot or Basie or anybody. Fantastic time. He swung better than anybody I ever played with. Oh man, and he was even better at his tempos. I don't care what tempo it is, either. 'Them There Eyes,' you can't have it too fast, you know. . . . Man, he was sailing. You could go as fast as you want and he was right on it, all the way. A whole 32-piece band and he'll lead 'em right in. I played everywhere with him—concerts, TV shows, on Broadway—for the last two years of his life [1975–77]. He hadn't worked live in public for years before then.

"Bing's show on Broadway was dull, because the show was so big, with his family and everything. What are you going to do, hit a golf ball on stage? I mean, one of his kids was good at golf, but—stop! You're liable to *injure* somebody. And his wife trying to sing—whew! Was that a tough one. But Bing could fix anything up with his singing; he was that good. Photographic memory, too. You know, he just looked at a thing like this, and he's got it.

"We went to Norway on a one-nighter. He got there, tired, and it was raining out. It was an open-air thing. He had to lead 50 of the old Scandinavian radio stars—it was the 100th anniversary of radio or something. They're all going to sing a song in Norwegian and he's going to read the lyrics. Well, he looked at it like this, memorized all the Norwegian lyrics, plus the melody. He did do it for about a half hour in the back room, rehearsing all the people, then went out and just did it, led the whole thing. He was the only one with a mike. Perfect. Can you believe that guy? Fantastic. Very relaxed guy. That's one singer that you don't mind working for."

What other singers did Hanna like working for?

"Jimmy Rushing. Great. Jimmy Rushing. And Rosemary Clooney, naturally. What a snap! Anything's OK with her. Sylvia Sims is like that. 'What key do you want, Sylvia?' 'Any key is OK with me.' 'What tempo?' 'Pick out your own tempo.' Jesus Christ, she's something else. She's great, you know. I like dealing with her.

"There's a lot of them I just cannot stand—I don't want to mention names because they're too famous. Some of them pay really good money, but it ain't worth it. Ulcer city. They're just crazy. I guess they're just not used to bossing people about, being the leader. Crosby never bossed anybody. But you don't have to do that! If you hire pros, it should take care of itself. They're trained for it. It's not a music school."

Hanna played a significant role in Clooney's comeback in the late '70s. He recalls: "I put together her first Concord album, *Everything's Coming Up Rosie*; I got the tunes and hired the musicians. The other ones, since then, she did herself.

"We were working with Bing Crosby when I got her. I told her, 'Jesus, you're a jazz singer, you're not a pop singer. You're a jazz singer that happened to have some pop hits.' 'No, no,' she said. 'Yeah. You were with Tony Pastor's band, he's a jazz musician—he had great time, swings like a bastard.' She said, 'I learned a lot from him, we had some good guys.' 'Honestly, you want to sing with a little jazz band?' 'I've never done it.'

"I told her, 'Nothing to it. Whatever songs you want to sing in the shower, that's what we'll do. So you don't have to look for a hit that will sell. You just look for songs that you like to sing.' 'Can you get me a date?' I say, 'Let me call this guy, Carl Jefferson [the president of Concord Records].' Carl goes, 'Rosemary Clooney? Absolutely.' I say to her, 'What do you want?' 'I'll do it for nothing.' I told her, 'No, no. You talk to the guy.' They made some kind of a deal and she had a good time." Clooney, after a stretch of relative inactivity, began recording for Concord in 1977. She's continued recording successfully for Concord since then, using small jazz bands including such musicians as Hanna, John Oddo, Warren Vaché Jr., and Scott Hamilton, using them in her live appearances (when they're available), as well. She's repositioned herself, as Hanna had believed she could, as a jazz-inflected pop singer.

Clooney's first Concord recording session was also the first Concord recording session for Scott Hamilton, who was not yet widely known. Hanna takes credit for bringing Hamilton into the Concord fold. "I told Carl Jefferson, 'I want to record this tenor player.' He says, 'Oh, we'll use Plas Johnson.' I said, 'Jeff, if you don't mind, use this guy. Because I promised him $1000 if I didn't record him by May first.' 'Jesus! What the hell did you do that for?' I told him, 'Well, that's one way to get you off your ass. I put my money in Scott's pocket.' Scott didn't have my money, really—he thought I was crazy when I gave him the money; he gave it right back. I gave him a $1000 bill that Bing gave me. (That's how Bing used to pay us. He used to pay us more than that, but he'd always give you a $1000 bill in your pocket at the end of the week.) But I told Jefferson I'd given Scott $1000."

Jefferson flew Hamilton out to California, heard him play, and was so impressed that he agreed to record an album under Hamilton's own name the same day they recorded Clooney. "So we did two whole albums in one day. We went out to eat and did another whole album. We just scribbled down the tunes Scott wanted to do, at the supper table. We kept the same band." Hamilton's debut album for Concord, *Scott Hamilton is a Good Wind Blowing Us No Ill*, had the same five musicians who'd backed Clooney on her album: Hamilton, Hanna, Nat Pierce, Monty Budwig, and Bill Berry. Since then, Hamilton has gone on to become one of Concord's most prolifically recorded artists. Hanna has played with Hamilton on such albums as *No Bass Hit* and *Major League* (both trio sessions with Dave McKenna as the third player), *Concord Super Band in Tokyo, Concord Jazz All Stars at the Northsea Jazz Festival*, and so on.

Hanna has been a ubiquitous presence on Concord albums, recording with artists as varied as Herb Ellis, Ernestine Anderson, Snooky Young, Marian McPartland, Tal Farlow, Dick Johnson, Jack Sheldon, Marshall Royal, Red Norvo, Emily Remler, Teddy Wilson, Warren Vaché Jr., Barney Kessel, Lorraine Feather, Bing Crosby, Buddy Tate, Rosemary Clooney, Sweets Edison, Al Cohn, and Woody Herman, among others.

He has also recorded several albums for Concord as a leader or co-leader: *Jake Takes Manhattan, Kansas City Express*, and *The Hanna-Fontana Band* (co-led by Carl Fontana). "*Jake Takes Manhattan* was an accident," he says. "We were supposed to record Rosemary Clooney but she got sick. So we went into the studio—the musicians that were going to have backed Rosie that day. We said, 'Who knows this tune? Anybody know this?' And we made the album."

Hanna was particularly pleased with the way *Kansas City Express* turned out. "I got my guys—Nat Pierce, Bill Berry, Monty Budwig, Richie Kamuca—and I got Mary Ann McCall to sing a couple of songs. Somehow we found her. We brought her back. It took the engineer about an hour and a half to set up. Then we recorded one side in about a half an hour—as long as it took to play it. And it all worked out. So we get out of there an hour and a half early the first date. The next day we did even quicker. That record came out good."

Some of the best albums he's done have been made in very little time. If you're dealing with jazz pros, Hanna believes, they've learned to make their statements efficiently. "Real jazz is about economy," he says. "That's what good music is. It's economy. Cutting out all the excess and the bullshit. Hitting the right chords and choosing the right notes.

"I did an album with Count Basie for Pablo once. It took one hour and 55 minutes for the whole album: Count Basie, Freddie Hubbard, J. J. [Johnson], Lockjaw [Davis], Joe Pass, and myself. That's the fastest thing I ever did outside of a live album."

Hanna recalls going into a recording studio once, around 1970 or '71, and seeing signs saying things like "No jazz recording allowed in this studio" and "Jazz is dead." The studio owner wasn't kidding either, Hanna adds. "There was a conspiracy against jazz. They make most of their money on rock stuff because those guys take so long to do a date. You know, with players like Jack Sheldon and Ray Brown, it's one take and you're out of there. The engineer just turns the machine on and goes and reads a magazine. . . . They say, 'I can't make any money on you guys. Bring me the amateurs. They never get anything right. I can put in three weeks here and make a bundle. Charge them so much a tape and so much for studio time.' A rock date takes a long time to make. Six months sometimes."

Hanna adds he doubts the engineers at that studio had recorded much jazz. When Ray Brown brought in his acoustic bass, one engineer placed the microphones at the top of the bass as if he imagined the sound emanated from there. "Ray looks at Herb Ellis and he goes, 'Hey fellas, I don't think these guys ever saw one of these before.' I think he was right, too!" Hanna adds that the engineer asked him if he'd remove the front head of his bass drum, perhaps so the drum could be muffled, as is common on rock dates. Hanna got the engineer to leave him alone by claiming he wasn't going to play the bass drum at all—only cymbals. Hanna is convinced that engineers can wreck the sound of any instrument if given half a chance. And he is very particular about the sound of his equipment. His Chinese cymbal, he notes with pride, was actually hand-hammered in China more than 100 years ago. His favorite cymbal, originally owned by the late George Wettling, was made in 1927. He uses a 1937 Slingerland Radio King drum, given to him by Frankie Ippolito, that was played in the Glenn Miller Army Air Force Band by both Ray McKinley and Ippolito, who was McKinley's alternate on drums in the band. It was trimmed down somewhat after World War Two when narrower drums came into fashion, but, with an old-style authentic calf-skin head, it still gets "a beautiful tone—a warm tone," he says. There's something fitting about Hanna having inherited some of that old drumming equipment, for he sees himself as continuing the tradition to which it belonged.

Hanna has little use for rock. He says bluntly: "Rock music itself is a big bore—the stupidest crap I ever heard. Write three chords, one chord, Jesus. How can you break an instrument and call that music, for Christ's sake? I can't believe it. That's the lowest. And that's the corniest group of humans I've encountered in my lifetime—rock 'n' roll people. Well, there are good guys in the recording studios that are playing the music well. But actually the people involved in rock 'n' roll are some of the most arrogant nitwits I've ever bumped into. And I find most of the people listening to it remind me of mentally retarded people. They're still listening to that crap? God! You're supposed to get rid of that when you're 14 years old. And move on, you know. Move on back to Beethoven. But this is—I can't see how music can regress like that and be called quality music.

"And these Grammys! That's where they give an award to a record that's sold over a million copies. That's all it is. It's redundant. They've already got their reward in their money. Why are they giving them a reward? There's no quality in the record, no musicianship involved."

When he's at home in Los Angeles, Hanna usually has the radio tuned to a station playing classical music. (There is one jazz DJ in Los Angeles whom Hanna likes, Chuck Niles, but Hanna's rarely at home when Niles is on, he says.) Hanna's not fond of a lot of what he says is "passed off as jazz" these days, anyway. For relaxation, he likes watching sports.

Any advice Hanna has to offer aspiring drummers?

"Get your ass up to Toronto and study with Jim Blackley! That's Terry Clarke's teacher. And he's the absolute best teacher I ever bumped into in my whole life," Hanna says.

And he has this advice to offer to aspiring jazz players of any instrument: "Listen like a bastard. Get all the Zoot records you can, all the Basie records you can, all the Louis Armstrong records you can, all the good Lester Young records you can. Listen. Listen to the melody guy playing. Never mind all the notes. Listen to the melody guy and you'll learn to play the instrument by doing that."

In listening to music himself, Hanna takes pleasure where he finds it. "I've been on some mediocre bands where Monty Budgwig's playing on bass—he's the best musician there—and man, you can't wait for that bass solo to come up, to hear some real quality music. He's my favorite on the bass," Hanna says. "I like individuals in music, that's what I like. And the more good individuals you see collected on one bandstand, you know you're going to hear some good music. You see Zoot Sims up there with a bunch of bums, you're going to hear one guy playing good and the rest of the song is going to be a waste of time. You'll hear Zoot playing. Or Al. But the more good guys you get, the more good music you'll have."

1985

Bibliography

Allen, Frederick Lewis, *Only Yesterday: An Informal History of the 1920s.* New York, Perennial Library/Harper and Row, 1964.

Armstrong, Louis, *Satchmo: My Life in New Orleans.* New York, Prentice Hall, 1954.

Balliett, Whitney, *American Musicians: Fifty-six Portraits in Jazz.* New York, Oxford University Press, 1986.

Basie, Count (as told to Albert Murray), *Good Morning Blues, The Autobiography of Count Basie.* New York, Random House, 1985.

Berger, Morroe, Edward Berger, and James Patrick, *Benny Carter: A Life in American Music.* Metuchen, N.J., Scarecrow Press and the Institute of Jazz Studies, Rutgers University, 1982.

Berton, Ralph, *Remembering Bix.* New York, Harper and Row, 1974.

Blesh, Rudi, *Shining Trumpets, A History of Jazz.* New York, Alfred A. Knopf, 1946.

Bruyninckx, Walter, *Sixty Years of Recorded Jazz, 1917–1977.* Mechelen, Belgium, n.p., 1978.

Carmichael, Hoagy, *The Stardust Road.* New York, Greenwood Press, 1969.

Case, Brian and Stan Britt, revised and updated by Chrissie Murray, *The Harmony Illustrated Encyclopeda of Jazz,* third edition. New York, Harmony Books, 1987.

Castelli, Vittorio, Evert (Ted) Kaleveld and Liborio Pusateri, *The Bix Bands.* Milan, Raretone, 1972.

In the Mainstream

Charters, Samuel B. and Leonard Kunstadt, *Jazz: A History of the New York Scene*. New York, Da Capo Press, 1981.

Chilton, John, *Who's Who of Jazz*, fourth edition. New York, Da Capo Press, 1985.

Clayton, Buck and Nancy Miller Elliott, *Buck Clayton's Jazz World*. New York, Oxford University Press, 1987.

Collier, James Lincoln, *Duke Ellington*. New York, Oxford University Press, 1987.

Condon, Eddie and Hank O'Neal, *The Eddie Condon Scrapbook of Jazz*. New York, St. Martin's Press, 1973.

Condon, Eddie and Thomas Sugrue, *We Called It Music*. New York, Henry Holt and Company, 1947.

Dance, Stanley, *The World of Count Basie*. New York, Charles Scribner's Sons, 1980.

Dance, Stanley, *The World of Duke Ellington*. New York, Charles Scribner's Sons, 1970.

Dance, Stanley, *The World of Earl Hines*. New York, Charles Scribner's Sons, 1977.

Dance, Stanley, *The World of Swing*. New York, Charles Scribner's Sons, 1974.

Deffaa, Chip, "The Sons of Bix Keep Blowing," in the *Princeton Alumni Weekly*. Princeton, N.J., May 2, 1984, pp. 30–35.

Deffaa, Chip, *Swing Legacy*. Metuchen, N.J., Scarecrow Press and the Institute of Jazz Studies, Rutgers University, 1989.

Deffaa, Chip, *Voices of the Jazz Age*. Urbana, University of Illinois Press, 1990.

DeLong, Thomas A., *Pops: Paul Whiteman, King of Jazz*. Piscataway, N.J., New Century Publishers, 1983.

Eberly, Philip K., *Music in the Air*. New York, Hastings House, 1982.

Ellington, Duke, *Music is My Mistress*. Garden City, N.Y., Doubleday, 1973.

Feather, Leonard, *The Encyclopedia of Jazz*. New York, Da Capo Press, 1985.

Feather, Leonard, *The Encyclopedia of Jazz in the '60s*. New York, Da Capo Press, 1986.

Feather, Leonard, *From Satchmo to Miles*. Briarcliff Manor, N.Y., Stein and Day, 1972.

Feather, Leonard and Ira Gitler, *The Encyclopedia of Jazz in the '70s*. New York, Da Capo Press, 1987.

Ferguson, Otis, *The Otis Ferguson Reader* (edited by Dorothy Chamberlain and Robert Wilson). Highland Park, Ill., December Press, 1983.

BIBLIOGRAPHY

Freeman, Bud, *If You Know of a Better Life*. Dublin, Bashall Eves, 1976.

Freeman, Bud, *You Don't Look Like a Musician*. Detroit, Balamp Publishing, 1974.

Giddins, Gary, *Rhythm-a-ning: Jazz Tradition and Innovation in the '80s*. New York, Oxford University Press, 1985.

Giddins, Gary, *Riding on a Blue Note*. New York, Oxford University Press, 1981.

Giddins, Gary, *Satchmo*. New York, A Dolphin Book, Doubleday, 1988.

Gitler, Ira, *Swing to Bop*. New York, Oxford University Press, 1985.

Goodman, Benny, and Irving Kolodin, *The Kingdom of Swing*. New York, Frederick Ungar Publishing Company, 1961.

Gourse, Leslie, *Louis' Children: American Jazz Singers*. New York, Quill, 1984.

Hadlock, Richard, *Jazz Masters of the Twenties*. New York, Macmillan, 1965.

Haskins, Jim, *The Cotton Club*. New York, New American Library, 1984.

Holiday, Billie, with William Dufty, *Lady Sings the Blues*. New York, Lancer Books, 1969.

Jewell, Derek, *A Portrait of Duke Ellington*. New York, W.W. Norton and Company, 1977.

Johnson, Grady, *The Five Pennies*. New York, Dell, 1959.

Keepnews, Orrin and Bill Grauer, Jr., *A Pictorial History of Jazz*. New York, Bonanza Books, 1966.

Kernfeld, Barry, ed., *The New Grove Dictionary of Jazz*. New York, Grove's Dictionaries of Music, 1988.

Kirk, Andy, as told to Amy Lee, *Twenty Years on Wheels*. Ann Arbor, The University of Michigan Press, 1989.

Larkin, Philip, *All What Jazz*. New York, Farrar Straus Giroux, 1985.

Lax, Roger and Frederick Smith, *The Great Song Thesaurus*. New York, Oxford University Press, 1984.

McPartland, Marian. *All in Good Time*. New York, Oxford University Press, 1987.

Miller, Tari, ed., *The Princeton Recollector*. Princeton, N.J., 1980.

Morgenstern, Dan (text) and Ole Brask (photographs), *Jazz People*. New York, Harry N. Abrams, Inc., 1976.

Pearson, Nathan W., Jr., *Goin' to Kansas City*. Urbana, University of Illinois Press, 1987.

Pleasants, Henry, *The Great American Popular Singers*. New York, Simon and Schuster, 1974.

Polic, Edward F., *The Glenn Miller Army Air Force Band: Sustineo Alas / I*

Sustain the Wings. Metuchen, N.J., Scarecrow Press and the Institute of Jazz Studies, Rutgers University, 1989.

Ramsey, Frederick, Jr. and Charles Edward Smith, editors, *Jazzmen.* New York, Limelight Editions, 1985.

Rust, Brian, *Jazz Records, 1897–1942.* Chigwell, England, Storyville Publications, 1982.

Sanford, Herb, *Tommy and Jimmy: The Dorsey Years.* New York, Da Capo Press, 1980.

Sanjek, Russell, *From Print to Plastic: Publishing and Promoting America's Popular Music (1900–1980).* New York, Institute for Studies in American Music, Conservatory of Music, Brooklyn College of the City University of New York, 1983.

Schuller, Gunther, *Early Jazz.* New York, Oxford University Press, 1968.

Schuller, Gunther, *Musing.* New York, Oxford University Press, 1986.

Schuller, Gunther, *The Swing Era.* New York, Oxford University Press, 1989.

Shapiro, Nat and Nat Hentoff, editors, *Hear Me Talkin' to Ya.* New York, Dover Publications, 1966.

Shapiro, Nat and Nat Hentoff, editors, *The Jazz Makers.* New York, Rinehart, 1957.

Shaw, Arnold, *52nd Street: The Street of Jazz.* New York, Da Capo Press, 1977.

Simon, George T., *The Big Bands.* New York, Schirmer Books, 1981.

Simon, George T., *Simon Says: The Sights and Sounds of the Swing Era, 1935–1955.* New York, Galahad Books, 1971.

Stearns, Marshall, *The Story of Jazz.* New York, Mentor Books, 1958.

Stearns, Marshall and Jean Stearns, *Jazz Dance.* New York, Schirmer Books, 1968.

Stewart, Rex, *Jazz Masters of the Thirties.* New York, Macmillan, 1972.

Stillman, Edmund and Marshall Davidson, *The American Heritage History of the 20's and 30's.* New York, American Heritage Publishing Co., Inc., 1970.

Sudhalter, Richard M. and Philip R. Evans, with William Dean-Myatt, *Bix, Man and Legend.* New Rochelle, N.Y., Arlington House, 1974.

Acknowledgments

I am greatly indebted to the Institute of Jazz Studies at Rutgers University, its director, Dan Morgenstern, and his associates, Ed Berger and Vincent Pelote. They have always been ready and able to give whatever assistance was desired. I have drawn upon the Institute's collection of jazz clippings, books, oral histories, and photos.

My thanks to the editors of the various publications for which I originally wrote articles about musicians in this book: Leslie Johnson of *The Mississippi Rag*, Rick Mattingly and Rick Van Horn of *Modern Drummer*, V. A. Musetto, Sue Byrom, and Clarence Fanto of *The New York Post*, W. Royal Stokes of *JazzTimes*, Bill Smith and John Norris of *Coda* (Canada), Ed Shanaphy of *Sheet Music*, Florence Kooistra of *The Ridgewood News*, Larry Marsheck of *New Jersey Monthly*, Warren Vaché Sr. of *Jersey Jazz*, and Dennis Matthews of *Crescendo* (England). Earlier, shorter versions of most profiles in this book originally appeared in *The Mississippi Rag*: Bucky and John Pizzarelli, October 1984 issue; Mahlon Clark, May 1985; Joe Wilder, August 1985; Bill Challis, December 1988 and January 1989; George Kelly, April 1990; Erskine Hawkins, May 1990; Doc Cheatham, June and July 1990 (a portion of my Doc Cheatham profile originally appeared in *Coda*, October/November 1990); Buddy Morrow, August 1990;

In the Mainstream

Andy Kirk, September 1990; Jake Hanna, November 1990; Ray McKinley, January 1991; Ken Peplowski, May 1991; Bill Dillard, July 1991. Earlier, shorter versions of my profiles of Sonny Igoe and Oliver Jackson originally appeared in *Modern Drummer*, November 1984 and August 1986 issues, respectively.

I'm highly grateful to Duncan Schiedt, Nancy Miller Elliott, Bill Walters, Zack Cullens, and Frank Driggs for making available photos from their extensive collections. My special thanks to Frank Jolliffe for his conscientious proofreading.

I appreciate the assistance in various ways provided by George T. Simon, Richard M. Sudhalter, Vince Giordano, Rich Conaty, Stan Hester, Lloyd Rauch, Ian Whitcomb, Phil Schaap, Joe Boughton, Alan Roberts, Evan Challis, Merilee Trost of Concord Records, Marilyn Lipsius of RCA, Michael Bloom of GRP, Didier Deutsch of Atlantic, Wendell Echols and George Buck of Jazzology, Charles Bourgeois of Festival Productions, Phil Evans, Jerry Mann, Earl Kunzig, Mary Lugo, Lewis Porter, Barry Barth, Will Friedwald, Edward Enck, Brian Gari, Ron Neal, George Boyle, Mary Beth McGeary, Herb Goldman, Len Kunstadt, and Deb and Alvin. Thanks, too, to Rebecca Reitz for her aid in connecting me with people, and to the indefatigable Bernice Doyle of *The New York Post* for many kindnesses. My appreciation, also, to Stanley Dance, not just for nudging me, some time ago, to collect my profiles into books but for originally coining the term "mainstream jazz" (he called it "a kind of jazz which, while neither 'traditional' nor 'modern,' is better than both"). The term is used more loosely today than when Dance created it in the 1950s, but it's still a useful one.

Many thanks to Princeton's Ferris Professor of Journalism Emeritus Irving Dilliard and Lanny Jones. My appreciation, also, to Randy Block, Jim Cortese, A. Scott Berg, and the late Robert Alexander for their early help—it's nice to have people who believe in you—and to Wil Wheaton, who provided more assistance than he realized in conversation one afternoon at the All-American Burger stand on Sunset Boulevard. And, of course, my deep gratitude to the musicians who made this project so pleasurable for me, and to my family.

Index

INDEX

INDEX

INDEX

Hammond, John, 139, 140, 155, 164
Hampton, Lionel, 5, 6, 249, 254, 261, 263, 271, 335
"Hangin' Around Boudon," 161
"Hangover Square," 109
Hanna, Jake, 6, 43, 333–357
The Hanna-Fontana Band, 354
Hannah and Her Sisters, 329
Hanratty's, 322, 329, 330
"Happy Go Lucky Local," 194
"Hard Hearted Hannah," 110, 226
Harlem Blues and Jazz Band, The, 203, 219, 220
Harlem Opera House, The, 139
"Harlem Twister, The," 156
Harmon, Dave, 50
Harmony Kings, The, 290
Harris, Barry, 264
Harris, Bill, 238, 244
Hart, William S., 152
"Hawaiian War Chant," 185
Hawkins, Coleman, 94, 162, 206, 207, 266, 267, 293
Hawkins, Erskine, 5, 137–149
Hayes, Clancy, 133, 136
Haymes, Joe, 169, 170
Haynes, Cyril, 208, 209, 212
Haynes, Roy, 299
Hayton, Lennie, 65
"He May Be Your Man But He Comes to See Me Sometimes," 188
"Heat Wave," 192
Heath, Percy, 244
Heath, Ted, 146
"Heebie Jeebies," 119, 120
Hefti, Neal, 335, 345
Heleny, Joel, 43
"Help Yourself to Happiness," 69

Henderson, Fletcher, 12, 18, 29, 30, 35, 52, 66, 69, 73, 94, 95, 113, 153, 162, 165, 194, 301, 311, 313
Henderson, Jimmy, 111
Henderson, Skitch, 276
Hendrickson, Al, 227
Henry, Heywood, 138, 142
Hentoff, Nat, 132, 135
Herbert, Arthur, 162
"Here Comes Cookie," 156
Herfurt, Skeets, 97, 177
Herman, Maxie, 192
Herman, Woody, 5, 6, 118, 172, 191, 235, 236, 238, 241–243, 246, 291, 335–338, 340, 341–343, 345, 348, 354
Hester, Mary Lee, 184
Hey Doc, 41
"Hey Lawdy Mama," 87
"Hey, Mrs. Jones," 194
Heywood, Eddie, 36
Hickory House, The, 337
Higginbotham, J. C., 114, 163, 266
Highlights in Jazz, 219
Hightower, Lottie, 18
Hi-Lo's, The, 338
Hill, Teddy, 154, 156, 157, 158, 161, 206
Hillman, Roc, 97
Himber, Dick, 70
Hines, Earl, 6, 43, 261, 271, 272, 312, 323
Hinton, Milt, 35, 318, 323
"Hip Hip Hooray," 87
Hirt, Al, 320
"Hit Parade, The," 70, 131
Hite, Les, 248, 249, 254
Hitz, Ralph, 119
Hodes, Art, 314, 315

INDEX

About the Author

Chip Deffaa, a jazz critic for *The New York Post* and England's *Crescendo*, has written for such publications as *JazzTimes*, *Living Blues*, *Down Beat*, *Modern Drummer*, *Sheet Music*, *Keyboard*, *New Woman*, *The Mississippi Rag*, *Video Review*, *The Philadelphia Inquirer*, England's *Storyville*, Canada's *Coda*, and Japan's *Swing Journal*.

He is the author of *Swing Legacy* (Scarecrow Press and the Institute of Jazz Studies) and *Voices of the Jazz Age* (University of Illinois Press), and is at work on *A Jazz Portrait Gallery*.